Cities and Citizenship at the U.S.-Mexico Border

The Paso Del Norte Metropolitan Region

Edited by
Kathleen Staudt,
César M. Fuentes,
and
Julia E. Monárrez Fragoso

CITIES AND CITIZENSHIP AT THE U.S.-MEXICO BORDER
Copyright © Kathleen Staudt, César M. Fuentes, and
Julia E. Monárrez Fragoso, 2010

All rights reserved.

First published in 2010 by
PALGRAVE MACMILLAN® in the United States – a division of
St. Martin's Press LLC, 175 Fifth Avenue, New York, NY 10010.

Where this book is distributed in the UK, Europe and the rest of
the world, this is by Palgrave Macmillan, a division of Macmillan
Publishers Limited, registered in England, company number 785998,
of Houndmills, Basingstoke, Hampshire RG21 6XS.

Palgrave Macmillan is the global academic imprint of the above
companies and has companies and representatives throughout the world.

Palgrave® and Macmillan® are registered trademarks in the
United States, the United Kingdom, Europe and other countries.

ISBN: 978–0–230–10031–2 (hardcover)
ISBN: 978–0–230–10032–9 (paperback)

Library of Congress Cataloging-in-Publication Data

Cities and citizenship at the U.S.-Mexico border: the Paso del Norte
metropolitan region/edited by Kathleen Staudt, Cesar M. Fuentes,
Julia Monarrez Fragoso.
      p. cm.
    ISBN 978–0–230–10032–9 (pbk.)
    1. Mexican-American Border Region—Emigration and immigration—
Social aspects—Case studies.   2. Mexican-American Border Region—
Social conditions—Case studies.   3. Mexican-American Border
Region—Economic conditions—Case studies.   4. Mexican-
American Border Region—Politics and government—Case studies.
5. Globalization—Mexican-American Border Region—Case studies.
6. Globalization—Mexico—Ciudad Juárez.   7. Ciudad Juárez
(Mexico)—Social conditions.   8. Ciudad Juárez (Mexico)—Economic
conditions.   9. Ciudad Juárez (Mexico)—Politics and government.
I. Staudt, Kathleen A.   II. Fuentes, César M.   III. Monárrez Fragoso,
Julia Estela.
    JV6565.C58 2010
    972'.16—dc22

                                                    2010002673

A catalogue record of the book is available from the British Library.

Design by MPS Limited, A Macmillan Company

First edition: September 2010

10 9 8 7 6 5 4 3 2 1

Printed in the United States of America.

To Juarenses and to borderlanders/*fronterizos/fronterizas*
everywhere!

Peace and Justice/*Paz y Justicia*

CONTENTS

List of Maps and Figures   vii

List of Tables   viii

Preface: "Living and Working in a Global Manufacturing
Border Urban Space: A Paradigm for the Future?"   ix
Kathleen Staudt

1 Globalization, Transborder Networks, and U.S.-Mexico
   Border Cities   1
   César M. Fuentes and Sergio Peña

SECTION I SECURITY AND SAFETY IN THE BORDER REGION   21

2 Death in a Transnational Metropolitan Region   23
   Julia E. Monárrez Fragoso

3 The Disarticulation of Justice: Precarious Life and
   Cross-Border Feminicides in the Paso del Norte Region   43
   Julia E. Monárrez Fragoso and Cynthia Bejarano

4 Surviving Domestic Violence in the Paso del
   Norte Border Region   71
   Kathleen Staudt and Rosalba Robles Ortega

SECTION II GLOBALIZED PRODUCTION, URBAN SPACE,
AND PUBLIC SERVICES   91

5 Globalization and its Effects on the Urban Socio-Spatial
   Structure of a Transfrontier Metropolis: El Paso,
   TX-Ciudad Juárez, Chih.-Sunland-Park, NM   93
   César M. Fuentes and Sergio Peña

6 World-class Automotive Harnesses and the Precariousness
   of Employment in Juárez   119
   Martha Miker Palafox

SECTION III LIVING WITH GLOBALIZED RISKS: POVERTY,
IMMIGRATION, AND EDUCATION   145

7 Centering the Margins: The Transformation of
   Community in Colonias on the U.S.-Mexico Border   147
   Guillermina Gina Núñez and Georg M. Klamminger

8 Schooling for Global Competitiveness in the Border
   Metropolitan Region   173
   Kathleen Staudt and Zulma Y. Méndez

9 *Alianza para la Calidad de la Educación* and the
   Production of an Empty Curriculum   195
   Zulma Y. Méndez

SECTION IV TOWARD NEW GOVERNANCE?   215

10 Crossborder Governance in a Tristate,
    Binational Region   217
    Tony Payan

About the Contributors   245

Index   247

LIST OF MAPS AND FIGURES

Map 1.1   U.S.-Mexico northern border: Cuidad Juárez,
          Chihuahua–El Paso, Texas   2
Map 3.1   Last place where victims were seen: Systemic
          Sexual Feminicide, 1993–2008   62
Map 4.1   Complaints attended by police in Ciudad Juárez,
          Chihuahua   83
Map 5.1   Dependency ratio for El Paso-Ciudad Juárez   109
Map 5.2   Population (15–64) employed in manufacturing
          in the Paso del Norte Region   111
Map 5.3   Public service access (Indoor Plumbing) in the
          Paso del Norte Region   112

Figure 1.1   Maquiladora workers in a plastic glove factory:
             a metaphor for the "hands" that produce for the
             global economy   9
Figure 2.1   Billboard: One in four employees in Mexico's
             manufacturing export-processing work in
             Ciudad Juárez   25
Figure 2.2   Billboard: Let us pray; we need it. Taken in
             Ciudad Juárez   32
Figure 2.3   Mexican military vehicles advancing into the
             interior of Ciudad Juárez   37
Figure 3.1   In search of the "missing" girls of Ciudad Juárez   47
Figure 3.2   Cross marking where one woman's body was
             found near Las Cruces, New Mexico   57
Figure 3.3   Systemic Sexual Feminicide 1993–2008, Number
             of Victims   61
Figure 4.1   El Paso Police District domestic violence
             incidents, 2007   85
Figure 8.1   El Paso Independent School District 9th grade pass
             rates in low-, medium-, and high-poverty schools 185
Figure 8.2   El Paso Independent School District completion
             and drop-out rates in low-, medium-, and
             high-poverty schools   187

LIST OF TABLES

Table 1.1   *Maquiladora* plants and employment by border
city (2000)   11

Table 1.2   Number of *maquiladora* plants and average
number of employees in Ciudad Juárez   12

Table 5.1   Participation of the economically active population
in Ciudad Juárez, Chihuahua, by sectors and
percentage of change in 1970 and 2000   99

Table 5.2   Employment in El Paso by sector (1970,
2001, 2006)   101

Table 5.3   Weekly income by occupation and gender of
maquiladora workers (2000–2006) (U.S. dollars)   102

Table 5.4   Land use change in Ciudad Juárez, Chihuahua
(1995 and 2001)   104

Table 10.1   Border typology: Coordination, cooperation,
and collaboration   230

Table 10.2   Comparative governance structures: Mexico
and the United States   235

PREFACE

"Living and Working in a Global Manufacturing Border Urban Space: A Paradigm for the Future?"

Kathleen Staudt

At the center of the 2,000-mile U.S.-Mexico border, a sprawling transnational urban space swells with over two million people whose livelihoods depend on global manufacturing, trade corridors, and government jobs. This tristate region includes Ciudad Juárez (Chihuahua), El Paso (Texas), and at their peripheries, Sunland Park and Las Cruces (New Mexico). In this volume, we analyze a large, sprawling, prototypical export-processing (*maquiladora*) global manufacturing urban space at an urbanized international border. Ciudad Juárez, the centerpiece of the space and this volume, contains two-fifths of its formal workforce employed in export-processing global manufacturing and as such, epitomizes the "*maquiladora* model" in Mexico and the "*capital mundial*" *en las Americas*—the world capital in the Western Hemisphere.

Dynamic as that description appears, in the region, there grows an underside of insecurity, poverty, and grim futures for youth given the shrinkage of the "state." Chapter contributors define the state as the historical set of institutions that govern space and shape society from top to bottom, center to periphery, including current governments. The Government of Mexico and its public institutions, laws, and public policies once promised decent, humane working conditions and qualities of life, but state shrinkage has implications both for citizens, their claims, and accountability from their own government, and for those people who cross the international border into the neighboring United States and experience conditions in another state, (i.e., set of institutions, laws and policies), which offer not only seeming opportunity but also precarious labor conditions and risks for their lives, freedom, and the futures of their children.

State size and state priorities in Mexico and the United States offer flawed contrasts, one of them shrinking in response to global capital and the other, swelling in the name of law enforcement and border security. Since the early 1990s, the immigration and border-control apparatus of the U.S. state has swollen rather than shrunk. The U.S. border wall, also called the border fence, is symbolically emblematic of the border as fortress, but a fortress through which authorized goods and people can pass and through which unauthorized goods and people continue to pass regardless of the fence/wall. The spatially segregated production and distribution of manufactured goods (produced with low-cost labor using world-class standards) is authorized, encouraged, and subsidized. While world-class standards often streamline production processes, raise the quality of production, protect industries in the ebb and flow of market demand, and standardize global procedures, such standards also challenge and/or erase national complexities, including hard-fought policy achievements for working people. World-class standards normalize capitalist discipline and institutionalize preference for capitalism's owners and managers rather than its workers who add value to the production process. Meanwhile, the existence of two sovereign states poses challenges for border people's abilities to organize around their common interests (Staudt and Coronado, 2002).

TRANSNATIONAL URBAN SPACE AT BORDERS

Scholarship on global and world cities, focused on global transnational financial and manufacturing connections, renders space less important. As is now commonly understood, globalization has made the nation-state less relevant and, as a result, less able to govern. Saskia Sassen says we learn about power through its absence, calling attention to denationalized space and reduced regulatory functions (2007a). Chapter contributors in this volume call this the relatively absent state (*el estado ausente*)—an intriguing concept well worth a full analysis. Sassen also identifies social features of these urban spaces: inequalities, immigrant labor, and informal economies, including gendered wage inequalities and increasing polarization between rich and poor. In issuing a call for analysts to decipher global places, Sassen calls for a "new geography of centrality and marginality," making borders one of her central themes: "new types of borderings" that "alter the meaning of what we think of as borders" (2007a: 213–4; Chapter 8).

In this volume, we provide pioneering and comprehensive analysis of the binational, tristate Paso del Norte region of denationalized space, particularly its underside and contradictory patterns. Here in this "tri-state" descriptor, we refer to states as subnational units of federal governments: Chihuahua, Texas, and New Mexico.

Historicizing the Border Region

Border Studies is an interdisciplinary field that focuses attention on the shortcomings of narrow, disciplined approaches to the study of society, space, and nation. Historically, borders can be viewed as ever-changing lines, redrawn after conquest, purchase, wars, and treaties. Benedict Anderson eloquently analyzes national spaces as once-imagined communities (1983). The Paso del Norte region—indeed, most of the U.S. southwest and west—was once part of northern Mexico until the U.S.-Mexican War of 1846–1848 and the 1848 Treaty of Guadalupe Hidalgo when Mexico lost approximately half of its territory to the United States. The latest border change occurred in the region during the 1960s under the Chamizal Agreement, fixing a meandering Rio Grande river boundary (known as the Río Bravo in Mexico).

The Paso del Norte region is a centuries-old region along the river, surrounded by the great Chihuahua Desert, where Spanish colonizers established a religious mission. Alejandro Lugo provides insightful interpretation of the naming of this place and its people. In 1659, Spanish conquerors not only established a "resting place midway on the commercial trail between Parral (southern Nueva Viscaya) and Santa Fe (northern Nueva Mexico)," but also a mission to convert the indigenous peoples, the so-called Mansos (literally "the tamed") to Christianity (2008: 38). The Spaniards differentiated the so-called settled, tamed indigenous peoples from those they viewed as wild and nomadic. For Lugo and for the contributors in this book, the history and people of the region have been shaped by distantly national, binational, and global political-economic forces.

Paso del Norte became the name of the territory known since the mid-nineteenth century, but after the momentous U.S. conquest and Mexican loss of territory, codified in the 1848 Treaty of Guadalupe

Hidalgo, the territory eventually emerged as two distinctive locales: El Paso (1852) and Ciudad Juárez (1888), named after Mexico's much-beloved President, Benito Juárez (García Amaral and Santiago Quijada, 2007: 148). Historians have written about the region, including Oscar Martínez (1978), Mario García (1981), and González de la Vara (2002). Later, sociologists and political scientists analyzed the cities as related through crossborder and binational links (D'Antonio and Form, 1965; Staudt, 1998; Staudt and Coronado, 2002). While community activists collaborate over their common interests with some success, albeit limited (Staudt and Coronado, 2002), the dominant hegemonic relations occur among business leaders with enormous financial stakes in land and manufacturing development, one example of which is the Paso del Norte Group. Like the monarchies of feudal Europe, some of these binational relationships are cemented through crossborder marriages. Likewise, a century ago, Anglo settlers colonized the region, in part, through intermarriage with commercial families, but also through economic incentives, force, intimidation, and assimilation (Romo, 2005).

THE TWENTY-FIRST CENTURY BORDER: INTERDEPENDENT, INTEGRATED, OR ALIENATED (OR ALL OF THE ABOVE?)

Historian Oscar Martínez, with his four-fold typology of border regions, calls the Ciudad Juárez-El Paso borderlands an "interdependent border" (1996). This characterization is ruffled by three processes: (1) the rise both of globalized manufacturing industries that organize plants and working conditions according to "world-class" standards; (2) profit-driven motives that erase and shrink laws and policies of the Mexican space in which manufacturing operates; and (3) anxiety that bloats the U.S. security state.

On the one hand, economic and commercial relations resemble what Martínez might call in his typology an "integrated border." Despite considerable economic integration, there exist extensive delays at borders and the official ports of entry where trucks, people, and vehicles undergo checks for unauthorized crossing of people and (illegal) goods like drugs and guns.

On the other hand, another of Martínez's categories seems appropriate—that of an alienated border. The U.S. built a physical barrier, consisting of 670 miles of what residents call the border "wall" and the government calls the "fence," along with policy practices that inhibit crossing, the U.S. media's demonization of Mexico, and the very real fears that people have about moving about in a city like Ciudad Juárez with outlier murder rates. In 2008–2010, approximately 200 murders occur monthly in Ciudad Juárez, and petty criminals take the failed local and state law enforcement institutions as an opportunity to ratchet up ordinary theft to kidnapping, carjacking, and large-scale extortion. And violence against women continues unabated, as the weak rule of law renders low priority to domestic violence, attempted murder of women (minimized and normalized as "domestic violence"), and femicide, known as as *feminicidio* in Mexico to refer to the sexualized killings of women.

Perhaps interdependent or integrated labels make a better characterization of the border as a hybrid space of fissures, synergies, and mutations. Literary and cultural studies add insights to the study of border regions and spaces. Gloria Anzaldúa talks about the border like a scar from a wound ripping through a region (1987). Others write about the border as a place of mixing, a "hybrid" area of multiple languages and cultures (Bhabha, 1994). Filmmaker Lourdes Portillo narrates the documentary *Senorita Extraviada* (2001), making reference to Ciudad Juárez as a "city spinning out of control." Ominously, the late Robert Bolaño referred to this region as a killing place in his monumental novel *2666* (2008). The border metropolitan region is indeed a space of contradictions, segregation, and connectedness. Immigration researcher Joseph Nevins uses the striking term "global apartheid" to understand Mexican border crossings and the perils of immigrants' lives and labors (2008). Borderland spaces facilitate global capital-driven investments into segregated enclaves wherein workers' labor values reap ten-to-one wage differentials across national lines within a border zone, such as the Paso del Norte region (Staudt, 1998; Staudt and Coronado, 2002). The region is a juxtaposition between one of the safest and deadliest cities in their respective countries.

MAJOR CONTENTIONS IN THIS VOLUME

While space and states may no longer shape global manufacturing, our primary contention in all the chapters is that space and states do matter enormously in the Paso del Norte metropolitan region for the people who live in and migrate from there. Almost half the transnational border residents live in economically marginal circumstances as immigrants (or internal migrants) with limited power and/or rights within political institutions that often mute their voices. For the impoverished, the inability (or unwillingness) of the nation-state to govern has long been a reality. Many women (and men) live daily lives of insecurity and threat, given the rates of gender-based violence that make Ciudad Juárez infamous for its *feminicidio*/femicide and high homicide rates from well-armed and organized crime cartels, police impunity to an overall lawless atmosphere. In Ciudad Juárez, the relative absence of effective law enforcement institutions creates and sustains everyday insecurity, as shown in murder rates and residents' reluctance to denounce crimes to the widely distrusted police. The absence of effective law enforcement institutions produces multiple consequences: empowering those who commit crimes, aggravating insecurity, and encouraging federal militarization strategies, as has already happened in U.S. border security policies and practices (Dunn, 1996; 2009). Since taking office in 2006, President Calderón sent thousands of military troops and federal police to Ciudad Juárez and other states of Mexico—declared drug states of *feudos del narcotráfico*. This same strategy came to Ciudad Juárez in 2008, with little impact on the atmosphere of insecurity, yet with the military's own reputed human rights abuses. Borders themselves may be magnets for crime, given the existence of two or more sovereign states, the relatively easy escape through border crossing, and the "othering" or dehumanization of whole categories of people such as women (Ruiz Marrujo, 2009) and immigrants (selections in Staudt et al., 2009). And trade in unauthorized goods flourishes beyond human trafficking, whether gun smuggling from north to south, or drug smuggling from south to north.

In our volume, we utilized grounded analysis in transnational border urban space, refining, challenging, and advancing existing approaches to transnational urban space with comprehensive, interdisciplinary attention to security, economic, urban, spatial, and education patterns in the region. Each and every chapter offers the potential for partial predictive power for transborder cities elsewhere in the world. Chapter contributors address many missing empirical pieces in Sassen's analysis with a comprehensive and in-depth focus on the Paso del Norte transnational border region, including regional insecurity, gender-based violence, and nuanced attention to states, which, once unpacked, loom large or shrink small, depending on their priority and function in various territorial institutions.

While the state is relatively absent in the local law enforcement institutions that promise everyday security in Ciudad Juárez, the state has ample presence in immigration and border security enforcement, particularly on the U.S. side of the border. On both sides of the border, the state is visibly present in public education, with over half a million students enrolled in the Paso del Norte region. In the tristate, binational region, with their Mexico and U.S. variants, educational reformers tie policy and program changes to themes associated with global competitiveness and international standards using standardized assessments that create a class of students who fail standardized tests and leave school before graduation, which in Mexico is known as *deserción,* with desertion so starkly a referent in Spanish. Whether intentional or not, standardized schooling reproduces the polarized supply of laborers who toil in or migrate from transnational urban spaces. We also analyze particulars of spatial segregation across and within the transnational border region in housing, industrial location, and land speculation. In the Paso del Norte transborder region, location and space matter for the industrial plants, the residence of workers, and transportation costs.

In this volume, we tackle the challenges of comparative analysis at borders that use different units of measure and employ different questions in census indicators at borders (Staudt, 1998). These challenges have been elegantly referred to as "methodological nationalism" (Sassen, 2007a: 214). In our own collaborations over this volume, we encountered petty, even humorous crossborder challenges: for example, daylight savings time, which begins in different months in the "mountain zone"; the bureaucratic regulations over a Mexican work permit, itself a complex maze of *tramitología* (procedureology), specified a 4-by-4 picture, but the 4-by-4 inch submission offered a laugh given the 4-by-4 centimeter expectations! While some of this is funny, it can also be frustrating.

COMPARATIVE PERSPECTIVES: A PARADIGMATIC FUTURE?

This volume makes original and unique contributions to the study of transnational urban space in a border region of huge significance, not only for the United States and Mexico, but also for border regions elsewhere. Chapters provide heretofore unpublished, new empirical research, methodological challenges to existing ways of doing research, and theoretical advances to understand the region with vivid, accessible analyses of content.

We have assembled a distinguished, expert group of scholars, from multiple disciplines, on both sides of the U.S.-Mexico border in the Paso del Norte metropolitan region. The disciplines include anthropology, education, political science, sociology, and urban planning, along with the overlapping interdisciplinary fields that connect those disciplines: border studies, women/gender studies, Latin

American studies, and development and urban studies. A grounded study of transnational urban space at borders will produce important findings both for this region and for similar regions not only along the U.S.-Mexico border, (such as San Diego-Tijuana, the Laredos and *ambos* Nogales), but also in other transnational city spaces around the world. Together, the editors of this volume experience the lived reality of border space for approximately 100 years. We are *cruzadores*, crossers, who work, study, and teach across borders. Martínez categorizes people like these as "transnationals." In this volume, we worked toward creating a coherence rarely achieved in edited collections, given the interactive and collaborative process we used to develop chapter themes and present chapter drafts to one another thanks to the space provided by El Colegio de la Frontera Norte (COLEF), one of Mexico's major social science research think tanks (www.colef.mx). Our special collaborative process from July 2008–May 2009, at COLEF in Ciudad Juárez, involved collective dialogue and exchange in a space on a par with Italy's luxury Bellagio Center for distant scholars, but for us in a grittier locale, grounded, close, and immersed in our field of expertise—the U.S.-Mexico border. This volume features distinguished Mexican scholars, some of whom are publishing their original Spanish research for English-language readers for the first time. While this is a volume in English, we occasionally insert words or phrases in Spanish, for Spanish terminology sometimes clarifies the overtly political nature of some processes that the English language neutralizes with technical-sounding language. One good example is *expropiación* (expropriation) versus eminent domain—government land seizures.

ABOUT THE CHAPTERS

The rise of the global economy was accompanied with a parallel decline in the role of the nation-state, particularly the welfare or proactive state, in an atmosphere that prizes international competitiveness above all else. The Paso del Norte region exemplifies this denationalized space and the role of borders.

We use the paradigmatic case of the Paso del Norte transborder urban region of Ciudad Juárez-El Paso—that surpasses a population of more than two million residents—to analyze a global manufacturing region. The region facilitates global production processes with a plentiful, low-paid labor force. The region vividly illustrates the underside of global and global manufacturing cities: inequalities, challenges associated with the full rights of citizenship, insecurity, and informal economies.

The Paso del Norte region consists of migrants from Mexico's interior, seeking jobs, as well as immigrants who have crossed the international border and migrants to the sunny southwest from the mainstream United States. It contains a youthful population, with two national school systems; each responds to the discourse of international competitiveness and practices or aspires to practice to standards and standardized assessments that resonate with global business models. Studies of global cities have not yet addressed youth and education in their analyses. It is a region that exemplifies neoliberal commitment to "free trade," with extensive commercial exchange and traffic across the border as well as to other regions of production. It is also a region of extensive informal economic activity, generating income for informal workers (the quintessential free traders) who themselves get around state regulations (Staudt, 1998).

The region is beset with contradictions: a relatively absent state when it comes to regulating business or enforcing national labor and environmental regulations, but a heavy and present state when it comes to enforcing national border security policies. Others have called the border "militarized" (Dunn, 1996); the U.S. government established border blockades in the urban areas of El Paso and San Diego (the former of which is analyzed in Dunn, 2009). Since the spread of the drug trade from sea-border routes to the U.S.-Mexico border, the region has become a major gateway for international criminals to use in the illegal trade, ruthlessly responding to the dynamics of supply and demand (Payan, 2006). Mexico's military crackdown on drug cartels represents a parallel border militarization to that of the United States.

Curiously, this emphasis on border security and drug cartel crackdowns has little to no consequence for everyday insecurity (Staudt, Payan, and Kruszewski, 2009). Nowhere is this more evident than in the killing of women, known at the border as femicide or *feminicidio*, which has made the region internationally infamous since the 1990s. Domestic violence and attempted murder are part of this picture (Staudt, 2008).

This volume is divided into three parts, framed with an introductory chapter on global manufacturing and a closing chapter on governance at borders. In the introductory chapter, César Fuentes and Sergio Peña focus on the rise of global manufacturing, transborder networks, and the U.S.-Mexico border region.

In the first section thereafter, "Security and Safety in the Border Region," three chapters focus on death, insecurity, and crime. Julia E. Monárrez Fragoso, in "Death at the Border," analyzes murder, crimes, and drug-related violence in vivid detail. Her chapter is theoretically sophisticated, applying critical analysis to the widespread notion that El Paso and Ciudad Juárez are "two cities apart," showing their connectedness instead. Following that chapter, she and Cynthia Bejarano address the absent state notion in "The Disarticulation of Justice: Precarious Life and Cross-Border Feminicides in the Paso del Norte Region." The essay develops and analyzes a new concept for the region: crossborder feminicide (sexualized killings). They focus on the similarities of dissimilar spaces in the ways women have been murdered, displayed, and disposed of in desert regions. After that, in the chapter entitled "Surviving Domestic Violence in the Paso del Norte Region," Kathleen Staudt and Rosalba Robles Ortega examine spatial dimensions of this insecurity. They analyze patterns of domestic violence, drawing on reports from survivors and reports to police, illustrating these patterns with maps and charts.

The second section focuses on "Globalized Production, Urban Space, and Public Services." The section begins with another chapter from Fuentes and Peña, "Globalization and its Effects on Urban Sociospatial Structure in a Transfrontier Metropolis: El Paso, TX, Ciudad Juárez, CHIH, and Sunland Park, NM." In it, the increasing delocalization and the deepening commodification of real estate property seem to portend to a significant impact on the transborder urban sociospatial structure. The authors examine changing employment and spatial and public service segregation in both regions, illustrating quantitative data with maps. The clarity of north-south inequalities are reproduced in a singular globalizing city at the border. Following that, in "Global Production and Precarious Labor: Harness Production in Ciudad Juárez," Martha World-Class Automotive Harnesses analyzes a large sector of the export-processing industry associated with the production of automobile frames. She analyzes four global corporations, from Japan and the United States, whose capitalist discipline practices reveal more similarities than dissimilarities in production, management, and employee-control practices.

In the third section, "Living with Globalized Risks: Poverty, Immigration, and Education," chapter authors examine poverty, education, and organized civil society activism in everyday life in and near the globalizing Paso del Norte Metropolitan region. Guillermina Núñez and Georg M. Klamminger, titling their chapter "Centering the Margins: The Transformation of Community in *Colonias* on the U.S.-Mexico Border, analyze mostly immigrants in a *colonia* (an unplanned settlement) in southern New Mexico. Against all odds, residents establish a community, yet live with fear and risk associated with movement across the supposed free space of the U.S. southwest. After that, Kathleen Staudt and Zulma Y. Méndez begin their chapter, "Schooling for Global Competitiveness in the Border Metropolitan Region," with the pervasive discourse of international competitiveness and demonstrate its effects on changes in educational policies and practices in Mexico, the United States, and the border region with mostly Mexican-heritage youth, many of whom speak Spanish. The analysis focuses mainly on standardized test scores and graduation rates in El Paso, illustrating the connections between the "economically disadvantaged" (so labeled in the Texas Education System), low pass rates, and noncompletion of high school. Despite noble efforts to change aspects of the high-stakes accountability system, analyzed in ethnographic form, organized civil society activists express political voices but gain little in face of the relentless business model in education. In the following chapter, Méndez interprets her lengthy observations of the third year of secondary school at a public school in Ciudad Juárez in "Alianza para la Calidad de la Educación and the Production of an Empty Curriculum." Based on extensive observation of the enacted curriculum, she analyzes the rhetoric of education reform—purporting to improve quality, but actually producing an empty curriculum.

Reflecting on both education chapters, one can only wonder if impoverished youth on either side of the border will gain the skills necessary to compete in the globalizing city. These chapters suggest that educational practices are more likely to reproduce the polarized inequality of the transborder region. And despite transborder, transnational NGOs on violence, environmental and other issues, no such connections exist to change the nationalist education systems (Rippberger and Staudt, 2003). Unlike the compelling business discourse of international competitiveness, civil society activists and residents can hardly articulate change that influences their own governments, much less multiple governance systems across borders. Yet crossborder activism produces some successes (see Staudt and Coronado, 2002).

Tony Payan, in the final, closing chapter, asks what sort of governance occurs now and in future years, given the dominance of global production and the contradictory aspects of governance in the region. He advances to the next stage of border typology development, focused on coordination, cooperation, and collaboration at the border. Both Mexico and the United States offer the trappings of democracy in their federal systems of government, with opportunities to participate at the national, state, and local levels. Growing civil society activists in the urban region open political space for some border voices, but people confront a massive global system working hand in hand with notions of "limited government" (United States) and the shrinking or absent nation-state (Mexico) in territorial spaces like the border region.

As for the question of Ciudad Juárez as the paradigmatic future, contributors in this volume hope academics, (faculty members and students), civil society activists, and policy analysts—including, and especially, the readers of this collection—will raise questions and exercise their allied power to sound analytic warnings about clone-like cities elsewhere in the world before those populations face the kinds of threats that Juarenses undergo daily. Some wonder what would have happened to the region without global manufacturing, and others may wonder what would happen if it disappeared. The real questions involve how to halt dangerous practices or intervene to address the horrifying insecurities and poverty that states, in cooperation with global manufacturing, constructed for huge populations who produce goods for all of us consumers in the global economy.

*Thanks to Julia E. Monárrez and César Fuentes for their comments on this preface.

REFERENCE LIST

Anderson, Benedict. 1983. *Imagined Communities: Reflections on the Origins and Spread of Nationalism.* London: Verso.

Anzaldúa, Gloria. 1987. *Borderlands/La Fronera: The New Mestiza.* San Francisco: Aunt Lute/Spinsters Press.

Bhabha, Homi. 1994. "Narrating the Nation." In *Nationalism,* eds John Hutchison and Anthrony D. Smith. NY: Oxford University Press.

Bolaño, Robert. 2008. *2666.* NY: Farrar, Straus, and Giroux publishers.

D'Antonio, William, and William Form. 1965. *Influentials in Two Border Cities: A Study in Community Decision-Making.* University of Notre Dame Press.

Dunn, Timothy J. 2009. *Blockading the Border and Human Rights.* Austin: University of Texas Press.

———. 1996. *Militarization of the U.S.-Mexico Border.* Austin: University of Texas Center for Mexican American Studies.

García Amaral, María Luisa and Guadalupe Santiago Quijada. 2008. "Ciudades Fronterizas del Norte de México," in *Chihuahua Hoy 2007: Visiones de su Historia, Economia, Politica y Culture, Tomo V,* Victor Orozco, editor. Chihuahua, Chih: Universidad Autónoma de Chihuahua, Universidad Autónoma de Ciudad Juárez, and Instituto Chihuahuense de la Cultura, pp. 137–156.

González de la Vara, Martín. 2002. *Breve historia de Ciudad Juárez y su región.* México. El Colegio de la Frontera Norte. Center for Latin American and Border Studies, Universidad Autónoma de Ciudad Juárez, Ediciones y Gráficos Eón.

Lugo, Alejandro. 2008. *Fragmented Lives, Assembled Parts: Culture, Capitalism, and Conquest at the U.S.-Mexico Border.* Austin: University of Texas Press.

Mario García. 1981. *Desert Immigrants: The Mexicans Of El Paso, 1880–1920.* New Haven: Yale University Press.

Martínez, Oscar. 1978. *Border Boom Town: Ciudad Juárez Since 1848.* Austin: University of Texas Press.

———. 1996. *Border People.* Tucson: University of Arizona Press.

Nevins, Joseph. 2008. *Dying to Live: A Story of U.S. Immigration in an Age of Global Apartheid.* San Francisco: City Lights.

Payan, Tony. 2006. *The Three U.S.-Mexico Border Wars: Drugs, Violence, and Homeland Security.* NY: Praeger.

Rippberger, Susan and Kathleen Staudt. 2003. *Pledging Allegiance: Learning Nationalism at the El Paso-Juárez Border.* NY: Routledge/Falmer.

Romo, David. 2005. *Ringside Seat to a Revolution: An Underground Cultural History of El Paso and Juarez, 1893–1923.* El Paso: Cinco Puntos Press.

Ruiz Marrujo, Olivia. 2009. *In Human Rights along the U.S.-Mexico Border: Gendered Violence and Insecurity.* Staudt, Payan, and Kruszewski, eds. Tucson: University of Arizona Press.

Sassen, Saskia. 2007a. *A Sociology of Globalization.* NY: W. W. Norton.

———. 2000. *Cities in a World Economy,* second edition. Pine Forge Press.

Staudt, Kathleen. 1998. *Free Trade? Informal Economies at the U.S.-Mexico Border.* Philadelphia: Temple University Press.

———. 2008. *Violence and Activism at the Border: Gender, Fear and Everyday Life in Ciudad Juárez.* Austin: University of Texas Press.

——— and Irasema Coronado. 2002. *Fronteras no Más: Toward Social Justice at the U.S.-Mexico Border.* NY: Palgrave.

———, Tony Payan, and Z. Anthony Kruszewski, co-editors. 2009. *Human Rights along the U.S.-Mexico Border: Gendered Violence and Insecurity.* Tucson: University of Arizona Press.

CHAPTER 1

GLOBALIZATION, TRANSBORDER NETWORKS, AND U.S.-MEXICO BORDER CITIES

César M. Fuentes and Sergio Peña

This chapter presents a theoretical framework to bridge the understanding of quintessential global cities, such as London, New York, and Tokyo (Sassen, 2001) with cities essential to the lower circuits of globalization. One site to analyze globalizing cities is at the international borderline of Mexico and the United States. At the center point of the border, the Paso del Norte metropolitan region exemplifies the transborder networks that we analyze in this chapter and the entire edited collection.

The Mexico-United States border region is large and very dynamic. It is over 3,000 kilometers in length—that is, slightly less than 2,000 miles in a border zone—and uses two types of metrics that make comparative analysis difficult. In the border zone itself—within 25 miles of the border—the total population according to both national censuses in 2000 was 14 million people. If one added the population of all ten border states of Mexico and the United States, the region in 2000 consisted of over 80 million people (Staudt and Coronado, 2002). All along the lengthy border, one finds many cities and towns that form transnational conurbations, including one of the world's busiest transport hubs in Nuevo Laredo-Laredo, as well as two large urban areas that produce intensively for the global economy: Tijuana-San Diego in the western Pacific region, and Ciudad Juárez-El Paso

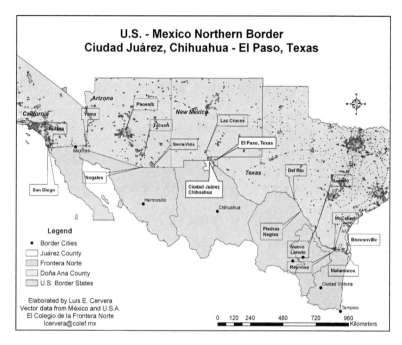

Map 1.1   U.S.-Mexico Border Region

in the central region (see Map 1.1). This volume focuses on the latter, for it is a paradigmatic case: the largest, with production most connected to the global economy.

Globalization is a process driven to great extent by economic forces to promote the sine qua non goal of the capitalist system—capital accumulation. This process not only transforms the economic, social, and political fabric of society, but it also revalues or devalues spaces, creating a worldwide system of interconnected urban places. Sassen (2007a) has referred to this process as the emergence of a "transnational urban system" that is hierarchical in nature. The transnational urban system is in part an organizational structure of transborder operations. To the degree that transborder transactions grow, so also does globalization by expanding the network that articulates particular urban agglomerations. As a result, we must reformulate the scales of strategic places that articulate the new system. Transborder regions are among these strategic places, and the Paso del Norte region is the quintessential site for this type of analysis. In transborder regions, the nation-state loses or weakens its capacity to govern; it surrenders its sovereignty to transnational governing bodies or global markets.

Maquiladora[1] (export-processing) production in U.S.-Mexican border cities exemplifies transborder networks among global cities and cities in a lower but crucial part of the hierarchy in transnational urban systems. Cities at the U.S.-Mexico border have experienced this globalizing process since the mid-1960s through capital flows in the form of foreign direct investment (FDI) in the manufacturing sector (*maquiladora*), the most important receptors of this type of investment in Mexico. The *maquiladora* industry links Mexican border cities and U.S. cities through the supply of raw materials, components, and specialized services. Through these relationships, U.S-Mexico border cities play key roles as production centers where the function of the Mexican *maquiladoras* is to assemble inputs into final products and the function of the U.S. companies is to provide the inputs, raw materials, components, and specialized services (Hanson, 1996). However, Mexican border cities play subordinate roles in the transnational urban system, depending on capital flows, technology, and specialized services from multinational corporations located mainly in United States. Given their functions, these cities have been defined as globalizing cities[2] in the sense that they are articulated to global cities but in the hierarchical scale are functionally subordinated (Heineberg, 2005).

The growth of the transborder networks between global cities and globalizing cities involves not only economic spheres, such as transborder industrial park developers (see Fuentes and Peña Ch. 5, this volume), but also other crossborder network spheres: nongovernment organizations (NGOs—environmental, human rights, feminist), and international criminal organizations (drug cartels, human smuggling) (Sassen, 2007a; Naím, 2005; Staudt and Coronado, 2002; Brooks and Fox, 2002; see also in this volume: Monárrez, Staudt and Robles, Payan). These processes call into question the extent to which governments are absent or present in mediating and representing interests in the region. However, Jackie Smith says that global corporate networks may equal or surpass the power of the nation-state and transnational NGOs (Smith, 2008; see Miker in this volume). In sum, globalization affects not only economic processes but also various social, political, and criminal processes that are important to unpack and uncover.

In this chapter, we focus on economic processes, framing the Paso del Norte metropolitan region at the border into global perspectives. The chapter is divided into four sections. The first section presents a general discussion of the process of globalization. After that, we discuss the ideas behind the hypothesis of global cities (Friedmann, 1986).

Following that, we analyze the transnational urban system. The fourth section discusses in more detail how globalization has affected the U.S.-Mexico border—particularly how transborder networks in the region are connected to the global. The idea behind the organization of the chapter is to start from a macro scale and then zoom in on lower layers and scales to begin uncovering all the dimensions of globalization. The idea of scales comes from Brenner (2000) and Sassen (2007a) who argue that globalization is a multiscalar process. Border regions are prime spaces in which to "unbundle" these multiscalar processes.

I. The Globalization Process

Since the end of the 1970s and the beginning of the 1980s, the world economy started a series of structural adjustments that affected levels of production, disposable resources, and the wealth of countries. From a domestic perspective, these adjustments reflect the way in which regions and cities around the world emerge and articulate with global processes, generating an intense competition among them (Gilbert, 1998). During this period (1970–1980), the world underwent important transitions, moving from an international economy, where the goods and services were commercialized by individuals and companies of different countries through national barriers, to a more global scale where goods and services are produced and purchased in a network of global corporations, whose operations extend beyond national borders (Knox, 1995).

It is important to distinguish between internationalization and globalization. Internationalization is related to the geographic expansion of economic activities reflecting qualitative changes. Globalization includes the functional integration of dispersed economic activities reflecting quantitative changes. In other words, the way economic activities are organized is what makes the difference. Globalization of the production process has generated a greater degree of interdependence between national economies and economies of the rest of the world. The accelerated increment of international commerce and the process of regional integration offer clear evidence of the new international dynamic that the world is facing. The acceleration and intensification of technological changes, along with the emergence of transnational companies with internal and external networks, assure that events that happen in one place will be rapidly transmitted to the rest of the world (Dicken, 2003). The integration of the economic activities, the interdependence of countries, and the emergence of regional economic blocks define the globalization process (Lo and Marcotullio, 2001).

Over the past 30 years, the world economy has become more and more integrated. International trade and investment have increased, and the spatial distribution of industrial activities has become more diffused. Advances in communications, computer technology, and logistics have revolutionized the way business is conducted and financial capital is invested. The advances in telecommunications have not ended nineteenth century forms of work; rather, technology has shifted a number of activities that once were part of manufacturing into the domain of services. Many traditional production tasks in manufacturing have been mechanized, automated, and computerized, making production more capital-intensive and less dependent on manual labor.

The transfer of skills from workers to machines, once epitomized by the assembly line, has a present-day version in the transfer of various activities from the shop floor into computers, attended by technical and professional personnel. Also, functional specialization within early factories finds a contemporary counterpart in today's pronounced fragmentation of the work process both spatially and organizationally. This fragmentation process has been called the "global assembly line": the production and assembly of goods from factories and depots throughout the world, wherever labor costs and economies of scale make an international division of labor cost-effective (Sassen, 1991).

Earlier studies of globalization, including the one by Friedmann (1986), pointed toward the notion that the world was becoming "flat;" that is, spatial differentiation no longer mattered to capitalism. This technologically deterministic argument assumed that technological changes, particularly in telecommunications and transportation, made space ubiquitous (see also Hambleton and Simone, 2007). Another argument that is commonly found in the literature is that globalization made the nation-state irrelevant. The argument goes along the line that the nation-state lost its capacity to govern and surrendered its sovereignty to transnational governing bodies, such as the International Monetary Fund (IMF) and the World Bank to mention two. Thus, democratic values and governance have been undermined.

Regarding the argument that the nation-state has lost its ability to govern, here, we argue along the same lines as Friedman and Wolff (1982) and Brenner (2000) who see globalization as a dialectical and contradictory process. Brenner (2000) eloquently argues that globalization should be viewed in scale terms, because globalization creates and superimposes multiple scales of socioeconomic spaces and political-institutional spaces. The argument of scales is the key to understanding globalization and governance. Every political institution has a scalar component, and "there exist several nested scales interacting in a geographic space; the interaction process could involve cooperation or conflict, homogenization or differentiation, empowerment and disempowerment" (Swyngedouw, 2000: 70–71). This globalization process is associated with structural changes, where world production, exchange, and investment continue to be dominated by capital from developed economies.

II. GLOBAL CITIES

The city is the place where economic globalization is constituted. In this sense, global cities (Friedmann, 1986; Sassen, 1996; 2001) are defined as command points in the organization of the world economy, key locations for finance, specialized services for firms, and major sites for producing innovations. As a result, these cities had been experiencing declining manufacturing employment and significant increases in service jobs. Industrial activities do not disappear, but rather are relocated to other points in the world, establishing a new international division of labor (NIDL). In this new division, the specialized activities of the tertiary sector are developed in cities considered to be nodes of control and organization. Meanwhile, the manufacturing activities are displaced to other regions within the urban hierarchy that do not implement control functions, but are nevertheless active participants of these global processes.

The combination of spatial dispersal and global integration has created a new strategic role for major cities. These cities, which are part of the global network, function in four new ways (Sassen, 1991):

First, as highly concentrated command points in the organization of the world economy.
Second, as key locations for finance and for specialized service firms, which have replaced manufacturing as the leading economic sector.
Third, as sites of production, including the production of innovations in these leading industries.
Fourth, as markets for the products and innovations produced.

New York, London, and Tokyo are considered the premier global cities. These cities have undergone massive and parallel changes in their economic base, spatial organization, and social structure.

Global cities are not only nodal points for the coordination of processes (Friedmann, 1986) but also particular sites of production. They are sites for (1) specialized services needed by complex organizations for running a spatially dispersed network of factories, offices, and service outlets; and (2) the production of financial innovations and the making of markets, both central to the internationalization and expansion of the financial industry (Sassen, 1991).

The territorial dispersal of current economic activity creates a need for expanded central control and management. In other words, while, in principle, the territorial decentralization of economic activity in recent years could have been accompanied by a corresponding decentralization in ownership and hence in the appropriation of profits, there has been little movement in that direction. Though large firms have increased their subcontracting to smaller firms, and many national firms in the newly industrializing countries have grown rapidly, this form of growth is ultimately part of a chain (Sassen, 1991).

These geoeconomic transformations, according to Dicken (2003), are a product of three interconnected processes, as follows:

* The presence of transnational corporations that are the leading actors of the global economy because of their potential ability to control and coordinate production networks through some countries.
* States that continue to have an important influence in the global economy by continuing deregulation (i.e., facilitating) economic transactions under their territorial limits.
* Last but not least, important technology, considered the fundamental force that allows the globalization of the economic activities.

According to Harvey (1989), globalization has simultaneously compressed time and space. Spaces seem closer due to technological advances in communication, which have reduced the time that economic activities require to take place (e.g., financial transactions).

Transnational corporations continue to control much of the end product and to reap the profits associated with selling in the world market. The internationalization and expansion of the financial industry has brought growth to a large number of smaller financial markets, a growth that has fed the expansion of the global industry. But top-level control and management of the industry have become concentrated in a few leading financial centers, notably New York, London, and Tokyo (Sassen, 1991).

The increment in the exchange of capital flows in the form of FDI and the new telecommunications technologies are important elements that help us understand the evolution of the global system. Globalization still requires that capital be invested in tangible assets, such as plants and facilities to produce output whose demand is global. This internationalization of industrial activities is profoundly altering the world's urban economic landscape. Over the past two decades, cities benefiting from global restructuring have grown rapidly, while less economically competitive cities have stagnated and shrunk. Given their plentiful supplies of cheap labor and permissive regulatory environments, cities in developing countries have become important actors in global manufacturing (Dowall, 1999). In this context, Export-Processing Zones (EPZs) are places for manufacturing production. As a consequence, some tasks have been shifted to other parts of the world—mainly Asia and Latin America—where labor is less expensive. In the EPZs, there is a growing incidence of manufacturing jobs and frequently a declining share of service jobs, a trend that diverges from what has been typical in highly industrialized countries over the last two decades.

Sassen (2006) offered a new typology that responds to the issue of how globalization has impacted the geography of cities more than those defined as global cities. She identifies four types of places as "strategic" in the global system network: 1) EPZs; 2) offshore banking centers; 3) high-tech districts; and 4) global cities. Also, a fifth category must be added, cities unable to "hinge" to the circuits of capitalism. The network of these four types of places is what makes capitalism move forward in the era of globalization.

EPZs are special arrangements—typically, a distinct geographic area near a port or border—that are set up to promote export industries. These are often assembly plants that use low-priced labor to bring together components from different countries so that a new product can then be exported. The EPZs usually apply a different set of regulatory rules from the rest of the country. They are typically established by developing-country governments with the explicit purpose of attracting foreign investment. EPZs are also known as "free trade areas" in many countries, and in Mexico, the government established a 20 km-wide "development" zone that stretched along the entire length of the Mexico-United States border. The *maquiladora* plant program was born out of Mexico's industrialization efforts (Esparza, Waldorf, and Chávez, 2004).

III. GLOBALIZATION IN THE U.S.-MEXICO
BORDER REGION

FDI in the form of manufacturing capital flows has been the principal driving force of globalization (Dowall, 1999). As a result, the Mexican border region has been receiving important amounts of FDI in the form of export-assembly plants (also known as the *maquiladora* program[3]). The origin of FDI comes mainly from multinational corporations[4] based in the United States (78.9%), South Korea (8.96%), Canada (5.75%), Italy (3.65%), and Japan (2.1%). As a result, Mexican border cities had experienced a tremendous expansion in the number of *maquiladora* plants and workers over the last four decades (Fuentes, 2001).

Since the establishment of the *maquiladora* program in the mid-1960s, the U.S-Mexico border region has been integrated in a formal way into the globalization process (see Figure 1.1). The function

Figure 1.1 Maquiladora workers in a plastic glove factory: a metaphor for the "hands" that produce for the global economy
Source: Photo credit, like what is done for other photographs—see consent forms.

assigned to the region was that of a production center given its comparative advantages in terms of labor cost and also its locational advantages (i.e., transport costs), such as adjacency and distance to the U.S. market. Border regions are attractive locations to relocate industries due to long-haul economies; that is, the cost of transporting an additional unit declines as distance increases (Edwards, 2007). As a result, the region becomes a manufacturing production center, playing a key role among cities within the lower circuits of globalization. However, the region has been dependent in terms of capital flows and technology. Thus, the region plays a subordinate role in terms of production decisions given the advances in telecommunications systems that have enabled firms to more closely synchronize orders with inventories and sales—increasing efficiency and reducing operating cost—making the firm more profitable.

The role assigned to the region was that of a production center with very limited backward and forward linkages with national industry and totally articulated to companies located in developed countries—mainly the United States—which provide raw materials, components, and specialized services. The *maquiladora* industry incorporates only 2 percent of national raw materials (Fuentes, 2001). In contrast, it is estimated that 26,000 companies with headquarter in the United States supply raw materials and components to the *maquiladoras*, and between 1990 and 2002, more than 500,000 new jobs shared a common supply chain with Mexican *maquiladoras* (Cañas, Coronado, and Gilmer, 2004).

The importance of this economic activity can be measured for its impact in the employment and value added generated. In 1970, there were only 120 plants that employed 290,327 people; by 2000 the number reached 3,590 plants and employed almost 1.3 million people. In 2006, the number of plants decreased to 2,810, and the employment reached 1.2 million (INEGI, 2007). At the outset, the assembly-line labor force comprised a female majority. By the late 1980s, the workforce became more gender balanced. The value added of manufactured goods by the *maquiladora* industry has become the country's main source of foreign exchange (US$8.1 billion); it went from 4.96 billion in 1995 to 19.2 billion in 2004 (INEGI, 2005).

The evolution of the *maquiladora* industry in the Mexican economy is astonishing; in 1985, it had become Mexico's second-largest source of income from foreign exports, behind oil (Stoddard, 1987). And in 2006, the *maquiladora* industry accounted for 45 percent of Mexico's manufacturing exports.

In the *maquiladora* industry located along the U.S.-Mexico border, the first plants were established almost simultaneously in Ciudad Juárez, Chihuahua, across from El Paso, Texas, and Nogales, Sonora, across from Nogales, Arizona. Tijuana and Mexicali across from San Diego and Calexico, California, respectively, and Reynosa and Matamoros across from McAllen and Brownsville, Texas, followed. The cities of Ciudad Juárez and Tijuana are the ones that now have the largest share of *maquiladora* plants and employment; both account for almost one-third of the plants (29%) and employment (33%) in 2000. (see Table 1.1)

In this industrialization process, a transfrontier metropolis (Herzog, 1991) has become one of the most important players: El Paso-Ciudad Juárez-Sunland Park (New Mexico). El Paso-Ciudad Juárez-Sunland Park is an example of global landscapes that coexist side by side, performing a different function in the "new transnational urban hierarchy. Ciudad Juárez has had success in the new global market as an export-processing zone or *maquiladora* hub. El Paso's economy depends, in part, on the *maquiladora* activity in Ciudad Juárez, and it functions as a supplier of raw material and components. In 2006, it was estimated that the *maquiladora* industry located in Ciudad Juárez purchased US$8 billion in components, new material and specialized services from U.S. companies" (REDCO, 2007). The El Paso-Ciudad Juárez-Southern New Mexico region is one of the largest manufacturing centers in North America with more than 267,000 persons employed in manufacturing (REDCO, 2005).

Ciudad Juárez is the city that had received the highest percentage of the FDI in the manufacturing sector in Mexico. As a result,

Table 1.1   *Maquiladora* plants and employment by border city (2000)

City	Number of Plants	Percentage	Number of Employees	Percentage
Matamoros	119	3.2	66,023	4.9
Reynosa	130	3.5	69,378	5.2
Nuevo Laredo	54	1.4	22,603	1.7
Piedras Negras	38	1.0	14,546	1.1
Acuña	56	1.5	32,130	2.4
Ciudad Juárez	308	8.3	249,509	18.6
Tijuana	779	21.0	184,756	13.8
Other cities	2,219	59.9	700,045	52.3
National	3,703	100.00	1,338,990	100.00

Source: Estadísticas de la Industria Maquiladora de Exportación (INEGI), 2006.

Table 1.2 Number of *maquiladora* plants and average number of employees in Ciudad Juárez, Chihuahua (2000–2006)

Year	*Maquiladora* Plants	Average Number of Employees	Value Added (Thousand of U.S. dollars)
2000	308	249,509	3,259,555.6
2001	307	228,445	3,537,984.1
2002	279	200,891	3,571,835.1
2003	271	194,642	3,413,269.4
2004	286	204,022	3,420,662.6
2005	290	218,022	3,821,732.5
2006	284	239,166	4,615,626.1

Source: Estadísticas de la Industria Maquiladora de Exportación (INEGI), 2007.

Ciudad Juárez has the largest concentration of *maquiladoras* than any Mexican city, with 239,166 positions in 2006 (see Table 1.2). In 2000, nearly 45 percent of the urban employment of the city was related to *maquiladora* production; in other words, global activities. The value added of the *maquiladora* output reached US$3.4 billion and represented almost 20 percent of the value added produced by the *maquiladora* industry at the national level in 2006.

As a part of the transborder networks, El Paso provides myriad specialized services to *maquiladoras* in sectors, such as real estate, warehousing, transportation, logistics, computer systems, management, and other services. These sectors of El Paso's economy have received some benefits in terms of employment. The general rule of thumb is that a 10 percent increase in production in a neighboring Mexican city will increase employment in the bordering U.S. city by 1 to 2 percent (Cañas, Gilmer, and James, 2007).

The intensity of the transactions between these cities, specifically in terms of finance, investment and services, has been increasing. Between them, one can detect the formation of transnational urban systems.

IV. THE TRANSNATIONAL URBAN SYSTEM

Sassen (2007a) proposed five hypotheses to explain the importance of cities in the institutionalization of the global economic processes. The first hypothesis addresses the geographical dispersion of economic activities that characterize globalization, together with the simultaneous organizational integration of such activities that constitute a key factor to the growth of the central corporative functions. The second hypothesis states that these central functions are transformed into tertiary activities by a large number of global companies. The third hypothesis concerns itself with specialized service companies that take part of more complex global market benefits from city agglomeration economies. The fourth hypothesis is a derivative of the previous: the more companies develop tertiary functions, the more complex the decision-making processes about location get. These four hypotheses seek to modify the dominant discourse about globalization and technology that argue the end of the city as an economic unit (Sassen, 2007a). The fifth hypothesis argues that specialized service companies need to provide global services, but they end up creating a transnational network of branches that strengthen transborder transactions among cities. The provision of services from companies located in global cities to manufacturing production centers creates a network between global cities and cities with limited global functions. Sassen (2007a) refers to this as the emergence of a "transnational urban system" that is hierarchical in nature.

Sassen (2007a) introduced transborder operations as part of the transnational urban hierarchy. In the economic compounds of transborder networks, we can find an increase in the number of mergers and international acquisitions, the widening of foreign branches, and the increase in the number of national financial centers that are incorporated into the global financial market, such as Miami, Sao Paulo, Mexico City; Sidney, and Toronto (Sassen, 2006). These city cases strengthen the case for the hypothesis that specialized service companies need to provide global services and end up forming an international network of branches and strengthening networks of transborder transactions. Among the elements that prove the existence of a series of transborder networks of cities are the growing global financial markets and specialized services. Transborder network transactions require a reduction of the state's supervisory and regulatory functions to operate, generating an increasing importance of other nongovernmental organizations that aim to regulate the global markets—NGOs that are, however, voluntary and lacking the force of state authority.

The result is the reformulation of scales in terms of strategic places that articulated the new system. The weakening or partial disarticulation of the national into spatial units provides the necessary conditions to come up with new scales and spatial units (Sassen, 2007b). Among them we can mention subnational scale and, more specifically, region, cities, transborder areas that include two or more subnational entities and the supranational entities, such as the global electronic markets and economic free trade communities (Sassen, 2007b).

The transborder networks between global cities and cities with limited global functions are not only limited to economic issues but also to various other dimensions—not only political, cultural, and social but even legal and criminal systems (Sassen, 2007b). The form of extrastate articulation shows multiple empirical referents that can be divided in different components. The fact that a

"process or entity [is] located within territory of a sovereign state does not necessarily mean it is a national process or entity; it might be a localization of the global or a denationalized instance of the national. Though most such entities and processes are likely to be national, there is a growing need for empirical research to establish a range of instances which are not from materiality or imaginaries"

Author's translation, Sassan, 2007a: 44

An empirical referent is the variety of transborder networks between immigrant communities and communities in the countries. Also, there has been an increase in the use of transborder networks with cultural activities, such as international art markets. At the same time, other informal political networks have been created, such as transborder networks of environmentalists, human rights activists, and organizations against violence toward women, among others. We can say the same about international crime organizations (drugs, human smuggling), such as that analyzed by Monárrez in this volume. This contributes to the formation of transborder specific geographies where different cities interact (Sassen, 2007a). Also, transborder groups of industrial park developers, real-estate investors, and construction contractors have been created that operate transnationally, such as that analyzed by Fuentes and Peña in this volume. Other chapters in this volume examine the extent to which the educational systems mesh with these changes or reproduce inequalities that aggravate conditions for large numbers of youth soon to be employed in or fleeing from the region (this volume: Staudt and Méndez; Méndez).

VI. Conclusions

Globalization has been defined as the functional integration of dispersed economic activities (Dicken, 2003). In this process, participation occurs not only through the core "circuits" of globalization, which the majority of the scholarly works focus on, but also on the lower circuits of globalization, such as the U.S.-Mexico border region focused upon in this book. Four types of places have been defined as strategic in the global system network; (1) global cities; (2) offshore banking centers; (3) high-tech districts; and (4) export-processing zones (Sassen, 2006). Each place has different functions and global urban hierarchy, yet together they give meaning to the concept of globalization. Global cities are considered centers for servicing and financing international trade, investment, control and management of the industrial operations. While New York, London and Tokyo are considered the premier global cities, in recent years more cities have been incorporated to this list, such as Hong Kong, Singapore, and Shanghai. It is high time that the multi-scalar reality is also examined, such as what we do in this volume at the Paso del Norte metropolitan region.

This process occurs in a context whereby globalization reduces the relevance of the nation-state. That argument goes along the line that nation-state lost its capacity to govern and surrendered its sovereignty to transnational governing bodies, such as the International Monetary Fund (IMF) and World Bank and to global manufacturing industries.

The U.S.-Mexico border cities do not escape from parallel processes, given their integration into globalization as production centers. Border cities that participate in the transnational network of cities provide global services to the production centers, strengthening transactions among them all. But in this global layout, residents grapple with security, safety, and settlement issues. Inequalities among people are extreme, and international borderlines pose challenges to immigrants with limited citizenship claims on both their own country and their national border neighbor. Global production can deal devastating blows to the social and political fabric of a region, blows that make everyday life insecure for all, including young people undergoing increasingly standardized education for uncertain futures.

NOTES

1. A *maquiladora* is a labor-intensive assembly operation. In its simplest organizational form, a Mexican *maquiladora* plant imports inputs from a foreign country—most typically the United States—processes these inputs, and ships them back to the country of origin for finishing and sale.

2. Other authors use the concept of globalizing cities considering that globalization is a not a state but a process, a process that affects all cities in the world—if to varying degrees and varying ways—not only those at the top of the global hierarchy (Marcuse and Van Kempen, 2000; Staudt, 1998 on the region).

3. In 1965, the Mexican government established the Border Industrialization Program that sought to employ the large reserve of labor by promoting industrialization. To accomplish this, Mexico established a 20-kilometer wide "development" zone that stretched along the entire length of the U.S.-Mexico border. Binational agreements provided substantial incentives that encouraged U.S. plants to locate within the development zone. The *maquiladora* plant program was born out of Mexico's industrialization efforts (Esparza et al., 2004).
4. Multinational corporations have been the principal driving forces of globalization. Multinational manufacturing corporations have increasingly shifted production from developed to developing countries to exploit the advantages of inexpensive labor (Dowall, 1998).

Reference List

Beauregard, R. and A. Haila. (2000). "The Unavoidable Continuities of the City," in P. Marcuse and R. Van Kempen, eds., *Globalizing Cities: A New Spatial Order*. Malden, MA: Blackwell Publishing.

Bell, W. (1968). "The City, the Suburb and a Theory of Social Choice," in Greer S., ed. *The New Urbanization*, NY: St Martins.

Brenner, N. (2000). The Urban Question as a Scale Question: Reflections on Henry Lefebvre, Urban Theory and the Politics of Scale. *International Journal of Urban and Regional Research* 24.2, pp. 361–378.

———. (2002). Decoding the Newest "Metropolitan Regionalism" in the USA: A Critical Overview. *Cities* 19.1, pp. 3–21.

Brooks, David and Jonathan Fox, eds. (2002). Cross-Border Dialogues: U.S.-Mexico Social Movement Networking. La Jolla, CA: Center for U.S.-Mexican Studies, University of California, San Diego.

Cañas, J. and R. Coronado. (2002). "Maquiladora Industry: Past, Present and Future," *Business Frontier* 2. Federal Reserve Bank of Dallas.

Cañas, J., R. Coronado, and B. Gilmer. (2004). "Maquiladora Downturn: Structural Change or Cyclical Factors?" *Business Frontier* 2. Federal Reserve Bank of Dallas.

Cañas, J., B. Gilmer, and James. (2007). "El Paso Economy Sluggish in 2007: U.S. Slowdown Outweighs Fort Bliss Expansion." *Business Frontier* 2. Federal Reserve Bank of Dallas.

Castells, M. (1991). *The Informational City: Information Technology, Economic Restructuring and the Urban Regional Process*. Malden, MA: Blackwell Publishers.

Chakravorty, S. (1994). "Equity and the Big City." *Economic Geography* 70, 1, January.

Christopherson, S. (1983). "The Household and Class Formation: Determinants of Residential Location in Ciudad Juarez." *Environmental and Planning D: Society and Space* 1, pp. 323–338.

Davis, D. (2005). "Cities in a Global Context: A Brief Intellectual History." *International Journal of Urban and Regional Research* 29.1, pp. 92–109.

Dieleman, F. (1994). "Social rented housing; valuable asset or unsustainable burden?" *Urban Studies* 31, pp. 447–463.

Dicken, P. (2003). *Global Shift Reshaping the Global Economic Map in the 21st Century*, NY: Sage Publications.

Dowall, D. (1999). "Globalization, Structural Change and Urban Land Management." Lincoln Institute of Land Policy.

Edwards, M. E. (2007). *Regional and Urban Economics and Economic Development*. NY: Auerbach Publications.

Esparza, A., B. Waldorf, and Chavez Javier. (2004). "Localized Effects of Globalization: The Case of Ciudad Juarez, Chihuahua, Mexico. *Urban Geography* 25.2, pp. 120–138.

Friedmann, J. & G. Wolff (1982). "World City Formation: An Agenda for Research and Action." *International Journal of Urban and Regional Research* 15.1, pp. 269–283.

Friedmann, J. (1986). "The world city hypothesis." *Development and Change* 1, pp. 69–83.

Fuentes, C. (2001). "Urban Function and its Effect on Urban Structure: The Case of Ciudad Juárez, Chih." *Journal of Borderlands Studies*, XV(2).

Gilbert, A. (1998). "World Cities and the Urban Future: The View from Latin America in Lo. F and Yeun Y. (eds.) *Globalization and the World of Large Cities*. Tokyo, Japan: United Nations University Press.

Grunwald, J. and Flamm, K. (1985). *The Global Factory*. Washington, DC: Brookings Institution.

Hambleton, R. & Jill Gross. (2007). *Governing Cities in a Global Era*. NY: Palgrave Macmillan.

Hanson, H. G. (1996). "Economic Integration, Inter-industry Trade and Frontier Regions." *European Economic Review* 40, pp. 941–949.

Harvey, D. (1989). *The Condition of Postmodernity*. Oxford: Blackwell.

Heineberg, H. (2005). "Las Metropolis en el Proceso de Globalización." *Revista Bibliográfica de Geografía y Ciencias Sociales* X.563, pp. 1–24.

Herzog, L. (1991). Cross-national urban structure in the era of global cities: The U.S-Mexico transfrontier metropolis. *Urban Studies* 28.4, pp. 519–533.

INEGI. (2007). *Estadísticas de la Industria Maquiladora de Exportación*.

INEGI. (2005). *Estadísticas de la Industria Maquiladora de Exportación*.

Knox, P. (1995). "World Cities in a World System." in: Knox, P. and Taylor P. (eds), *World Cities in a World System*. Cambridge: Cambridge University Press.

Lo, F. and Marcotullio P. (2001). "Globalization and Urban Transformations in the Asia Pacific Region," in Lo and Marcotullio (eds.), *Globalization and the Sustainability of Cities in the Asia Pacific Region*. Tokyo: United Nations University.

Marcuse, P. (1989). "Dual City: A Muddy Metaphor for a Quartered City." *Journal of Urban and Regional Research* 13.4, pp. 697–708.

Marcuse, P. and Van Kempen R. (2000). "Introduction" in Marcuse P. and Van Kempen R. (eds.), *Globalizing Cities: A New Spatial Order*. Malden, MA: Blackwell Publishing.

Merton, R. (1968). *Social Theory and Social Structure*. Glencoe, London.

Mollenkopf and Castells M. (1991). *Dual City: Restructuring New York*. NY: Russell Sage Foundation.

Naím, Moises. (2005). *Illicit*. NY: Random House.

Patrick, J. (1996). "A Preliminary Assesment of NAFTA's Impact on the Texas Border Economy." *Journal of Borderlands Studies* 11, pp. 23–50

Phillips, K., and Cañas J. (2008). "Regional Business Cycle Integration Along the U.S.-Mexico Border." *Annals of Regional Science* 42.

REDCO. (2007). *Where the World Gets to Work*. El Paso: El Paso Regional Economic Corporation.

Sassen, S. (1991). *The Global City: New York, London, Tokyo*. Princeton: Princeton University Press.

———. (1998) *Globalization and its Discontents: Essays on the New Mobility of People and Money*. NY: The New Press.

———. (2001). "Global Cities and Global City-Regions: A Comparison," in Allen S. (ed.), *Global City-Regions, Trends, Theory, Policy*. NY: Oxford University Press.

———. (2006). *Cities in a World Economy*. Thousand Oaks, CA: Pine Forge Press.

———. (2007a). *Una Sociología de la Globalización*. Buenos Aires: Katz Editores.

———. (2007b). "Introduction" in Sassen (ed.), *Deciphering the Global*. NY: Routledge.

Sklair, J. W. (1989). *Assembling for Development*. Boston, MA: Unwin Hyman.

Smith, Jackie. (2008). *Social Movements for Global Democracy*. Baltimore: Johns Hopkins University Press.

Smith, C. (2000). *Inevitable Partnership: Understanding Mexico-U.S. Relations*. Boulder, CO: Lynne Rienner Publishers.

Staudt, Kathleen. 1998. *Free Trade? Informal Economies at the U.S.-Mexico Border*. Philadelphia: Temple University Press.

———, and Irasema Coronado. 2002. *Fronteras no Más: Toward Social Justice at the U.S.-Mexico Border*. NY: Palgrave USA.

Stoddard, Ellwyn R. 1987. *Maquila: Assembly Plants in Northern Mexico*. El Paso: Texas Western Press.

Storper, M. and Walker, R. (1983). The Spatial Division of Labour: Labour and the Location of Industries, in: L. Sawers and W. Tabb (eds.), *Sunbelt/Snowbelt; Urban Development and Restructuring*. NY: Oxford University Press.

Swyngedouw, E. (2000). Authoritarian Governance, Power, and the Politics of Rescaling. *Environment and Planning: Society and Space* 18, pp. 63–76.

Van Kempen, R. and Priemus, H. (1999). Revolution in Social Housing in the Netherlands: Changing Social Function and Legal Status of Housing Associations. Paper for the ENHR-CECODHAS-NETHUR workshop on Social Housing Policy.

Wright, M. (1997). "Crossing and Factory Frontier: Gender, Place and Poverty in the Mexican Maquiladora." *Antipode* 29, pp. 278–302.

Section I

Security and Safety in the Border Region

CHAPTER 2

DEATH IN A TRANSNATIONAL
METROPOLITAN REGION

Julia E. Monárrez Fragoso

Power is possible only if death is no longer free.

Jean Baudrillard, *Symbolic Exchange and Death*

Boundaries that once delimited nation-state territory are now inside the city, dividing, inscribing, and incubating new ways of action that have the ability to structure everyday life in quite different ways.

Anne Bartlett, *The City and the Self*

Since the year 2008, Ciudad Juárez is once again, nationally and internationally, capturing attention by the extreme, atrocious, and continuous violence that its citizens experience in various degrees and forms on a daily basis. One of the most well-known expressions of this violence is homicide: 1,607 people were killed that year.[1] This carnage, which left decapitated, dismembered, burned, mutilated bodies abandoned in humiliating positions, is mostly the result of the war between drug cartels that manifests itself in daily public gun battles. Other violent crimes include extortions, kidnappings, carjacking, and armed robberies, to name the most notorious. Even though the intensity of violence has been present in this city for at least two decades, inhabitants of Juárez speak about their life before and after 2008 (Turati, 2009: 8) when President Felipe Calderón declared the

War against the Drug Cartels in the years 2006–2007. Within this frame, Ciudad Juárez is presented as a city that has "always been rough" and is compared with El Paso, Texas: the Mexican side is violent and the United States side is peaceful (McKinley, 2009). In this vision and I may say in the vision of many people: *these two cities are two worlds apart.*

With these last words in mind, I want to reflect on what is behind the verdict—two worlds apart—concerning these recent increases in homicide.[2] It appears that space and the state are strangely distant and set apart from the kind of violence produced by the Mexican cartels. It also appears that violence is a Mexican border phenomenon that stops once you cross the Río Bravo (Rio Grande in the United States). It looks as if violence is part of the local character of the *juarenses,* and in this light, the bloodshed has converted the *"capital mundial de las maquiladoras"* (world capital of export-processing factories) into the *"tiradero nacional de muertos"* (national dump of corpses) (Turati, 2009: 11). One in every four "executions"[3] in México took place in the state of Chihuahua. This northern border region has emerged in 2008 as the most violent state in the whole country with a total of 2,006 murders, 80 percent of which were committed in Ciudad Juárez (Ortega, 2009a).[4]

President Calderón has been congratulated by his U.S. counterparts, ex-President George W. Bush and recently President Barack H. Obama, for his firm stand against drug trafficking. Paradoxically, this case of Juárez has been used not only to praise but also to shame other nations, for e.g., in a *Foreign Policy* article, Caracas was cited as having an average of 130 murders per 100,000 inhabitants, topping that of Ciudad Juárez. Hugo Chávez, the Venezuelan President, declared it "infamous" to classify a city in his nation as the most dangerous in the world (El Mañana, 2009). And nobody wants to be compared with Ciudad Juárez or México, especially when some U.S. security experts warn that México comes closer to becoming a "failed state" (Althaus, 2009).

ARGUMENT AND THEORETICAL PERSPECTIVES

This chapter investigates the premise of "two worlds apart," taking into consideration the togetherness of these two worlds. If this statement prevails—following Baudrillard—then, "each term of the disjunction excludes the other, which eventually becomes its imaginary"(1993: 133). On the subject of this "new" violence in this transborder geography, it is important to link the two parts together; if not, it reawakens the antagonism of the opposite principles of good and evil. A general definition of murder is "when a human being kills another on purpose and intentionally" (Centro Nacional para Víctimas del Crimen, 2002). Homicides are also classified as violent deaths. Drawing from Baudrillard's Marxist heritage, death deserves a social definition: that is why "the real materiality of death . . . lies in its *form* which is always the form of a social relation" (1993: 131). This social relation involves criminal networks of drug traffickers in an illegally organized global economy.

Saskia Sassen (1998) affirms that economic globalization reconfigured two basic properties of the nation-state: territoriality (territorial organization of economic activity) and sovereignty (the organization of political power). In relation to the first property, Ciudad Juárez has been transformed since the late 1960s into an industrialized city of export-manufacturing zones; in fact, one in every four employees in México's export-processing sector is from this city (see Fig. 2.1). With regard to the second property, violence and public insecurity are two of the Mexican nation's main concerns.[5] Sassen also states that the nation state as a "social container" is no longer its firmest attribute, because in the globalization process, the state is becoming

Figure 2.1 Billboard: One in four employees in Mexico's manufacturing export-processing work in Ciudad Juárez
Source: Photo by Elvia Liliana Chaparro Vielma, Ciudad Juárez, February 20, 2009.

disarticulated, partially but with intensity and *different degrees of disarticulation* (Sassen, 2007: 11–12). She also illuminates this situation when she explains that it is important to move beyond the consideration of globalization in terms of interdependence and formations of exclusively global institutions. Globalization must be reexamined in terms of the national; in this way, we can open new avenues to investigate unexplored multiple possibilities (Sassen, 2007: 12). At present, there is an increase in the variety of transborder ties for economic transactions that in the past were thought of as practically impossible to achieve; this applies to international criminal networks as well (Sassen, 2007: 40). So, to live in a city means to be part of circuits of high intensity and density and to be part of international networks (Sassen, 2007: 39). With these theoretical guidelines in mind, the crossexamination would be as follows. Although the fact that extreme violence is located in the Mexican state does not necessarily mean that it is only a national process, could it be that the Mexican territory is a localization of a more global phenomenon? To synthesize, we can ask how national and international elements interact together as "two worlds apart" or as the togetherness of two worlds in the Ciudad Juárez–El Paso metropolitan region.

On March 28, 2008, the three levels of government—federal, state, and municipal—launched in Ciudad Juárez the Operativo Conjunto Chihuahua (Joint Operation Chihuahua). To a community tired of violence, it promised to weaken the financial infrastructure of drug traffickers, to recover public spaces for the inhabitants of Juárez, and to offer security for the population and their families. Also, they spoke—in this war against the cartels—about coordination, intelligence, and the arrival of special groups. In reality, the only truly organized people were the cartels fighting against the other cartels, the cartels against the State, and the cartels against the population.

For organized crime expert Carlos Flores, the deterioration of the financial structure seems unrealistic. He mentions, as an example, one element of this fallacy that cocaine impounded by México is only 3 percent of the total that has been captured according to the 2007 World Drug Report of the United Nations. Even Spain, geographically far from the United States, procures 7 percent of this drug. For Flores, the violence has been transformed into a variety of criminal behaviors and threats displayed in many ways (such as in videos or text messages, the use of military arms), authorities worn out with the fighting between opposing criminal organizations, and the feudalization of the cities by organized and disorganized criminal organizations, who "charge protection" for illegal and legal business

(2009). Under these circumstances, public spaces—instead of being recovered—have diminished but insecurity has increased in private and semiprivate spaces. From August 2008 to February 2009, the Director of the Junta Municipal de Aguas y Saneamiento (Municipal Water and Sanitation Department) declared that 15,000 houses have been abandoned in Ciudad Juárez (González, 2009: 3b). People are deserting the city; some go to southern México and others to El Paso, Texas.[6] As a matter a fact, houses for sale exceed the demand for them.

José Reyes Baeza, the Governor of Chihuahua, was attacked by a commando who killed one of his bodyguards in February 2009. José Reyes Ferriz, the Mayor of Ciudad Juárez, has been threatened (see Text Box 2.1 below). Terror prevails in the streets of Ciudad Juárez—declared the most violent city in the Mexican Republic—and it also affects the surrounding areas of El Paso, Texas, the third-safest city in the United States. And as Professor Tony Payan declares of these two cities, "[t]he contacts from citizen to citizen, and from group to group, are practically suspended and, from my point of view, that affects the community, because people begin to feel that we are already not a binational community, but two completely closed communities" (personal translation in Rodríguez Nieto, 2009a).

2.1   The threat

REYES FERRIS
TOMASTE BUENA DECISION
AL DEJAR QE SE FUERA EL
MUGROSO DE ORDUÑA PERO
SI SIGUES SOLAPANDO A MAS
CULEROS COMO EL ATI NO TE
VAMOS A PEDIR LA RENUNCIA
TE VAMOS A CORTAR LA
CABESA JUNTO CON TU FAMILIA AUNQUE ESTE EN
EL PASO TEXAS[7]

In this context, my focus of investigation is on the meaning and implications of death in a transnational metropolitan region. For this analysis, I use a combination of theories that study death and globalization developed by Jean Baudrillard and Saskia Sassen. My objective is to show how death in Ciudad Juárez is part of "international geography." To do this, I organize my discussion in two main sections: the first one will show how these deaths are a process of the disarticulation of Latin American democracies; the second will discuss death as a symbolic interchange, as a matter of giving and receiving between different actors and nations. My analysis attends to the importance of the concept of space for the flow of drugs and other criminal activities and presumably the impediments to violence crossing over into the United States.

LATIN AMERICAN POROSITY

Pierre Salama says that violence in most Latin American countries is very severe and its intensity more manifest. Although it is very difficult to measure the various degrees of violence, homicide is a very reliable indicator. Also, in every country violence has a spatial distribution. Two forces produced this spatial distribution: the absence of the state in the 1980s and the neoliberal coercion of the 1990s. Under these economic restrictions, states privileged the market and reduced its role in functions such as urban infrastructure, schools, and health care for its population. In this scenario, "the State controls the Nation even less; the territory then turns *porous*" (2008: 4).

This permeability, following Salama, in which the State abandoned some *barrios* (neighborhoods) or regions, causes the presence of a parallel power personified in the guerrillas—the *maras* or the *mafias*—with no official power but de facto power. They control drug trafficking, kidnapping, and unlawful gambling. They are generators of extreme violence. But this is not all; in these countries, there is deep public distrust of institutions. Access to rights is an illusion, and gaps exist between citizens, with some excluded, subject to inequalities without compensation, and "an incomplete control of the maintenance of the national territory by the State" (2008: 4).

The problems of violence and public insecurity that prevail in Latin America are part of the Mexican experience. According to the Fifth National Survey of Insecurity (Quinta Encuesta Nacional sobre Inseguridad, or ENSI-5), in the year 2007, 11 percent of the Mexican population over 18 years of age were victims of one act of crime. The national rate of victimization was 10,480 crimes per 100,000 population. This figure is markedly higher than what some countries, such as most members of the European Union, Australia, Canada, Chile, and Japan, consider an acceptable level of public safety. By the same token, the rates of victimization in México are higher compared to the United States, Canada, and Australia. Within the Mexican nation, the Distrito Federal (Federal District), Estado de México, Tamaulipas, Baja California, and Chihuahua comprise the major crime entities. This refutes the thesis that crime is generated by poverty, because these states are not the poorest in the country (ENSI-5, 2008). Ciudad Juárez is a complex phenomenon. It has many facets, and it approaches international infamy with its record of female homicides— known as *feminicides*—and the "executions" of men tied to drug trafficking. Nevertheless, these violent deaths are not the only ones that happen in this frontier-city setting. Since the 1980s, violence and public insecurity have affected the coexistence and the harmonious development in this border city of the north of México (Monárrez, 2005). An injured, aggrieved, fearful, and distrustful citizenry experiences, on a daily basis, generalized violence, corruption, impunity, organized crime, drug trafficking, murders, robbery, criminal juvenile conduct, frustrated programs of security, distrust in police bodies, and discretional procedures in the application of the law. The institutions in charge of justice at the three levels of government—municipal, state, and federal—have not been able to provide a safe, secure place at this frontier (Monárrez and García, 2007).

TO DIE IN CIUDAD JUÁREZ

Ciudad Juárez resembles a public cemetery; it is a modern necropolis. Yet these are not natural deaths but artificial ones, and we experience them as socially symbolic events, like a sacrifice *"through the will of the group"* (Baudrillard, 1993: 165). The executed—the ones that are connected to the criminal groups—will sooner or later die, because in Ciudad Juárez, social memory has been engaged through personal experiences or through the eyes of newspapers and mass media that report the killings. This is not a new phenomenon; the rate of murder in this city has been very high and continuous since the mid-1980s. But the sheer scope and size of murder totals have changed. Civil society has experienced these atrocities under the umbrella of war. War is not a new word for this frontier, given the use of assault weapons and warlike discourse: the city's homicides are described as executions; and the parties to deaths are sometimes called troops, commanders, chiefs, or traitors.

The state of Chihuahua has experimented with democracy for at least three decades, with transitions of two political parties in power: Partido Acción Nacional (PAN) and Partido Revolucionario

Institucional (PRI). Neither party has been able to provide security or eradicate organized crime; on the contrary, crime flourishes. When ex-Governor Francisco Barrio was in power (1992–1998), his Deputy State Attorney General, Jorge López Molinar, offered a solution to civil society regarding violence against women and the slaughter between the drug cartels—"to apply a curfew so all good citizens stay in their homes with their families, and the bad ones stay on the street" (Najar, 1998: 3).

In the year 2003, when Amnesty International presented its report *Intolerable Killings* regarding *feminicide* in Chihuahua, Governor Patricio Martínez (1998–2004) refused to accept its recommendations. With cynicism, he made it seem as though Amnesty International was responsible for carelessness around the reporting of homicides. He asked the organization "How many of them [the assassinated] have been massacred by the mafias? And, what has Amnesty International done to stop it? Or is it that the executed dead persons have no human rights?" (Ulate, 2003). He forgot that he was the one responsible and accountable for the answers to these questions. On this matter, these public men need to create the "Other" so they can mercilessly condemn the object of their indifference and can be judged as good, law-abiding citizens.

This kind of discrimination did not only emanate from those in political power, but also from some segments of society—especially the business elite—who cared little about these killings, as long as they didn't affect the city's image and ability to attract international investment. During these years, I have heard expressions from common citizens such as: "Let them kill themselves; they are drug dealers"; "If they continue this slaughter, the city will be cleaned up;" "Please, '*malandros*,' [bad guys], kill yourselves out of the city"; and "We don't have to worry or pity them; they are poisoning the very young." This rhetoric is a genealogy of discrimination on the basis of the "Inhuman" compared to the "normal human" (Baudrillard, 1993: 125–126). The rhetoric also implies the winning or losing of territories and the distinction of good and bad zones: provinces that are designed for living and, others, for dying.

With these discourses, law-abiding citizen dismissed the constant homicides perpetuated before 2008, and "little by little, *the dead cease to exist*" (126). That is why they were buried as unknown or unidentified persons in the *fosa común* (common grave), simply leaving them as "natural residues" (Baudrillard, 1993: 165). Justice did not trouble to identify them or prosecute or dismantle the groups. Justice did not care about those canned bodies in cement, or those bodies wrapped in plastic bags as trash; neither did justice concern itself with those countless numbers of skeletons buried in the *narcofosas* (narco-graves). Authorities and some segments of society categorized values associated with life and death: which bodies are worthy of importance; what lifestyles are considered to be a "life"; what lives are worth protecting; what lives are worth saving; and what lives deserve to be mourned? (Butler, 2002). Even though these confrontations—killing innocent people in the streets, restaurants, and bars—occurred a long time ago, the sediments of an absent and disarticulated State continue growing in Ciudad Juárez. Consequently when war was declared, this border was ready to receive more disarticulated bodies:

> This is precisely the way in which power will later be instituted between the subject separated from its body, between the individual separated from its social body, . . . the archetype of this operation is the separation between a group and its dead, or between each of us today and our own deaths.
>
> Baudrillard, 1993: 130.

Supposedly, this was a segmented violence; not all citizens suffered directly the consequences of these killings. Supposedly, drugs were just for the "Americans." As a result of this indolence, the newspaper *Reforma* estimates that 9,000 persons were executed from 2000 to 2006 in the whole country (Flores, 2009). And statistics from the Encuesta Nacional de Adicciones [National Survey of Addictions], sampling more than 50,000 homes between 2002 and 2008, reveal that in only six years, the number of persons addicted to illegal drugs increased by 50 percent, and the number of those who had consumed illegal drugs within Mexican territory increased by 30 percent (Encuesta Nacional de Adicciones, 2008). Despite patrols in Ciudad Juárez by 2,000 soldiers plus the police and new recruits from campaigns offering higher salaries, crime increased by 500 percent in 2008.

Many were killed including police officers, lawyers, thugs, and others. Those who refuse the euphemistic "protection charging" for their business were killed. Restaurants, discos, and bars were burned, presumably by criminals related to the drug business. Gangs such as HBO, Madre del Silencio (Mother of Silence), Doble AA, and Bufones *y* Cacos 90 [Buffoons and Thieves 90] were identified as the ones who provide *sicarios*[8] and sell and distribute drugs (Villalpando,

2008). These young men reside in poor settlements. Police killings were traced to *sicarios* in one or another cartel. In their *narco*messages, they presented themselves as members of two different groups called *"monta perros"* (mounted dogs) or *"marranos"* (swine). Authorities remained absent and mute.

Villapando also mentions that 3,000 persons from Ciudad Juárez went to live in El Paso, Texas.* At the same time, both the University of Texas at El Paso and New Mexico State University in Las Cruces, New Mexico, transmitted U.S. State Department messages warning students, faculty members, and staff about the dangers of going to Ciudad Juárez. Meanwhile, billboards from political parties and religious groups flooded the city. (see Figure 2.2)

The Greens, Partido Verde Ecologista de México (PVEM), offered the death penalty as a solution to death and terror. Religious groups presented prayer and the figure of Christ as a solution for the violence: We pray for Ciudad Juarez; it's what we must do. Not only was Ciudad Juárez distanced from adjacent U.S. cities, but it was also out of favor with God.

Figure 2.2 Billboard: Let us pray; we need it. Taken in Ciudad Juárez
Source: Photo by Elvia Liliana Chaparro Vielma, Ciudad Juárez, February 20, 2009.

* The El Paso Police Department in 2010 estimates that this number has increased to at least 30,000.

Two Worlds Apart, not at all: Space Matters and It Is Geographically Determined

Space matters. México is situated between the countries of the Andean[9] region that produce cocaine and the United States, which is the most lucrative market in the world for the consumption of illegal drugs and the largest consumer of cocaine; 90 percent of the cocaine consumed in the United States passes through México (WOLA Director's Testimony before Congress, 2007).

In this testimony, Joy Olson evokes history and explains that México was an important route for marijuana in the nineteenth and twentieth century. Cocaine was viewed as a problem for the United States. In México, it was neither a challenge for public security nor was there a problem of consumption. All this changed in the 1980s when the U.S. government decided to interdict the entry of drugs through cities of Florida, such as Miami. Colombian traffickers made alliances with the Mexican traffickers and used their routes to introduce cocaine to the United States. Since then, northern Mexican states, especially the border cities, started to play an important role (ibid).

Homicides—the focus of analysis—increased rapidly in Ciudad Juárez. For example, the number of men who died violently from 1985 to 1991 was 421; this number represents a weighted rate of 15.9 men killed per 100,000 of the male population of 415,157. In those same years, with 38 women murdered, the numbers represented a weighted rate of 0.47 per 100,000 inhabitants in a population of 422,052 females. In 1992, the number was 55; this figure represents a rate of 6.3 men killed per 100,000 male populations. In 1993, 125 homicides were registered; these cases doubled the rate to 13.6 in a male population of 458,023. Intriguingly, in those same years, women's murders went from 6 cases with a rate of 1.4 per 100,000 of the female populations to 24 killed. These cases quadrupled the rate to 5.2 of a female population of 462,129 (INEGI: 1994). Death established its route too.

But drug-related killing also cost the lives of American citizens. Drawing on data from the U.S. Department of State about the six U.S.-Mexican border states, from 2005 to 2008, 140 American citizens were killed. But in Ciudad Juárez alone, in 2008, 30 persons were violently killed (Rodríguez Nieto, 2009b). From the tactics adopted, those deaths appeared to be drug-related murders and, in this context, relationships between the two cities have worsened. The city of El Paso, too, has been experiencing, through the killing of its citizens, violent acts inflicted upon the bodies of the executed—though to a lesser degree.

Once again, Professor Payan provides insight on these killings: "Drug trafficking networks are not necessarily of Mexican citizens; in many of them, American citizens or those with double nationality are involved too. If there is a war between cartels, sooner or later north American citizens will be involved in that matter" (personal translation, Rodríguez Nieto, 2009a). According to the National Gang Threat Assessment 2009, international drug cartels are increasing their dependence on U.S. gangs to distribute drugs in the country, whether cocaine, marijuana, or heroin. Gang members who operate on the Mexican-U.S. border have established more connections with the major drug organizations. The names of some of them are Fresno Bull Dogs, Florencia 13, Tango Blast, Latin Disciples, and United Blood Nation (National Gang Intelligence Center, 2009).

The corridor of the death runs the same path as the corridor of the drugs, and as Baudrillard states: "Power is established on death's border. It will subsequently be sustained by further separations (the soul and the body, the male and the female, good and evil, etc.) that have infinite ramifications, but the principal separation is between life and death" (Baudrillard, 1993: 130). That is why it is not unexpected that the Texan Governor Rick Perry declared in February, from the very city of El Paso, the need for military forces to impede drug violence that spills over the U.S. border. Katherine Cesinger, Governor Rick Perry's spokesperson, declared to FOXNews.com that Texas is preparing a contingency plan in case murders cross the border and in case thousands of Mexicans seek refuge in the United States. One of their major concerns was the alliance of transnational gangs that work in combination with the Mexican drug cartels (Agencias, 2009: 8A).

But how is it possible to contain the spillover of violence to the other side of the border if this is a symbolic interaction, a matter of giving and receiving between the two nations? It is true that when the U.S. diverts the drug routes through México, Mexican political leaders continue to share responsibility for this drug corruption and the growth of a considerable number of addicts in its population. However, as Joy Olson questions:

> How can México succeed in reducing corruption and confronting violence when the drug trafficking organizations are awash in drug-related profits and have ready access to guns from U.S. markets? What steps is the U.S. taking to expand and improve the nation's addictions treatment system? What measures are being taken to strengthen

enforcement of regulations governing U.S. gun sales, particularly in border areas, to make it more difficult for weapons sold in our country to be illegally trafficked into México? What is being done to more effectively combat money laundering in the United States?

WOLA Director's testimony before Congress, 2007

The Bureau of Alcohol, Tobacco, Firearms and Explosives (ATF) has declared that *narco*-violence along the border and in México's interior is supported with arms. This same agency acknowledges that 90 percent of arms recovered at crime scenes are from the United States (U.S. Embassy, México City, 2009). Buying arms from U.S. civilians is a very easy transaction. In México, Mexican civilians require a permit from the military forces, and high caliber guns are prohibited. More than 6,600 licensed[10] gun dealers sell weapons along the U.S.-Mexican border. The Mexican ambassador Arturo Sarukhan, in a lecture given at the Institute of the Americas in the University of California in San Diego, asked the administration of President Barack Obama to stop the flow of arms that support organized crime in México (El Universal, 2009: 16A). Even though media campaigns (radio, television, and poster) in some cities of Texas warn the population not to buy arms for third persons as a way to combat illegal introduction to México (Milenio.com, 2008), arms trafficking continues.

In 2005, the United Status become aware of growing drug consumption among persons aged 12–17 in the border states of Arizona, New Mexico, and Texas, along with an increase in cocaine trafficking from México in these same areas and California as well (United Nations, 2007).[11]

Money laundering in the United States has been declared a national threat, because the volume of this "dirty money circulating through the United States is undeniably vast and criminals are enjoying new advantages with globalization and the advent of new financial services" (Working Group, 2005: i). Globalization has made the financial system vulnerable by incorporating new technologies of saving, investing, and circulating money. Such vulnerabilities are exploited with the use of the Internet to open accounts and the loss of face-to-face customer-bank relationships. Paradoxically, domestic payment networks do not connect with each other; these transactions are hard to track; and criminals have found that money service business such as paper checks, money orders, and cashier's checks are easier to move internationally and less likely to be detected (Working Group, 2005). This circulation of illicit money is geographically concentrated in some cities of the United States, such as New York,

California, Florida, Colorado, New Jersey, Massachusetts, Georgia, Illinois, Arizona, and Texas. And with respect to laundered money, México is its principal destination, followed by Russia, Colombia, the Dominican Republic, and some sites in Central and South America (Working Group, 2005). Cash associated with illicit narcotics flows from the United States to México, especially through the southwest border, and it follows the same route through which narcotics enter the U.S. market. On the Mexican side of the border, *casas de cambio* (money exchanges) are attractive places to launder money (Working Group, 2005).

In Washington, during a seminar at the Heritage Foundation, Retired General Barry McCaffrey, ex-U.S. drug czar, asked President Obama for immediate help for México because this country is living a national emergency (Díaz Briseño, 2009: 16A). On the other side, Chihuahua Governor José Reyes Baeza requested the federal government to intensify its efforts because "we are living a war." He claimed that kidnapping was eradicated in this region, but with this fight between cartels, it started again, as had other crimes, such as extortion and the selling of protection (Figueroa, 2009: 1A, 4A).

Operación Conjunta Chihuahua was reformulated on February 26; military and judicial staff from México City came to Ciudad Juárez. The secretaries of National Defense, of the Navy, and of the Interior (*Gobernación*), promised to send 5,000 soldiers to combat organized and disorganized crime. Interior Secretary Fernando Goméz Mont said "We are not going to yield even one centimeter of the plaza" (Ortega, 2009b). (see Fig. 2.3).

In this international and national frame, President Felipe Calderón on February 27, 2009, expressed discomfort because the United States. was not doing its part in this war (AP, 2009). The United States answered through its Director of National Intelligence, Admiral Dennis Blair, who stated that his country was eroded by corruption and *narcos* from México and that President Calderón was unable to keep his territory under control (La Jornada, 2009a). Interior Secretary Fernando Goméz Mont replied that "there is not a single space of the Mexican territory that escapes to the direction of the State" (La Jornada, 2009b). But this is precisely the key issue: Mexican territory is becoming disarticulated and the United States is afraid of the effects of this disarticulation in its own territory. They are not two worlds apart; they are united by the organized crime and its diverse manifestations and ramifications. México, and consequently Ciudad Juarez, is a national entity that has been denationalized by this component—organized crime—of the global economy, with the

Figure 2.3   Mexican military vehicles advancing into the interior of Ciudad Juárez
Source: Héctor Dayer, Periódico Norte De Ciudad Juárez.

power of the organized crime that manipulates and administers death as living proof of the unbundling of the nation-state. But at the same time, the U.S. border also is becoming porous. Its peace lies in the exchange of drug routes, the lucrative business of drugs, and the violent deaths on the Mexican side.

CONCLUSION

As this chapter has shown, death is a form of social relation. This form is organized crime with spatial distributions of criminals and crimes associated with drug trafficking. Ciudad Juárez is for México, if not yet a failed state, surely an example of its disarticulation. Yet it is important to clarify that this unbundling is also characterized by national structures of social abandonment for its citizens and by corruption, corroded further by drug trafficking. But also this chapter has also demonstrated how U.S. criminal drug trafficking elements interact with those in México and are part of the same system: money laundering, drug addiction, and affiliation with gangs. That is why violence can spill over to the other side—the United States. Homicides are part of the history of Ciudad Juárez; this terminal and unstoppable violence is moving the two nations together. Cadavers carry with them a political message (Scabuzzo, 2008): they are not worthy of the civilized ritual of death, they are dumped like the debris of a fragmented war between cartels as reminders of decisions that are taken outside the nation and of residues of an absent state and city behind its dead persons. They are sacrificed in order to monopolize and strengthen the transnational economic benefits of this shadow economy. Even though the main networks of drug trafficking are inserted in Mexican national territory, "this does not imply that regulatory existing frames at national levels will be able to regulate them" (Sassen, 2007: 44). It seems that the functions of regulation are increasingly transferred to a set of regulatory crossborder emergent networks in the United States because "[so] long as the U.S. market for illicit drugs remains so large and lucrative, successful disruption of drug production and trafficking displaces trafficking operations and the devastation they entail to new areas" (WOLA Director's Testimony before Congress, 2007: 2). Ciudad Juárez is devastated. Could it be possible that this public cemetery, this new necropolis, can change the rules of the drug market instead of accepting the disarticulation of one nation and the porosity of the other because one side is violent and the other peaceful?

Acknowledgment: I would like to thank the Fondo Mixto CONACyT-Chihuahua for its support for the research project "Estrategias para la prevención e intervención del feminicido juarense" clave CHIH-2007 CO1-79934 and to Diana L. García Salinas and Liliana Chaparro for their assistance in this chapter.

NOTES

1. 97 of them were *feminicides* (femicide). Here, I am using the term regardless of the absence of a gender motive for the killing of a woman.
2. The first two months of year 2009, more than 300 persons were killed.
3. To execute, means to kill a condemned culprit (Real Academia Española de la Lengua, 2009). These killings are also known as the "ajuste de cuentas"—"War between cartels."
4. Ciudad Juárez surpassed 11 times the national rate and more than 25 times the international rate of murders for every 100,000 inhabitants, with a complete estimation in 123.61 cases. Killings that occurred in the first month of 2009 on this border represent a

proportional increase projected for 2009 that raises the figure to 148.61 murders for every 100,000 inhabitants (Ortega, 2009a).
5. ENSI 2002–2007 (National Survey of Insecurity)
6. It would be very interesting to know how many Mexicans have abandoned the Mexican side of the border to live on the United States side of the border.
7. Newspapers from Ciudad Juárez didn't grant permission to use this photograph, that is why I cite the threat to the mayor. Reyes Ferris [sic]. You made a good decision letting go of the "dirty" Orduña [police chief]. But if you continue overlapping more fuckers and helping people that you know, we are not going to ask you for your resignation. We are going to cut off your head along with your family even though they are in El Paso Texas. http://www.mexicowebcast.com.mx/index. php?loc=l&inner=article&id=22446 Consulted February 23, 2009.
8. Wage-earning killer.
9. Colombia, Perú, and Bolivia. 2
10. Illegal sale is another channel to obtain arms.
11. The United States is not the only country with increasing numbers of drug addicts. Canada and Europe have a significant rise in this number as well. Also, cocaine is only one among the various illicit drugs that people produce, sell, buy, and consume.

REFERENCE LIST

Agencias. (February 13, 2009). "Prepara Texas plan de contingencia." *El Diario*, Ciudad Juárez, Chih., p. 8A.
Althaus, Dudley. (January 25, 2009). "Darkening days is Juarez." *Houston Chronicle.* http://www.chron.com/disp/story.mpl/headline/world/6228949.html, consulted January 25, 2009.
Amnesty International, Mexico. (2003). Intolerable killings: Ten years of abductions and murders in Ciudad Juárez and Chihuahua. http://web.amnesty. org/library/Index/ENGAMR410272003, consulted August 2003.
AP. (February 27, 2009). "México: Estados Unidos debe combatir el tráfico de armas al país." http://noticias.aol.com/articulos/_a/México-estados-unidos-debe-combatir-el/n20090227192609990003, consulted March 11, 2009.
Baudrillard, Jean. (1993). *Symbolic Exchange and Death.* Sage: London.
Butler, Judith. (2002). *Cuerpos que importan.* Alcira Bixio (trans.). Paidós, México.
Centro Nacional Para Víctimas del Crimen. (February, 2002)."Víctimas secundarias al homicidio." http://www.nm-victimsrights.org/pdf/HomicideCovictimization_sp.pdf, consulted August 20, 2007.
Díaz Briceño, José. (February 14, 2009). "Alarman narcos en EU." *El Diario*, Ciudad Juárez, Chih., p. 16A.

El Mañana. (February 4, 2009). "Acentúa Chávez inseguridad en México." http://www.eluniversal.com.mx/notas/574038.html.

El Universal. (February 14, 2009). "Insisten en frenar armas." *El Diario,* Ciudad Juárez, Chih., p. 16A.

Encuesta Nacional de Adicciones. (2008). *Boletín Informativo,* Premedi Test, México. http://www.premeditest.com.mx/?cont=boletin&id=31, consulted March 2, 2008.

ENSI-5. (2008). Quinta Encuesta Nacional sobre Inseguridad, ICESI. http://www.icesi.org.mx/documentos/encuestas/encuestasNacionales/ ENSI-5.pdf, consulted February 14, 2009.

Figueroa, Martha Elba. (February 13, 2009). "Estamos viviendo una guerra: Baeza." *El Diario,* Ciudad Juárez, Chih., pp. 1A, 4A.

Flores, Carlos. (February 23, 2009). "La seguridad nacional, narcotráfico y fuerzas armadas." paper presented at the session Iniciativa Mérida y el crimen organizado: diagnóstico y desafío en las Américas. Under Seminario Seguridad y desarrollo en la relación México Estados Unidos Canadá, El Colegio de la Frontera Norte, Tijuana, B. C. http://www. colef.mx/streaming/endemanda.asp?video=5.

González, Félix A. (February 8, 2009). "Abandonan 15 mil casas en los últimos seis meses," *NORTE de Ciudad Juárez.* pp. 1A, 3B.

INEGI. (1994). Mortalidad, Estadísticas Sociodemográficas, Vol. III, CD, México, (1985–1993).

La Jornada. (March 11, 2009). "Corrupción y narco en México erosionan a EU: Denis Blair." http://www.jornada.unam.mx/2009/03/11/index. php?section=politica&article=003n1pol#texto.

La Jornada. (March 11, 2009). "Desafortunadas, las declaraciones del director de inteligencia de EU: Gómez Mont." http://www.jornada. unam.mx/ultimas/2009/03/11/desafortunadas-las-declaraciones-del-director-de-inteligencia-de-eu-gomez-mont.

McKinley Jr., James C. (January 23, 2009). "Two sides of a border: One violent, one peaceful," *NewYork Times.* http://www.nytimes. com/2009/01/23/us/23elpaso.html, consulted January 23, 2009.

Monárrez Fragoso, Julia E. (2005). Violencia e (in)seguridad ciudadana en Ciudad Juárez," *Diagnóstico Geo-socioeconómico de Ciudad Juárez y su sociedad,* Luis Cervera (coord.). Instituto Nacional de las Mujeres y El Colegio de la Frontera Norte, Ciudad Juárez, CD. pp, 273–315. http:// cedoc.inmujeres.gob.mx/documentos_download/100882.pdf.

Milenio.com. (September 30, 2008). "Buscan reducir venta de armas de fuego en ciudades de Texas." http://www.milenio.com/node/88191, consulted March 11, 2009.

Monárrez Fragoso, Julia E., and Jaime García. (2007). "Violencia inseguridad pública en la frontera norte de México." Article submitted for consideration to be published.

Najar, Alberto. (January 25,1998). "Violadas y asesinadas en Ciudad Juárez. Impunidad en el desierto. La normalidad de la violencia, según Barrio." *La Jornada,* México, D. F., p. 3.

National Gang Intelligence Center. (2009). *National Gang Threat Assessment 2009*, Washington, D. C. January. http://www.fbi.gov/publications/ngta2009.pdf.

Ortega, Luis Carlos. (February 10, 2009a). "Aumentan asesinatos en enero 392% más que el año pasado," *NORTE de Ciudad Juárez*.

———. (March 1, 2009b). "Juárez: ingobernabilidad y sin jefe civil policíaco." *NORTE de Ciudad Juárez*. http://www.nortedeciudadjuarez.com/paginas/frontera/fta2.html. http://www.nortedeciudadjuarez.com/paginas/seguridad/seg7.html, consulted February 10, 2009.

Rodríguez Nieto, Sandra. (February 10, 2009a). "Destruye la violencia la vida binacional, alerta académico." *El Diario*, Ciudad Juárez, Chih. http://www.diario.com.mx/nota.php?notaid=1bb5ce5c88e2895df9d57 96310f4e363.

Rodríguez Nieto, Sandra. (February 8, 2009b). "Fueron asesinados 30 estadounidenses aquí en 2008; el año anterior, sólo tres." *El Diario*, Ciudad Juárez, Chih. http://www.diario.com.mx/nota.php?notaid=19c1 d98f3b8c7961b6c00aace9cc8d3e, consulted February 8, 2009.

Salama, Pierre. (January 28, 2008). *Informe sobre la violencia en América Latina*. Informe para el Consejo de Europa DG IV, Paris, March 1, 2008. Paper presented at the Seminario Seguridad y desarrollo en la relación México Estados Unidos Canadá, El Colegio de la Frontera Norte, Ciudad Juárez, Chihuahua. http://www.colef.mx/streaming/endemanda.asp?video=5.

Sassen, Saskia. (1998). *Globalization and Its Discontents*. The New Press, New York.

Sassen, Saskia. (2007). *Una Sociología de la globalización*. María Victoria Rodil (trans.) Katz, Buenos Aires.

Scabuzo, Claudia. (July 14, 2008). "La sociedad de los muertos vivos." *La terminal*. http://laterminalrosario.wordpress.com/2008/07/14/la-sociedad-de-los-muertos-vivos/. I thank my colleague Luis Cervera for this document.

Turati, Marcela. (January 18, 2009). "Ciudad Juárez, vivir y morir en la capital del crimen." *Proceso* México, D. F. No. 1681. pp. 8–11.

Ulate, Angélica. (August 13, 2003). "Truena Patricio contra Amnistía Internacional," *El Diario*, Ciudad Juárez. http://www.diario.com.mx, consulted August 13, 2003.

United Nations, Office on Drug and Crime. (2007). 2007 World Drug Report. http://www.nacionesunidas.org.mx/prensa/especiales/2007/informe_drogas/WDR_2007.pdf, consulted March 15, 2009.

US Embassy, México City. (February 2009). U.S. México at a Glance. Combatting Illicit Firearms. http://México.usembassy.gov/eng/eataglance_illicit_firearms.pdf, consulted March 11, 2009.

Villalpando, Rubén. (November 17, 2008). "La violencia en Ciudad Juárez provoca éxodo de 3 mil familias." *La Jornada*, México. http://www.jornada.unam.mx/2008/11/17/index.php?section=estados&article=02 4n1est, consulted January 2009.

Washington Office on Latin America on U.S. Security Assistance to México. (2007) Testimony of Joy Olson, Executive Director of the Washington Office on Latin America, before the House Committee on Foreign Affairs, Subcommittee on the Western Hemisphere, October 25, 2007. http://www.wola.org/media/Microsoft%20Word%20-%20Testimony%20Olson %20HWH%2010%2025%2007.pdf, consulted October 30, 2007. http://www.nacionesunidas.org.mx/prensa/especiales/2007/informe_drogas/WDR_2007.pdf.

Working Group. (2005). U.S. Money Laundering Threat Assessment. http://files.ots.treas.gov/480215.pdf, consulted March 12, 2009.

FURTHER READING

Gaceta. Es. (March 1, 2009). "Estados Unidos fabrica y vende las armas, México pone los muertos." http://www.gaceta.es/01-03-2009+estados_unidos_fabrica_vende_armas_México_pone_muertos,noticia_1img,8,8,48941, consulted March 11, 2009.

Ponce de León, Alberto. "Son pandillas, clave para narcos en EU," *El Diario*, Ciudad Juárez, Chih., February 13, 2009, p. 7A.

Chapter 3

The Disarticulation of Justice: Precarious Life and Cross-Border Feminicides in the Paso del Norte Region

Julia E. Monárrez Fragoso &
Cynthia Bejarano

The analysis of murders of girls and women immediately directs us to the term feminicide and to the city of Ciudad Juárez. Our investigation of extreme violence against women, however, encompasses a vast desert of a geographical area called the Paso del Norte region that includes: Ciudad Juárez, Chihuahua, México; El Paso, Texas; and Las Cruces, New Mexico. Since 1993, feminicide (*feminicidio*) is a concept that has referred mainly—although not exclusively—to the sexual killings and unsolved cases of the women in this Mexican border city. While authorities documented the murders of its citizens in Juárez, it was women's rights groups that identified an ostensible pattern in these killings, and began denouncing them along with victims' families, feminist activists, filmmakers, poets, artists, painters, and academicians. This proliferation of violence toward women accounts for nearly 571 crimes from 1993 to 2008.

Among these various representations of the 571 murders committed by husbands, lovers, friends, and clients, one of the most compelling forms of crimes against women was the systematic and specific assassination of girls and women committed by unknown killers. The murders of more than 117 impoverished young women bore a signature of torturous kidnappings, rapes, and mutilations; the murderers then dumped their bodies on the outskirts of the city or in empty lots within the city. Out of this figure, authorities claimed that they solved ten cases. These systemic sexual feminicides (Monárrez, 2009) are constant atrocities that have had no precedent in the history of Ciudad Juárez, yet they continue; and since 2000, the murders have even extended into the state capital, Chihuahua City.[1] Victims' families, who cry for justice, have gained the attention of national and international human rights organizations for several years, and entities like the United Nations have given recommendations to the Government of Mexico about how to address these long-tolerated atrocities and injustices against women.

Within this essay, we aim to build on Saskia Sassen's work on state disintegration under globalization. We address how globalization influences gender violence, and, in particular, feminicide. We further explore how globalization has ripple effects throughout the transnational border area called the Paso del Norte region. Our analysis primarily focuses on the feminicides, the impact these murders have had on the region, and the proliferation of feminicide across space through what Foucault calls *convenientia*: how things that are close to each other begin to resemble one another. We use this concept to examine the growth of feminicide in the Paso del Norte region and expand on this thinking through the term *cross-border feminicides*[2] that examines how the Juárez feminicides have catalyzed imminent threats to victims of gender violence and spread such threats throughout the region. Through this lens of crossborder feminicides, we explore its duality of meaning that includes how feminicide on one side of the border seemed to "inspire" feminicide and gender violence on the other. In addition, we document how the entire region is framed as a space to unleash violence against women, even though Juárez becomes "the" singular site to discuss feminicide while other violence in the region is overlooked. Finally, we also discuss state responses to feminicide throughout the region and access to justice or the lack thereof for victims' families within this transnational border corridor: a border region characterized by the disarticulation of justice and state impunity.

FRAMING SEXUAL VIOLENCE AND FEMINICIDES WITHIN AN ERA OF GLOBALIZATION

Throughout this essay, we reflect on sexual murders, globalization and its effects, and elusive notions of justice within the transnational border corridor called Paso del Norte. Violence affects men and women;

however, its impact changes according to the sex of the victim (Rico, 1996). In this sense, the particular aggressions that men direct toward women allow us to identify these as gender violence, which is linked to the unequal distribution of power and to the asymmetric relationships between men and women in patriarchal societies. According to Nieves Rico (1996: 5; personal translation from the authors), gender violence:

> can adopt diverse forms, which allows [us] to classify the crime, in accordance with the relationship in which it is framed and the exercise of power that it supposes, in the following categories: sexual violation and incest, sexual harassment in the work and in the institutions of education, sexual violence against arrested or imprisoned women, acts of violence against rooted out women, and trafficked women and victims of domestic violence.

This list is by no means an exhaustive one for violence against women. Abuse against girls and women is diverse, including verbal and physical abuse, torture, child pornography, prostitution, child abuse, unnecessary gynecological operations, female genital mutilation, forced heterosexuality, penalization of abortion, and women's suicide in situations of maltreatment and femicide (Caputi and Russell, 1992: 5). Violence emerges in the family, in the school, in the workplace, in the public and private spaces of the city, in the street and within the home. It is implemented by relatives as much as well-known men and completely unknown men. Law enforcement institutions are also implicated when they do not guarantee the safety and freedom of women. Violence against women has ultimately focused on their genital organs—symbols of their sexuality and their femininity—which are then raped, tortured, and abused.

Lisa Sharlach explains that rape is one of the most traumatic and widespread of human right abuses; some scholars of violence analyze it as a consequence of war rather than a component of it (Sharlach, 2002). Sexual murder is a part of the continuum of sexual violence against women, and Jane Caputi defines it as an act where sex and violence meld, where an intimate relationship between manliness and pleasure is established. These kinds of murders do not lack motivation: "kidnapping, rape, torture, mutilation and extermination of victims are the elements, the impulse and the inspiration of a sexual murder" (Caputi, 1987). For Cameron and Frazer, this is an irrational fusion of sex and violence, and the killers find it "erotic" to kill the object of their desire. These brutal assassinations reflect sadistic sexual tendencies and the way patriarchy socializes men—the other can be female or male, but the victimizer is always male. For these authors, rape and sexual assault are not sufficient or necessary conditions to label a crime as sexual; what is important is the "eroticization of the act of killing"[3] and this way of murdering women is the product of a certain social order (1987: 18–19, 33). This social order is gender, ethnic, or class discrimination and the material and political conditions of a given society. The Juárez sexual murders do not break away from this conception.

They have been equated to it as a consequence of the process of export-oriented manufacturing that made Ciudad Juárez a city immersed in the globalization process, that created jobs yet diminished security and labor conditions for young women and men who work there. Julián Cardona explains that women's murders—of which many were committed against immigrants—are the side effects of two main factors: the low wages that the maquiladora industry[4] pays to its employees, and what he calls the "exorbitant dividends and devastating violence affecting the daily lives of the inhabitants of the city" (2004) (see Monárrez, this volume). Despite the global shame heaped upon the Mexican state for not investigating crimes against women (Fregoso, 2006), the "disappearances of girls" continues in this city now under siege by multiple forms of violence. (see Photograph 3.1).

For Mexicans in the Paso del Norte region, the global attention around violence against women and girls has served as a tragic illustration of how impunity and gender violence, left unchecked, can have systemic repercussions for surrounding cities. This in no way claims that gender, sexual violence, and murder did not exist in the Paso del Norte region prior to 1993. Making such claims would be preposterous, considering the legacy of colonization, exploitation, degradation, and violence that affected this region. This area represents dangerous immigrant crossings, border corridors for trafficking in arms, drugs, and humans, and embodies a growing reputation as a globally/regionally cheap workplace where the poor are simply exploited. The photo (Fig. 3.1) shows a common scene in the anti-violence movements that peaked in the last decade.

It is then demonstrably important for us to investigate how in two deeply connected yet different countries, globalization produces different articulations or disarticulations of the implementation of justice concerning sexual murders of girls and women. As this examination has shown, impunity prevails in México. And as Saskia Sassen (1998) explains, economic globalization has reconfigured two fundamental properties of the nation-state: territoriality (territorial organization of economic activity) and sovereignty (the organization of political power). Sassen also sheds light on this situation when she explains that

Figure 3.1 In search of the "missing" girls of Ciudad Juárez
Source: Photo by Elvia Liliana Chaparro Vielma, Ciudad Juárez, February 20, 2009.

it is important to discard the consideration of globalization in terms of interdependence and formations of exclusively global institutions; globalization must be reexamined in terms of the national. In this way, she says, we can open new avenues to investigate unexplored multiple possibilities of social problems (Sassen, 2007: 12). In specific cases of feminicides within Chihuahua, the Mexican State has become an anorexic/absent/unattendant state regarding women's human rights, and in particular the most important right: the right to live.

With this argument, we can affirm and agree with Sassen's theory that globalization has restructured the economies of Ciudad Juárez and its surrounding cities. In this region, there is a growing demand for low-wage workers and deskilled jobs, because they are partly related in one way or another to the export-processing zone of Ciudad Juárez. Women of color and immigrants make these kinds of jobs and wages possible, yet despite their status as hardworking, they will never have the opportunity to climb any kind of social ladder. Even if workers are incorporated into the leading sectors of their city's global economy, they remain an "invisible" workforce (Sassen, 2006: 178–180). Across the river from Ciudad Juárez is the sprawling city of El Paso, Texas, with a population of almost 800,000. Like Ciudad Juárez, El Paso has relied on women to fulfill neoliberal economic policies. In their work, Morales and Bejarano discuss the violence besieging women in El Paso and Ciudad Juárez stating,

> violence is gendered because girls' and women's bodies have become tools to achieve political-economic aims of nation-states and transnational corporations. As a result, the politics of work and the politics of sexuality have both fed into how different groups (e.g., women vs. men; poor vs. affluent; white vs. brown; and intersections thereof) experience violence
>
> Morales and Bejarano, 2009.

Sassen contends that immigrant women are incorporated into this new system in two ways: documented or undocumented; so besides being low wage workers, they are "low-valued-individuals," especially for the "shadow economy" that incorporates them into the illegal trafficking of women for prostitution and other forms of the sex industry, such as tourism enclaves and the entertainment business (Sassen, 2006: 187). Economic and sexual exploitation, and, in some cases, the murder of these women—following Hannah Arendt's logic—is seen as the killing of "primitive" and "cultural" people (Arendt, 1992: 96).

In Ciudad Juárez, one argument made about the access to maquiladora jobs and the wages earned there is that women gain power since they earn money and are able to buy things. David Harvey postulates that the worker, besides being a productive body, is also a consuming one (Harvey, 2003). The argument is that women are now able to buy and pay for goods and can even, for instance, purchase a car. All these emancipative actions permit them to transition from the private to the public sphere, but this new way of occupying private and public spaces also stigmatizes them. Consequently, a discourse emerged: they were women who worked in cabarets and as prostitutes, so the maquiladoras were the redeemers of these contaminated women (Balderas, 2002). These types of cultural productions created by masculine institutions to disempower women are one of the main sediments of the nexus between globalization and violence.

According to Sassen, a key response to the unbundling of the state has been the involvement of nonstate actors, civil society organizations, human rights organizations, and feminist activists that have taken a national and international leading role representing and making visible women and other subjects that have become too small to be seen by the state. Globalization not only has transformed the economy, but it has also disrupted the organization of political power. Nevertheless, the unbundling of sovereignty that has been relocated in "supranational, nongovernmental or private institutions" have become the "alternative subjects of international law and actors in international relations" that speak out their grievances in the international fora (Sassen, 1998: 92–93).

Our work is the product of a long process of political and activist participation and academic research with victims' families, Mexican and U.S. civil organizations, members of the Mexican and United States congresses at the state and federal levels, and through years of involvement in the social movement against feminicide as feminist activists and academics. Our collective experiences have prompted us to raise questions around these crossborder phenomena, and how each instance of feminicide has been addressed or overlooked in the tristate region. As women and academics working in this region, we are compelled to raise these pressing questions of injustices that impact not just women but society on both sides of the line. It is critical for us to show how in two deeply connected yet different countries, globalization has different articulations or disarticulations of the implementation of justice concerning the sexual murders of girls and women. We raise issues around the similarities, differences, and even nuances in the states' approaches to feminicide across the region. In other words, "a woman is a woman is a woman," but what differentiates women are their social, class, racial, and even nationalized hierarchies as we will disentangle in this essay.

THE *CONVENIENTIA* OF FEMINICIDES IN LAS CRUCES, NUEVO MEXICO AND EL PASO, TEXAS

We combine a feminist standpoint regarding sexual crimes against women with Saskia Sassen's analysis of state disintegration under globalization. We link our points of view regarding crimes against women with representations made by "societies of discourse" (Foucault, 2005: 42). For this Foucauldian analysis of discourse's production, we make use of a technology of discourse: *convenientia*, which is similarity and resemblance in linking space in the form of "closer and closer." It implies that in the vicinity of places, things come together, they join, and their extremities touch each other. As a result of this contact, new similarities emerge and a common regime is imposed (Foucault, 2001: 26–27). In other words, *convenientia* is the "adjacency of dissimilar things, so that they assume similarities by default through their spatial juxtaposition" (Velibeyoglu, 1999: 14).

To organize our discussions, we first highlight the *convenientia* of violence against women and the social orders in El Paso, Texas, and Las Cruces, New Mexico, and their relationship to the violence in Ciudad Juárez. In this sense, it is important to highlight Saskia Sassen's words where she explains that "cities are the nexus where many of the new organizational tendencies of economies and societies come together in specific localized configurations" (Sassen, 2006: 180). Second, for El Paso, Texas, we will discuss the well-known murder of a little girl in 2001 that took place during a string of the most gruesome discoveries of feminicide in Juárez. Third, we will discuss the cases of five women killed between 1998 and 2005 in Las Cruces, New Mexico. And finally, for Ciudad Juárez, we would like to focus on 117 victims of paradigmatic cases of sexual murder,[5] their occupations, their place of origin, and the places where they were last seen alive before their dead bodies were located. State responses varied in each city, but strong racialized and social and class hierarchies exist across the Paso del Norte region. Explaining the cases of the three cities, and the authorities' failure to serve justice, our objective is to observe how—independently of borders—sexual murder is an experience that women and girls suffer. It is also important to highlight that no matter the extent to which justice is served in these two countries, women and girls are oftentimes objects of sexualized violence.

We recognize that feminicide in Juárez does not mark the inception of violence against women and girls within the region. Clearly, violence against girls and women has existed in every society worldwide. What we argue is that feminicide marked a painfully visible and tragic display of misogyny in Ciudad Juárez, where state actors and powerful segments of society like businessmen along Avenida Juárez, a popular tourist attraction, and others with a stake in revitalizing the image of Juárez as a pristine city for industry, were both duplicitous in their investigations of murder and their advocacy for justice for these women and girls. This conversely has had a ripple effect across the region where, as mentioned earlier, the "contact [of] new similarities emerge and a common regime is imposed" (Foucault, 2001: 26–27). The brutality and proliferation of feminicide is fostered by state failures to identify patterns in behavior and modus operandi of killers.

The crimes against humanity, coupled with the failure to investigate, are unconscionable.

In Las Cruces, New Mexico, only 45 miles from the El Paso, Texas and Ciudad Juárez border, twenty-one women have been killed since 1998.[6] From what we know, five of them were students: four in college and one in high school. Of these cases of sexual murder,[7] labeled as such due to the erotic killing and manner in which the women and the girl were disposed of, three have been solved. Four of the five women's bodies were dumped in the desert near or just outside the city limits; the high-school girl's skeletal remains were slowly discovered over a week floating in the Rio Grande near a city park. Although much time passed between each of these five murders, every woman killed was found in the Eastern, Northeastern, and Southern regions of the city limits or nearby the city limits and all were located in desolate desert areas, except for the girl's remains found in the Rio Grande who authorities believe was killed elsewhere. These women were disposed of in the desert like debris where the "new similarities" of *convenientia* emerged just like many of the girls and women of Juárez. Also, like the women and girls of Juárez, the families of these young women blanketed the city and local region with fliers of the women's photos and a loved one's contact information. The women's mothers mourned and pled with the media to help them find their daughters. However, the level of attentiveness in each case ranging from the media, law enforcement, and local communities differed, and race, class, age, and social hierarchies were visibly present with each case, including that of El Pasoan Alejandra Flores in 2001. This case demonstrated that El Paso was not immune to gendered and sexual violence against little girls or women.

Women experience domestic violence and other forms of gendered and sexual violence in El Paso, despite its status as the third safest city (for its size) in the U.S., which is ironic when considering its geographic location and strong social, cultural, and binational ties to the most dangerous city in the region (see Staudt and Robles, this volume). El Paso's safe status though clearly does not reflect the paralyzing fear that women live with daily when they confront forms of gendered or sexualized violence, or if they are the recipients of violent threats. For example, Cynthia Morales, former program director for the Center Against Family Violence in El Paso, claims that women are forcibly transported to Juárez by their male partners when they have intentions of killing them (Morales and Bejarano, 2009; Staudt, 2008: Ch. 5). Men's threats to murder women are an everyday occurrence in Juárez and in many cases the threats are followed through with while advocacy groups and researchers take note of this trend.[8] Feminicide and impunity in Ciudad Juárez have served as an instrument of *convenientia* for men to threaten women with physical, psychological, and sexual torture or death. This signature of violence is also evident in Las Cruces, NM, which also comprises the Paso del Norte border region.[9] These instruments of *convenientia* are salient to point out because a common language of violence against women is developing due to the impunity that men witness in this region. The message relayed is: women can be killed, and little is done to stop feminicide. What is formed through this impunity and the politics of misogyny is a climate that cultivates a perpetual threat to women in the Paso del Norte region along with recurrent attempts at feminicide in Juárez and *crossborder feminicides* throughout the area. What takes shape is an erosion of justice, a disarticulation of justice where a safe corridor for, literally, "getting away with murder" emerges.

EL PASO

It is impossible to analyze each case of feminicide in the region in great detail or to understand the psychosis of a murderer, but one case that sent shock waves throughout El Paso was that of the abduction and murder of five-year old Alejandra Flores whose naked body was found underneath a carport in downtown El Paso on November 18, 2001. She was strangled with a plastic bag and was partially burned after she had been killed (Molina Johnson, 2008). Alejandra's death occurred two weeks after the discovery of eight girls' bodies in a cotton field across from El Paso in Ciudad Juárez. Their ages ranged from 14 to the early 20s. The horrifying details that emerged about those girls' abductions and murders in Juárez were atrocious and intolerable, yet this one case of a child murdered rallied an entire city on the U.S. side of the border to find her murderer. It is difficult to say whether Juárez's "cotton field murders" incited terrorizing fear in the people of El Paso that then prompted their immediate response, or if the murder of 14 girls, aged 3–13, between 1993 and 2001 played a role in mobilizing support to find Alejandra's murderer (Washington Valdez, 2001). In Juárez, feminicides were covered up and cases of victims who were accused in the local Juárez media of being prostitutes or girls who ran off with their boyfriends were dismissed. Conversely, in El Paso, efforts to find Alejandra's killer even stirred the local newspaper—the *El Paso Times*—to donate ten cents for each of its copies sold between December 3 and December 8, 2001, to a reward fund (this included two bank accounts and the

El Paso Crime Stoppers, who offered up to US$1000 for information on Alejandra's case).[10]

Conceivably, due to economic resources in El Paso, which translate into social resources (i.e., media: major franchise support as from Wal-Mart and smaller franchises like the local newspaper), more seemed to be done in this one case collectively in El Paso than for all the girls missing and murdered in Ciudad Juárez. Americans are noted for their volunteerism and donations (perhaps due to more expendable resources) and their protection of childhood (which is clearly a class issue since many societies globally cannot afford their children the same privilege). This does not make Americans more sympathetic or heroic through their visible protection of children than others globally. Alejandra's case merely symbolizes access to resources within a global economy where national, social, and class hierarchies are evident in the Paso del Norte region.[11] For example, a child emergency system, Amber Alert, was immediately mobilized in El Paso, and this community with resources rallied together to find one murderer, while its neighbouring twin city mourned the loss of several girls' lives whose murders are still unresolved.[12]

At the time, this case was the focal point for El Paso law enforcement and within two weeks, Alejandra's murderer, David Rentería, was arrested and since then has been sentenced to death twice, once in 2003 and again in 2008. The murderer was an El Paso native described as a quiet, mild-mannered man, but one who had a previous conviction of indecency with a minor (Molina Johnson, 2008). People speculated widely whether Alejandra was sexually assaulted, and during her autopsy and the collection of evidence, fingerprinting, and palm-print gathering, the doctor who conducted the autopsy testified that she died of strangulation and there were no signs of sexual assault. He did however indicate that "he could not determine whether she had been touched" (Molina Johnson, 2008). Although it is unclear whether she was sexually assaulted, the nakedness of her body represents sexual abuse, and her case, as Cameron and Frazer would define it, is a sexual murder because of the "eroticization of the act of killing" (1987: 18–19, 33).

Much of the early focus with Alejandra's investigations pointed to Juárez and costly human resources were mobilized. Within weeks of Alejandra's abduction and discovery, El Paso police "checked in" with Chihuahua state police in Juárez and their unsolved child murders (Washington Valdez, 2001). Canadian criminologist, Candace Skrapec, who was helping Chihuahua state police investigate the cases of murdered women, was considered for consultation by the El Paso

Police Department and two FBI profilers even flew to El Paso from
Virginia to create a criminal profile of her murderer. Another former
FBI profiler, Robert Ressler, was quoted in this same newspaper as
saying "The border makes it easy for killers to commit a crime in
one country and flee or escape to the other country" (Washington
Valdez, 2001). This comment punctuates our argument that the Paso
del Norte region is becoming a borderless crime scene for feminicide
across the area and a haven for these murderers. Washington Valdez
explained, "For some criminals, possibly even child killers, the border
has become a safe harbour" (2001).

LAS CRUCES

One could argue that Juárez has become a "scapegoated" city, where
all the social ills of the region are blamed on the rampant violence and
lack of infrastructure and resources in that city. It becomes facile to
place the blame entirely south of the line where state disintegration
due to globalization and impunity and corruption seems to have its
most strident impact. In the case of Las Cruces, this small city that
forms part of the tristate region of Chihuahua, New Mexico, and
Texas is recognized more as a college and retirement community
than an expansive global metropolis. Yet, this city forms part of the
border region that is affected by and reflects the patterns of work,
trade, mobilization, and violence within its neighboring sister cities.
Las Cruces is a community bordered by two major interstate corridors into the United States, which is ideal for trade. However, a transborder development initiative has been in motion since the 1990s.
Santa Teresa, New Mexico, a small town bordering the outskirts
of Juárez, serves as a port of entry from the U.S. into Chihuahua.
Because of this port of entry, a new industrial town is developing
across from Santa Teresa that is now called its sister city, Jerónimo.
These urban expansions will host foreign trade zones and an anticipated 100,000 residents in the next ten years, surely influencing Las
Cruces. Yet little is mentioned about the "disposable" residents living
close to this area in the Juárez neighborhood, Lomas del Poleo, who
are being displaced and forcibly moved out of their neighborhoods.
They are perceived as an obstacle for this new and vigorous economic
expansion plan for a super export highway to be built between the
two countries and whose entrance, strategically, is the San Jeronimo
point of entry. The binational landlords of this area in Chihuahua and
New Mexico are violently and physically forcing these inhabitants of
Lomas del Poleo out of their homes. Less is revealed about how the

two intersecting, interstate corridors in Las Cruces coming from El Paso and near Santa Teresa serve as major nationwide transportation hubs for arms trafficking, drug trafficking, and human trafficking, including sex trafficking.[13]

Other more common forms of gendered and sexualized violence than feminicides are referenced even less in Las Cruces, like the pervasive cycle of domestic violence that afflicts this city and the surrounding small towns within the county seat. In 2007, La Casa, a nonprofit organization that offers comprehensive services and shelter to victims of domestic violence, reported serving 2,361 adults and children from Las Cruces and the surrounding area.[14] Like the Center Against Family Violence in El Paso, La Casa's executive director, Gina Orona-Ruiz has also confirmed that batterers have threatened their partners with transporting them across the international border to Ciudad Juárez in order to kill them. These alarming statements are now rampantly made across the Paso del Norte region. The batterers' argument is that the Mexican police and public will believe that the women from the United States. are Juárez feminicide victims, and the institutionalized impunity practiced in Juárez will never lead to the discovery of a woman's body or investigation into their crimes.[15]

Comparatively speaking, Las Cruces is dismissed as a quiet town, far-removed from feminicide. It is perceived as having fewer problems than its metropolitan sister cities of El Paso and Juárez. In Las Cruces, however, the threats of murder made by batterers to their partners, along with the young women's bodies discovered in nearby isolated areas of Las Cruces and its surrounding desert, point to the overwhelming impact feminicide has had on the tristate region. The cases of young women murdered in Las Cruces and whose bodies were found in the surrounding region can be called (un)paradigmatic murders, yet the five cases share alarming similarities that we argue are an element of *convenientia*, which influenced the patterns of disposability of women in Juárez as much as how women are disposed of on the U.S. side of the desert.

Unlike most of the women of Juárez who were poor or living in abject poverty and working in maquiladoras or engaged in other related activities, these five women in Las Cruces were students. It is not known what their median income was, but four of the five were university students, two of whom were graduate students and one was a high school student. Of the five, two were from smaller cities in New Mexico; one was from Las Cruces, another from El Paso, and one woman's city of origin was unknown. Four of the five women and girls ranged in age from 16 to 20 when they were killed, and one woman was 53 years old. Three of the five women were of Mexican descent and two were white.

All victims' remains were found in the desert, two of which were found near a landfill in the same general vicinity outside of Las Cruces. Another young woman was also found in an area that was previously a landfill but within Las Cruces city limits. These sexual murders point yet again to Cameron and Frazer's "eroticization of killing women" regardless of their social, class, or racial status and goes against what Sassen argues about low-waged individual women. These cases more strongly point to the spread of *convenientia* in the region, where the comment, "a woman is a woman is a woman" is unmistakable and women become disposable beings, a discarded human category. The desert is a vast, devouring space and the murderers' intentions were to avoid having these women's bodies discovered. The common phrase born from feminicide for this desert region is a *fosa común*, a common pauper's gravesite to throw women away. Through the transnational corridor that is forming for violence against women, a nascent message is conveyed to potential and actual murderers that the state does not respond—helping to cultivate a safe-haven for murderers.

Despite these emerging frameworks, in order to articulate justice in these feminicide cases, women are still blamed for their own deaths. For instance, three of the five women in Las Cruces were killed the evening they were known to be "partying" with men in the area, and public judgment ran high as to what the young women were doing "partying" and staying out late into the evening. This is reminiscent of girls and women and their families being blamed in Juárez for their own deaths, because they were out after dark. A memorable Juárez billboard once read, "Parents, do you know where your daughters are?" The youngest of these five victims from Las Cruces ran away from home, and it was unknown what the fifth, older woman was doing before she was killed; her body, however, was found in a remote part of the desert across from an unpaved road a quarter mile from a landfill along with the young woman who had gone to Juárez the night she died. One woman was killed in 2004 and the other was killed in 2005.

In 2004, the younger woman mentioned above had gone to Ciudad Juárez to celebrate her twentieth birthday, and shortly after her disappearance, people speculated whether she went missing in Juárez and if she would be the next victim of feminicide in that city. A Las Cruces–based organization, Amigos de las Mujeres de Juarez, actually posted fliers of the missing young woman throughout the Juárez downtown area; her body was discovered a week later. A large pink cross similar to those staked throughout Ciudad Juárez where women and girls' bodies were found now marks where her body was discarded outside of Las Cruces.

The mechanisms employed to kill these women are suggestive of how women were murdered in Ciudad Juárez. Some of the women in Las Cruces were either stabbed several times or strangled; in one case, a victim was found fully clothed with no visible trace of foul play, even though her case is still unresolved and her body was thrown in the middle of nowhere (see Fig. 3.2); another woman was burned and sexually assaulted.[16]

Law enforcement detectives were unable to determine how the young girl whose remains were found in the grassy area near the Rio Grande (and in the river itself) was killed.

Although these cases are nuanced, together they mark a significant likeness to feminicide in Ciudad Juárez. We do recognize, however, the vast cultural, social, political, and national differences within these cases. Despite strong collaboration between local law enforcement agencies in Las Cruces and the county sheriff's office, some of these cases are still unsolved. Families still struggling for answers clearly feel a disarticulation of justice, and those with fewer resources who

Figure 3.2 Cross marking where one woman's body was found near Las Cruces, New Mexico
Source: Photo by Cynthia Bejarano.

were from out of town found it difficult to see advocacy for or thorough advancement in their daughter's cases; different cases were not treated equally by media outlets or even communities. Two of the cases received national media attention from internationally recognized shows like *America's Most Wanted*, while others quietly faded into the last pages of newspapers and people's memories. The two cases receiving most of the attention were perhaps the most gruesome and unfortunately demonstrate what draws the most vigorous attention from the public. The two young women in these widely recognized cases were very attractive and came from prominent and established families within their communities. Their families and community members were able to raise significant amounts of reward money for evidence in their daughters' cases, and eventually the widespread attention to their murders influenced local and state legislation around DNA laws and felons, and local awareness campaigns addressing violence against women.

Although nuanced, this segment explores the similarities and differences in the feminicides across El Paso and Las Cruces to describe the commonalities shared with the Juárez feminicides. Violence against women is no longer coincidental or random but manifests as a systemic issue plaguing the Paso Del Norte region. It is critical to examine feminicide within each city to understand how each location has resolved to address or overlook this endemic violence. Clearly, Juárez is not the singular site for the finality of death; the Paso del Norte region is becoming a space where feminicide and cross-border feminicides are propagated often, state impunity is limitless and a murderous haven for killers is facilitated.

CROSSBORDER FEMINICIDES AND SAFE-HAVEN CORRIDORS

Feminicide in Ciudad Juárez has come to represent much more than the horrific atrocities of murders of countless women and girls. What is developing in the Paso del Norte region is a climate of fear of feminicides and a normalized landscape of sexualized and gendered violence that is tolerated and often minimized. Feminicide now represents murder, the threat of murder, and the misogyny and *terrorization of women* (Fregoso and Bejarano, 2010) practiced by murderers, batterers, and laymen. The rhetoric of violence is now rationalized by violent men and justified as a viable option to control and kill women with impunity, regardless of what nation-state they represent or what citizenship they possess. The Paso del Norte region, which shares an international border, is becoming a sociocultural, political, and economic landscape ripe for *crossborder feminicides.* The cases of *crossborder feminicides* have up to this point been discussed independently from one another. However, this analysis extends its discussion to broadly examine the impact of feminicide, and now its discourse, rhetoric, and the larger influence that violence across borders has had throughout this marginalized Paso del Norte region.[17]

The ostensible duality within the meaning of crossborder feminicides is palpable. On one hand, feminicides on one side of the border (Juárez) are potentially influencing or inciting gender or sexualized violence and even (un)paradigmatic feminicides on the opposite side of the line (Texas or New Mexico); in other words, these murders seem unorganized and random yet they share very similar patterns or traits. On the other hand, crossborder feminicides also represent for some misogynist killers an easy alibi to cross effortlessly into Juárez to kill or to transport a woman into Juárez from the U.S. and to dispose of her in that Mexican border desert. All these possibilities are viable options for murderers because they perceive the deficiency in the application of law in the city of Juárez. For example, Anabel Calzada Alvarado who was a Juarense and was living in Ruidoso, New Mexico, was stabbed several times and killed on December 2007 by Guillermo Ruiz Armendáriz from El Paso. He killed her because she refused to have sex with him. He decided to cross her body to Ciudad Juárez and burn it. He then abandoned her son, a two-year-old infant, who was found wandering around downtown Juárez. This feminicide was called by the Juarez press "*homicidio transfronterizo*" (Felix, 2007; Gilot, 2008). Another example is the deportation from El Paso to Ciudad Juárez of Felipe Jesús Machado Reyes, presumably a drug dealer, who killed his wife and three more women in Ciudad Juárez between 2001 and 2003 (Villalpando, 2003). These crossborder feminicides seem to be minimalized or completely overlooked by the media on the U.S. side of the border. Thwarting any kind of linkage to the feminicides on either side of the border by authorities and others invested in avoiding making these comparisons or responding to the change that the Paso del Norte region and its communities and inhabitants are facing at the hands of global and structurally violent forces that are shaping a climate of violence seems to be socially, culturally, and politically prudent. Hence, Ciudad Juárez has served as the catalyst to examining violence against women more broadly and at a global level.

THE PARADIGMATIC CASES OF CIUDAD JUÁREZ AND THE EMERGENCE OF NONSTATE ACTORS

In Ciudad Juárez in 1993, organized groups of victims' families and women and feminists identified a pattern of sexual murders, mostly among the young and poor and maquiladora workers who were kidnapped, tortured, and raped and whose bodies were disposed of in empty lots and in the desert encircling the city. The same patriarchal codes with which they were *subjetivizadas* (subjectivized) when they were alive were also encoded in their killing. They were referred to as weak women, and as girls with a dissolute life who deserved to be murdered; prevention campaigns oriented their messages to confine women to the private space and to decrease their autonomy (Tabuenca Córdoba, 2003). Families clamored that there was an unattended justice around their loved one's cases, yet the feminicides continued (see Fig. 3.3). The graph represents sexualized killings, rather than all women killing; the annual rate of women killed in 2008 was high at 98 murders but higher yet in 2009 with 184 murdered.

As shown in graph 3.3, feminicides have been ongoing. In Ciudad Juárez, as a result of the struggles for justice initiated by the victims' families and activists in reaction to these heinous murders, the Governor of Chihuahua and law enforcement officials were urged to stop the killing (Comisión Nacional de Derechos Humanos, 1998). They rejected the National Human Rights Commission's recommendations, so nothing happened, and the murders continued. The Mexican state was urged by the international community to stop the killings, to enforce security procedures for vulnerable women, and to present the assassins to the national and international communities in order to serve justice for the victims and their families.[18]

In 2002, recommendations were given by La Comisión Interamericana de Derechos Humanos (Inter American Commission on Human Rights) denoting a specific type of murder—the multiple or serial killing that appeared to be present in some crimes against women. In 2003, Amnesty International centered its recommendations on crimes committed under the rubric of sexual violence and whether they were serial or not in Ciudad Juárez and Chihuahua. The dead were young, poor, humble, and disenfranchised women. From El Colegio de la Frontera Norte's database, "Feminicide 1993–2008," victims shared a variety of occupations, from bar workers (3) and maquiladora workers (19) to students (8) and student employees (8), but most (44) had unspecified occupations. The U.N. High Commissioner for Human Rights' office in Mexico (U.N. 2003) called these crimes paradigmatic examples

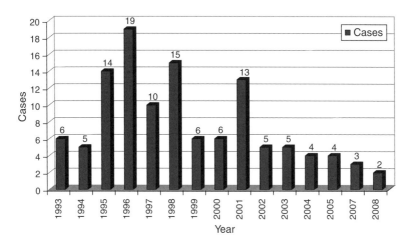

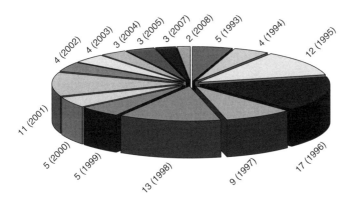

Figure 3.3   Systemic Sexual Feminicide 1993–2008, Number of Victims
Source: Data Base "Feminicide 1993–2008," El Colegio de la Frontera Norte.

of groups that experience vulnerability and discrimination, linked to an economic model and vicinity with the United States. In other words, the two global cities, linked by an international border and economy, have served as a discrepant paradox between the poor and even poorer and the few who make an earning off their meager wagers. This tristate border and its lure for a better future for migrants make this region one of the most vulnerable in the world. Consequently, urgent recommendations were made by the UN Commissioner to improve material conditions within the areas in which these victims and other potential subjects of feminicide live (see Map 3.1) (Comisión Interamericana de Derechos Humanos, 2002; Amnesty International, 2003; (Naciones Unidas, 2005).

Although we only have information for 47 victims' residences, this map shows that they lived on the west side of the city. This is the area in which a deficit of urban infrastructure prevails, where workers of the maquiladoras live, and where immigrants settle (Monárrez and Fuentes, 2004). Also, the places where they were last seen alive show a pattern identified as "missing persons zones." Eleven of them disappeared from the industrial parks, 20 of them from the downtown area, 12 from the *colonias* of the west zone, and 4 of them from the east side. Unfortunately, we do not have information for the other 70 cases, because we have no reports for the 42 unidentified bodies and because authorities do not disclose this information, not even for academic purposes.

Some studies have claimed that only migrant women are killed, but this is not true since out of 55 cases where the victims' place of origin is known, 28 are from Chihuahua, 16 from Ciudad Juárez,

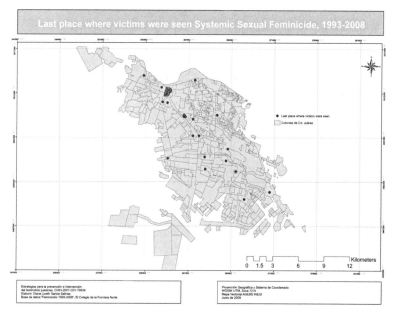

Map 3.1 Last place where victims were seen: Systemic Sexual Feminicide, 1993–2008

Source: Data Base "Feminicide 1993–2008," El Colegio de la Frontera Norte.

and 12 from other municipalities of Chihuahua. We say this cautiously since there are still approximately 42 unidentified womens' remains. Questions continue as to the origins of these women: are they from Ciudad Juárez or from other states of México or are they from Central America? Another poignant question is if these killings are part of sexual trafficking organizations. In this analysis, we have demonstrated that the Mexican State is the prime example of paradigmatic gender violence against girls and women in the Paso del Norte region. Also, evidence displays the disarticulation of justice based on the relations of power, which hinder justice for women. Our scrutiny of these atrocities began over a decade ago, after witnessing the social control of women as exercised through the murder of girls and women in vulnerable conditions with total impunity. It is important to remark here that in Ciudad Juárez, Sassen's arguments about the disarticulation of the state through the organization of economic activities and the organization of political power is a fatal reality for those "invisible," "low-valued" individuals: the missing, the unidentified—the murdered women and girls of Juárez

Conclusion

As our research has shown, impunity prevails in the case of Ciudad Juárez's sexual feminicides. Some factions see an intangible notion of justice is present in the sexual murders committed against the girls and women in Ciudad Juárez. But as we said before, this injustice is not against all women, only to those described by Sassen as low-valued individuals. They are the poor citizens or the "*ciudadanas x*" of a denationalized city (Schmidt, 2007). And even though we have 42 unidentified women still in Juárez, we can say their murders have no connection to their place of origin. What is unquestionably demonstrable is their poor place of residence and the places where they were kidnapped, both of which underscore that they came from vulnerable communities, and although the data clearly shows a pattern of abductions here, the state does little to implement safety measures. For these reasons, we emphasize how critical it is for nonstate actors to articulate an agenda of justice to those who have been absent in their advocacy for justice or who have compromised this process. The Mexican state has become anorexic, absent, and not attendant to these cases. Thus, we can say that "under certain conditions, economic restructuring engenders new subnational forms of political community that effectively claim the right to make and enforce penal law over and against opposition from recognized state institutions"

(Johnson, 2007: 265–266), the nonstate actors. The answer given by Mexican authorities and hegemonic groups that feminicide is a "myth" (Cruz, 2007) reinstates the impunity of feminicide and the tolerance for gender violence in service of the city's image as an attractive destination for international investment based on low wages and poor jobs in order to exploit marginal people.

Through our analysis of the Paso del Norte region, we examine Sassen's dual properties of globalization: the territoriality of economic activity and the sovereignty and organization of political power that are present with economic globalization. What occurs are paradigm shifts throughout the region where not only economic activity but people—especially women—are territorialized, because they are women and there are few safeguards to stop this action. Territorializing women becomes a by-product of economic advancement and the attendant shifting of city growth and development. Women are exploited in this process and become the object of desire, to threaten, harass, abuse, rape, and ultimately, destroy.

Even though the Paso del Norte region is celebrated as a tristate region where sociocultural and economic borders evaporate, questions of sovereignty and political power are invariably used as an excuse to avoid creating binational and bilateral initiatives to investigate, identify, and address violence against women; nation-states on both sides of the line are guilty of this. Our analysis makes evident the need to immediately address feminicides on both sides of the border, and how crossborder feminicides display the imminent threat posed toward all communities involved. Sassen (2006) argues that economies and societies come together in specific, localized configurations and, as a result, what the cities in this Paso del Norte region now share are feminicides and a climate of fear for women. It will take communities of women and men to end this rampant violence, and for nation-states to set aside their claims to sovereignty to achieve the common goal of addressing these murders. Otherwise, the Paso del Norte region will be known globally as the border region where women and girls are killed without consequences.

Approaches to ending feminicides often proliferate from the margins. It is important to emphasize how this geographical region, especially the city of Ciudad Juárez, is "a vital space in the emergence of new political practices. As a communications circuit, as a space where rights can be fought for, as a bulwark against authoritarian regimes" (Bartlett, 2007: 222). The Mexican state appeared in the Corte Interamericana de Derechos Humanos in Santiago, Chile, April 2009, to address the case of Ciudad Juárez. The protests and manifestations

have made "the invisible seem visible, not just in the immediacy of
the protest but also in marking out who deals with whom [and],
where the social and linguistic markers are" (Bartlett, 2007: 232). We
applaud the Court's verdict of justice for the assassinated in finding
Mexico guilty of negligence and impunity; we hope that this verdict
will curb the sexual murders and disappearances of women and girls
in Ciudad Juárez , otherwise the region will resemble *convenientia* for
crossborder feminicides in the Paso del Norte region.

Acknowledgment: Julia E. Monárrez wants to thanks the funding
received from Fondo Mixto CONACyT-Chihuahua for the reserarch
project "Estrategias para la prevención e intervención del feminicido
juarense" clave CHIH -2007 CO1-79934 and to Liliana Chaparro,
and Diana L. García Salinas research assistants from El Colef, and
student Ivette Rosas for her assistance in this paper. Cynthia Bejarano
thanks Emilia Bernal for her assistance and to Molly Molloy for helping
her to obtain information from the library.

NOTES

1. Although the capital city of the State of Chihuahua is not part of
   this analysis because it is not a component of the Paso del Norte
   Region, it is important to mention since several murders of poor
   young women have occurred there; several more are still missing.
   Like Ciudad Juárez, women's bodies were found in empty lots, on
   the roadside on interstates, and in one set of cases, a cluster of bodies
   were discovered close to the state police headquarters.
2. Concept developed by Cynthia Bejarano.
3. On December 15, 2008, the cadaver of a woman approximately
   31 years old was found naked and sexually assaulted. She had marks
   written on her body stating, "The devil walks freely in Juárez, do not
   go out alone and sexy." Kathleen Staudt told us that she supposes
   this legend makes reference to the woman's presentation of self, her
   clothing, etc. For her, this case represents the eroticization of the killing or also some of the killers enjoy these sexual killings as eroticized
   or if some of the killers are repressed, reactionary individuals who kill
   and leave messages to restore a burqua-type world: where women
   who "'invade' men's public space must do so on conservative terms:
   covering their bodies fully" (Personal communication, January 18,
   2009).
4. Most assembly plants in Mexico, near the United States border, are
   where assembly parts are shipped into Mexico and the finished product is shipped back across the border. The arrangement allows plant
   owners to take advantage of low-cost labor and to pay duty only on

the "value added of the finished product." http://www.britannica.
com/EBchecked/topic/363663/maquiladora, consulted February
22, 2009

5. There are several more cases of sexual murders but they don't fit the
same pattern as these.

6. Most of these cases were domestic violence murders with others that
included death during a robbery or car jacking; this however, does
not minimize how these women were killed but goes beyond the
scope of this paper.

7. Only the skeletal remains were found, so authorities were unable to
identify whether she had been sexually assaulted.

8. From 1993 to 2008, 110 women were killed by their partners in
Ciudad Juárez. "Feminicide" Data Base

9. Las Cruces is not a newcomer to violence against women or even
murder. The case of Ovida "Cricket" Coogler in 1949, a local eigh-
teen year old whose body was found weeks later in the desert after
she went missing on March 31, 1949, is one poignant example that
feminicide did not start or end in contemporary history. This year will
mark this feminicide's 60th anniversary. Strong ties of alleged murder
linked the local sheriff, police officers and state police as well as judges
and politicians to her disappearance, cover-up and untimely murder,
but the case remains unsolved (Moore, 2008). Ironically, her body
was also discovered in the same adjacent desert near Las Cruces where
two other women's bodies were found in 2006.

10. Wal-Mart was also offering $50,000 for information since she
was abducted from their parking lot, and Alejandra's family collected $12,900 for information leading to any arrests (Gilot: 2001
pg.1B[0]).

11. It is worthwhile to mention that 42 girls from ages 0 to 5 were killed
in Ciudad Juárez from 1993 to 2008, "Feminicide" Data Base.

12. In Juárez in the year 2005 a similar system like the Amber Alert was
implemented after the abduction, torturous and sexual killing of a
little girl Airis Estrella Enríquez: the Estrella Alert.

13. In his New York Times magazine article, Peter Landsman described
how the I-10 interstate toward Deming, NM, a 45-minute drive from
Las Cruces, served as a transfer point for groups to trade trafficked
women at a local rest area (*The New York Times Magazine*, January
25, 2004).

14. Gina Orona-Ruiz is the Executive Director for La Casa, Inc. (E-Mail
Communication, September 30, 2008).

15. To date, no woman's body has been discovered by law enforcement authorities. Every discovery was made by a passerby in Ciudad
Juárez.

16. Both newspaper reports and police reports that were reviewed were
vague in discussing whether these women were sexually assaulted.

17. The murders of women and girls in Ciudad Juárez and Las Cruces, NM, were first discussed at the J. Paul Taylor Social Justice Symposium at New Mexico State University in 2006. The mother and father of two separate young women killed in Las Cruces in 1998 and 2004 were invited to participate in this conference focusing primarily on the femincides in Ciudad Juárez.

18. For a more detailed discussion about Mexican state's responsibility, international human organizations recommendations and sexual serial murders from 1999 to 2006 (see Monárrez, et al., 2009, forthcoming).

REFERENCE LIST

Amnesty International. (2003). Mexico. Intolerable killings: Ten years of abductions and murders in Ciudad Juárez and Chihuahua. Consulted August 2003. http://web.amnesty.org/library/Index/ENGAMR410272003.

Arendt, Hannah. (1970). *On violence*. NY: Harcourt Brace & Company.

Balderas Domínguez, Jorge. (2002). *Mujeres, antros y estigmas en la noche juarense*. Chihuahua: Instituto Chihuahuense de la Cultura.

Bartlett, Anne. (2007). "The City and the Self. The Emergence of New Political Subjects in London." In Saskia Sassen, *Deciphering the Global: Its Scales, Spaces and Subjects,* pp. 221–241. NY: Routledge.

Cameron, Deborah, and Elizabeth Frazer. (1987). *The Lust To Kill*. New York: New York University Press.

Caputi, Jane. (1987). *The Age of Sex Crime*. Ohio: Bowling Green State University Popular Press.

———, and Diana E. H Russell. (1992). "Femicide: Sexist Terrorism against Women." In Jill Radford and Diana E. H. Russell. (eds.). *Femicide: The Politics of Woman Killing,* pp. 13–21. New York: Twayne Publishers.

Cardona, Julián. (2004). "Ciudad Juárez: cinco historias." Griselda Gutiérrez Castañeda (coord). *Violencia sexista: Algunas claves para la comprensión del feminicidio en Ciudad Juárez*. Universidad Nacional Autónoma de México/Programa Universitario de Estudios de Género. México. pp. 25–46.

Comisión Interamericana de Derechos Humanos. (2002). *Situación de los derechos humanos de las mujeres en Ciudad Juárez, México: el derecho a no ser objeto de violencia y discriminación*. http://www.cidh.org/annualrep/2002sp/cap.vi.juarez.htm.

Comisión Nacional de los Derechos Humanos. (1998). *Recomendación No. 44/98 Caso de las mujeres asesinadas en Ciudad Juárez y sobre la falta de colaboración de las autoridades de la Procuraduría General de Justicia del Estado de Chihuahua*. http://www.cndh.org.mx/.

Cruz, Juan Manuel. (September 8, 2007). "Sigue haciendo daño 'mito de las muertas de Juárez.'" El Diario, Ciudad Juárez, http://www.cdn.com.mx/?c=129&a=8399, consulted March 1, 2009.

Felix, Guadalupe. (December 24, 2007). "*Conmociona a juarenses homicidio transfronterizo.*" El Diario, Ciudad Juárez. Section B.

Foucault, Michel. (2001). *Las palabras y las cosas: una arqueología de las ciencias humanas.Siglo XXI, México.*

Fregoso, Rosa Linda. (2006). "We Want Them Alive!: The Politics and Culture of Human Rights." *Social Identitites,* Vol. 12, No. 2, March. pp. 109–138.

———, and Cynthia Bejarano. *Terrorizing Women: Feminicides in the Américas.* Duke University Press, 2010.

Gilot, Louie. (November 27, 2001). "Police, FBI still searching for 5-year-old girls' killer,"*El Paso Times,* p. 1.

———. (December 25, 2008). "Man Linked to Ruidoso Slaying, Burned Body," *El Paso Times.*

Hannah Arendt. (1967). *Eichman en Jerusalén. Un estudio sobre la banalidad del mal.* Carlos Ribalta (trans.). *Editorial Lumen.* Barcelona.

Harvey, David. (2003). *Espacios de esperanza,* Cristina Piña Aldao (ed and trans), Madrid: Ediciones Akal.

Johnson, Jennifer L. (2007). "Deregulating Markets, Reregulating Crime. Extralegal Policing and the Penal State in Mexico." In Saskia Sassen, *Deciphering the Global: Its Scales, Spaces and Subjects,* pp. 265–282. New York: Routledge.

Kaplan, Josh. (2007). "The Transnational Human Rights Movement and States of Emergency in Israel/Palestine," In Saskia Sassen, *Deciphering the Global: Its Scales, Spaces and Subjects,* pp. 283–301. New York: Routledge

Landesman, Peter. (January 25, 2004). "Sex Slaves on Main Street." *New York Times Magazine.* New York City, Section 6.

Molina Johnson, Erica. (April 22, 2008). "Renteria jury hears child-slaying evidence," *El Paso Times.*

Monárrez, Julia E. (2009). *Trama de una injusticia: Feminicidio Sexual Sistémico en Ciudad Juárez,* El Colegio de la Frontera Norte/Miguel Ángel Porrúa Editores, México.

———, and César M. Fuentes. (2004). "Feminicidio y marginalidad urbana en Ciudad Juárez en la década de los noventa, Marta Torres Falcón (compiladora), *Violencia contra las mujeres en contextos urbanos y rurales.* El Colegio de México. México. pp. 43–70.

———, et al. *Violencia contra las mujeres e inseguridad ciudadana en Ciudad Juárez.* El Colegio de la Frontera Norte/Miguel Ángel Porrúa Editores, México. Forthcoming.

Moore, Paula. (2008). *Cricket in the Web: The 1949 Unsolved Murder that Unraveled Politics in New Mexico.* Albuquerque: University of New Mexico Press.

Morales, Maria Cristina and Cynthia Bejarano. 2009. "Transnational Sexual and Gendered Violence at the Borderlands: An Application of Border Sexual Conquest at a U.S.-Mexican Border" *Global Networks,* 9(3), 420–439.

————. (2008). "Border Sexual Conquest: A Framework for Gendered and Racial Sexual Violence." Angela J. Hattery, David G. Embrick, and Earl Smith (eds.). *Globalization and America: Race, Human Rights, and Inequality*. Boulder, CO: Rowman & Littlefield Pulishers, Inc.

Naciones Unidas. (2003). *Diagnóstico Sobre la Situación de los Derechos Humanos en México*, Oficina del Alto Comisionado de las Naciones Unidas para los Derechos Humanos en México, México.

Naciones Unidas. (2003). *Informe de la Comisión de Expertos Internacionales de la Organización de las Naciones Unidas, Oficina de las Naciones Unidas contra la Droga y el Delito, sobre la Misión en Ciudad Juárez, Chihuahua, México*, Oficina de las Naciones Unidas contra la Droga y el Delito, noviembre. http://www.comisioncdjuarez.gob.mx/Portal/PtMain.php?& nIdPanel=38&nIdFooter=40.

Naciones Unidas. (2005). *Informe de México producido por el Comité para la Eliminación de la Discriminación contra la Mujer bajo el Artículo 8 del P rotocolo Facultativo de la Convención*, CEDAW/C/2005/OP.8/ MEXICO.

Radford, Jill and Diana E. H. Russell. (1992). *Femicide: The Politics of Woman Killing*. New York: Twayne Publishers.

Rico, Nieves. (1996). *Violencia de género: un problema de derechos humanos*, CEPAL, Serie Mujer y Desarrollo, Núm. 16.

Sassen, Saskia. (1998). *Globalization and its Discontents*. New York: The New Press.

————. (2006). *Deciphering the Global: Its Scales, Spaces and Subjects*, New York: Routledge.

————. (2007). *Una Sociología de la globalización*. María Victoria Rodil (trans) Katz, Buenos Aires.

Schmidt Camacho, Alicia. (2007). "La Ciudadana X Reglamentando los derechos de las mujeres en la frontera México-Estados Unidos." Julia E. Monárrez Fragoso and María Socorro Tabuenca Córdova (coordinators). *Bordeando la violencia contra las mujeres en la frontera norte de México*. El Colegio de la Frontera and Miguel Ángel Porrúa Editores. México.

Sharlach, Lisa. (2002). "Sexual Violence as Genocide." In Rally Avery and Ungar Mark (eds.) *Violence and Politics*, pp. 107–123. Worcester, Kenton, Bermanzohn. New York: Routledge.

Staudt, Kathleen. (2008). *Violence and Activism at the Border. Gender, Fear, and Everyday Life in Ciudad Juárez*. Austin: Univeristy of Texas Press.

Tabuenca Córdoba, María Socorro. (2003). "Baile de fantasmas en Ciudad Juárez al final/principio del milenio," Boris Muñoz y Silvia Spitta (editors), *Más allá de la ciudad letrada: crónica y espacios urbanos*, Pittsburg, Universidad de Pittsburg, pp. 411–437.

Velibeyoglu, Koray. (1999). *Post-structuralism and Foucault*, 1999, http:// www.angelfire.com/ar/corei/foucault.html, consulted January 2009.

Villalpando, Ruben. (2003). "EU deporta a presunto asesino de cuatro mujeres en Ciudad Juárez.." *La Jornada*. México. http://www.jornada.

unam.mx/2005/06/06/esp_juarez/2003_juarez.htm, consulted March 5, 2009.

Washington Valdez, Diana (December 3, 2001). "Search for Child Killer May Turn to Juarez." *El Paso Times.*

Wright, Melissa. (1999). "The Dialectics of Still Life: Murder, women, and Maquiladoras." *Millenial Capitalism and the Culture of Neoliberalism*, pp. 125–146. Durham: Duke University Press.

CHAPTER 4

SURVIVING DOMESTIC VIOLENCE IN THE PASO DEL NORTE BORDER REGION

Kathleen Staudt and Rosalba Robles Ortega

The U.S.-Mexico border directs considerable media attention toward violence and drugs. Usually, this attention is oblivious to gender: whether victims and aggressors are male or female. However, with the shocking rise of femicide—the murder of 370 girls and women from 1993–2003—people began to consider borders as magnets for opportunities and threats to women (Staudt 2008). Olivia Ruiz Marrujo (2009) examines borders, both those dividing the United States. and Mexico and Mexico and Guatemala, as spaces of eroticized sexual violence. In this chapter, we examine women's experiences with grim, normalized, everyday violence in spatial terms at the Paso del Norte border, a large, two-million person metropolitan region of Ciudad Juárez, Chihuahua, and El Paso, Texas, which are immediately adjacent to each other.

Saskia Sassen's conceptions of global or world cities focus on metropolitan spaces as sites of global production and financial exchange and of informal and immigrant economies characterized by polarization and growing inequalities, including gender-based wage inequalities (2001). Ciudad Juárez is home to approximately three hundred *maquiladoras*, mostly U.S.-owned, export-processing factories, at their peak with 200,000–250,000 workers that pay US$25–50 weekly. The city has been called the "Maquila Capital

of the Americas." Women comprise a majority of the workforce
(Fernández-Kelly 1983; Kopinak 2004), earning Mexico's legal minimum wage that falls below its poverty line. El Paso, which is half the
size of Ciudad Juárez and was once the site of now-closed garment
factories, is home to military bases, a large public sector including
federal border security and drug control agencies, and businesses
linked to the maquila industry.

Here, "state" refers to government, law enforcement institutions,
and the governing ideologies that range from "minimalist" in Mexico
to "limited" in the United States, except for the bipartisan commitment to what the United States refers to as the "war on crime." In
this chapter, we unpack the layered state to focus on public safety in
local and state governments: the municipality of Ciudad Juárez in the
state of Chihuahua and both the city and county local governments
of El Paso. El Paso devotes a sizeable city budget to the police, and
most of county government is dedicated to law enforcement. Law
enforcement institutions in Mexico have a reputation of ineffective-
ness and impunity. In this chapter, we turn our attention to domestic
violence, an underreported crime wherein women and girls are generally the victims and survivors. We analyze the spatial dimensions of
domestic violence and the scope of this security problem, both in the
whole border region and within each city, paying particular attention
to police response.

Violence against women is a worldwide scourge, as many United
Nations conferences and resolutions have stressed. At the border,
both Mexico and the United States take national security policies
seriously; the United States. posts many Border Patrol, DEA, and
other federal agents along the border, and since 2008, the Mexican
federal government positioned thousands of its military troops in
Ciudad Juárez to quell the drug-related violence. The concept of
"human security," as opposed to nation-state security, embraces the
everyday security of people and freedom from violence, poverty, and
hunger (Enloe 2007; Staudt et al. 2009).

Saskia Sassen's analyses of denationalized spaces, global cities,
and inequalities therein have advanced understanding of the global
era. She notes the existence of gender inequalities in a global city's
labor market. When financial and manufacturing relationships reign
supreme, the role of government is reduced to facilitating such connections for market-driven development. In Chapter 3 of this volume,
Monárrez and Bejarano address the implications of an "absent state"
for strikingly high murder rates. Yet Sassen does not address public
security and gender-based violence. Alas, then neither Sassen nor law

enforcement and national security agencies deal with our concern in this chapter: everyday security against violence in the border region. In this chapter, we examine domestic violence in the Paso del Norte metropolitan region of El Paso and Ciudad Juárez—an urban border zone that merits consideration as a globalizing city in Sassen's terms (see Fuentes and Peña, this volume). We ask whether and to what extent these bordering states address women's everyday security and freedom from violence. The international borderline, running through both cities, is a magnet for violence due to its globalizing characteristics—both for legal commercial and the illegal drug trade (Payan 2006)—and its changing gender power relations (Staudt 2008: Ch. 2). We examine the extent to which the state nips domestic violence in the bud, before it becomes a preamble to murder. We also examine the spatial distribution of domestic violence, asking whether domestic violence incidence occurs primarily in impoverished regions or all over the city as well as how local law enforcement addresses the problem. Ultimately, solutions that reduce violence against women in border zones like the Paso del Norte Metropolitan region require transborder action both from civil society activism and governments (Staudt and Coronado 2002). Feminist and human rights civil society activists have vigorously challenged state inaction and the binational silence on violence against women (Staudt 2008: Ch. 4). As we ultimately conclude, however, despite transnational activism about violence against women in the Paso del Norte region, women's security from everyday violence is hardly guaranteed by local and state police, or by national border security efforts.

We draw from multiple methods of acquiring evidence and sources of evidence in this chapter. In Ciudad Juárez, we tap into in-depth interviews with women in 2002–2003 and large-scale surveys from 2004 to 2005. Moreover, we have participated in crossborder organizations since 2002, including the Organización Popular Independiente (OPI—Independent Popular Organization), a large coalition of neighborhood organizations in the densely populated, high-poverty Poniente region of west and southwestern Ciudad Juárez (Robles), and the Coalition against Violence toward Women and Families at the U.S.-Mexico Border (Staudt), focused on the femicide in Ciudad Juárez, resulting in the deaths, by 2009, of more than 500 women and girls in the region (see Monárrez and Bejarano in this volume; Staudt 2008). We also secured crime-report data from both the El Paso Police Department and the Municipal Police in Ciudad Juárez on the spatial locations of reported domestic violence incidents. Finally, we live and teach in the border region, where people cross frequently to visit friends and relatives, shop, and work; many of our students and their families have been touched by the violence. This chapter is organized into the following sections. First, we affirm but also challenge and extend theoretical traditions that provide global frameworks for understanding power and ideologies at borders—traditions that fall short of incorporating patriarchy into understanding women's everyday insecurities in governments with selective commitment to enforcing laws prohibiting domestic violence. Second, we analyze domestic violence at the border, a crime in both countries, which involves partners within households. The terms "family violence" or "domestic violence" seem to minimize these crimes—sometimes better labeled attempted murder. We analyze the incidence of such crime, provide poignant reminders of its terror, and outline spatial manifestations in the region. We compare the role of the state in counting reports and engaging with abusers and survivors. Finally, we close on a somewhat more optimistic note. Local, national, and transnational organizations have expanded awareness of violence against women, and more women seem to speak out against and report the crimes. Yet, individual women, human rights/feminist, and transnational organizations exercise limited capability to influence the still-patriarchal United States and Mexican states and their militarized drive to control the border in the name of border security, oblivious to women's everyday insecurities.

I. THEORETICAL PERSPECTIVES: SPATIAL ANALYSIS AT BORDERS

The Paso del Norte region of Ciudad Juárez-El Paso is situated at the global frontlines of export-processing industrialization and national security institutions. It is a region where business, industrial, and political elites praise free trade and where governments subsidize crossborder commerce and trade (Staudt and Coronado 2002: Ch. 5). While postrevolutionary Mexico was once committed to the rhetoric of social democracy and responsive government, it has joined the ranks of nation-states with primary faith in the global market economy to address citizens' needs.

Writing about industrialized nations, the late Antonio Gramsci (1971) conceptualized "hegemony" to explain how the strong control the weak not only through material and economic power, but also through ideologies that influence popular culture and induce what is seemingly consent among people without the use of coercion. With this logic, people internalize dominant hegemonies that come to be normalized in everyday work and life. Dominant hegemonic forces in the 21st century consist of powerful global economic actors, their free-trade ideologies, and the minimalist state functioning primarily to facilitate commerce, law, and order. Gender is only visible in Gramscian analysis with feminist attention.

We fault Gramsci for omitting patriarchy and masculinist hegemonies in his conceptions of power and control. Historically, men have ruled governments; "manned" law enforcement institutions, such as the police, prosecutors, and judges; and controlled households, ostensibly protecting women therein. Laws to reduce violence against women emerged more recently around the world as women's movements pressed for human rights and the rights of citizenship (Weldon 2002). Yet the *existence* of domestic violence laws does not produce *enforcement* or priority implementation. In the United States, approximately 30 years passed before civil society pressed the government strongly enough to instigate law enforcement institutions to train police officers and to staff and subsidize once-voluntary nonprofit organizations to offer safety, counseling, and shelter to survivors of domestic violence (Staudt 2008: Ch. 5). In Mexico, the development of effective law enforcement institutions seems distant and elusive, for the human, material, and political resources necessary to transform corrupt police cultures are not yet in place.

We believe that it is imperative to address multiple hegemonic layers, from the global economy to what Gloria González-López calls "regional patriarchies" (2005; also see Pablo Vila and Alejandro Lugo on border hyper-masculinities in Staudt 2008: Ch. 2). In the Paso del Norte region, we identify complex bordered regional patriarchies, where men exercise privilege and power over most women's everyday lives, a power that is checked only partially: law enforcement institutions on one side of the border "contain" murder and femicide more effectively (United States) than their counterparts on the other side of the border (Mexico), but domestic violence is common throughout the border region and in the mainstream of both countries. We expect that regional patriarchies are especially forceful where professional police institutions are weak.

Anthony Giddens analyzes globalization both as distant economic processes with a new international division of labor and as political, technical, and cultural processes. He also argues that globalization influences intimate and personal aspects of our lives (Giddens 2000: 23–25). Feminists have nurtured such insights for decades, and this chapter deepens such insights with more detail than theorists' abstract generics. As we noted above, women comprise the majority of the

huge *maquiladora* workforce in Ciudad Juárez. But taking both cities of the Paso del Norte region together, women make up 35–40
percent of the total formal labor force and earn less than men—no
surprise, given the ubiquitous gender wage gaps globally (Staudt
and Vera 2006). Giddens notes how globalization changes family
systems, generating demands for greater gender equality (ibid: 14).
The conjuncture of women's struggle for human rights and equality
runs up against the patriarchal, shrinking state that exists primarily to
guarantee orderly markets for global manufacturing firms.

Sociologists have long been interested in how women's work
and earnings affect household dynamics. Women's growing economic independence from men in marriage threatens male control
in households and may allow women to exit relationships with less
difficulty, including dangerous relationships. But in globalizing cities,
will women's meager earnings provide enough resources to support
themselves and their children? Drawing on a large sample of low-
income households in Mexico City, Lourdes Benería and Martha
Roldán documented a woman's ability to exit relationships with the
leverage that income provided (in Staudt 2008: Ch. 3). Yet women's
limited incomes offer tenuous bargaining capability, fraught with
potential threats and violence.

Our own border research affirms such findings from Mexico City.
In Ciudad Juárez, Staudt found that women who work in formal
wage employment report higher experiences of physical violence from
partners compared with women who do unpaid work in the home
(2008: Ch. 3). Yet the vast majority of women in a large, representative sample understand their human and civil rights, even as some lack
the resources and wherewithal to exit dangerous relationships (ibid).
And in a large sample of workers at a major *maquiladora*, the Delphi
Plant in Ciudad Juárez, women report rates of physical domestic
violence that are double the rates in other studies (Carmona, Aguirre
and Burciaga [2005] in Staudt 2008: 69). In in-depth interviews from
2002 to 2003, a woman told Robles that she works and takes charge
of family expenses, occasionally hiding 50 pesos (US$5 at the time of
the interviews) for her daughter who is in school. Her husband's sister
and mother sent her husband to California and after he returned, he
wanted her to stop working. "Whether he works or not, it is the same,
because he did not give me anything; he spends his money on friends
and other women and I am always in charge of the expenses." Women
working, therefore, may provide some survival resources for the family and perhaps some leverage to reduce economic dependence, but it
hardly transforms gender relations.

II. Bordering Domestic Violence: From Murder to Domestic Violence

In two monographs about violence against women in Mexico, Amnesty International challenged law enforcement's institutional impunity and the political will to professionalize such institutions. *Intolerable Killings* (2003) offered a full analysis of the femicide, and *Women's Struggle for Justice and Safety* (Amnesty International, 2008) focused on violence in the family. We reiterate that phrases like "family violence" and "domestic violence" are all too often misnomers for attempted murder. The term "domestic" domesticates dangerous assaults that would be addressed between and among strangers in professional law enforcement systems.

In Amnesty's family violence monograph on Mexico, authors draw on official figures that show 82 percent of female murders occurring in homes, versus 12 percent of male murders (2008: 11–12). The police might be viewed as accessories to the crimes, given their indifference and lack of responsiveness to women's safety. In Mexico, police and prosecutor institutions are notorious, and many people use the word impunity/*impunidad* to describe the system.

National and Historical Perspectives on the Police

In Mexico, scholars have criticized municipal and state police corruption and complicity with criminals (selections in Cornelius and Shirk, 2007; Alvarado 2008). Although U.S. police corruption has been substantial historically, especially before and during the 1920s–1930s era of organized crime racketeering through the civil rights era of the 1960s and 1970s with embedded racism and sexism in police practices, international public opinion surveys now show high rates, approximately 85–90 percent, of public trust in the police compared to a near inversion in Mexico rates, such as in Mexico City studies where 73 percent believe that the police protect criminals or cover up crime (Giugale et al., reported in Staudt 2008: 119).

The Paso del Norte Border Region: Crime and Safety

Moving to the globalized border, El Paso and Ciudad Juárez offer contrasting profiles with regard to serious crimes, such as murder and felonies. El Paso consistently comes in second or third on lists of the safest cities in the United States (Congressional Quarterly annual updates, 2009), while murder rates in Ciudad Juárez have long been high, ranging from 200–300 annually but skyrocketing in 2008 to over 1,600 and 2,600 in 2009 (Staudt 2009; also see Monárrez, this volume). Domestic violence is categorized as a less serious misdemeanor crime, unless it is a repeat offense or a weapon is involved. The crime is muted: underreported, and undercounted, though evidence below shows report rates increasing.

Ciudad Juárez is considered one of the most dangerous cities in Mexico and the world, especially during the era of drug-based violence, fueled by U.S. consumer demand The atmosphere of police mistrust, crime, and fear has implications for official response to violence against women, including domestic violence. Moreover, a culture of "non-reporting" exists, given the historical, near-universal public-private divide, which lodges women in the private household sphere. This public-private divide is breaking down in both the United States and Mexico. Yet, abuser-threat levels often escalate after victim-survivors report them to the police. Thus, fear and intimidation must also be taken into account.

Domestic Violence: Laws, Enforcement, and Shelters

As for state criminal laws, domestic violence is defined somewhat differently in Texas and Chihuahua. Mexican laws offer a more expansive definition to include psychological abuse, while U.S. laws focus on physical and sexual violence. While psychological and verbal violence may be less actionable in legal terms, it is often the prelude to physical violence as the abuser "readies" his victim for crime by undermining her worth, value, and self-esteem.

Texas county-level courts offer a civil remedy to domestic violence in the form of a Protective Order, requiring the abuser to keep a specific distance from his target. While the violation of Protective Orders instigates more serious charges, some abusers are not deterred by a paper document order and go on to murder their victim or to commit a murder-suicide. Of the 32 women killed in El Paso between 1998 and 2006, 8 died just before their murderer committed suicide (Texas Council on Family Violence data base, www.tcfv.org).

Although domestic violence is against the law in Mexican states, many police officers and public prosecutors are indifferent or assign it a low priority. In Amnesty's legal case research, a victim with a history of broken bones and locked inside the home with severe bruises made ten complaints, but "each time was told that it was not a crime and they could do nothing; in the majority of cases, the prosecutor failed to even take an official statement from her" (2008: 16). In other cases, several women were told that "their cases did not amount to criminal offences" or that the Prosecutor simply could not take their complaint because "they did not have the time and violence in the family was not a priority" (ibid: 21). In yet another legal case in a city without a battered women's shelter, the prosecutor would not register the complaint and the complainant was told to leave the city: "when you have one foot in the grave and the other still, then come back here" she was told (bid: 31).

Nonprofit organizations in each border city offer shelter and counseling. Some thirty shelters operate in El Paso, three of them specializing in domestic violence for battered victim-survivors. In Ciudad Juárez, Casa Amiga opened a shelter in 2005 with space for ten families, but recently closed it; several other small shelters operate, called Sin Violencia/Without Violence (SINVIAC) and Albergue Centro de Protección de Mujer a Mujer/Woman-to-Woman Protection Center. In El Paso, battered women's shelters offer space without questions about citizenship, and shelter directors report that those women who crossed the border have sometimes said that their abuser threatened to kill and dump them in the desert, just like other femicide victims (Staudt 2008: 113).

Ciudad Juárez has become the infamous city since the documentation and local to global activism against femicide, known as *feminicidio*. Julia E. Monárrez and César Fuentes have documented tragic spaces of insecurity for femicide victims in Ciudad Juárez, mapping those areas of extreme inequality as having high rates of hate-based sexualized murders (2004). One area of extreme poverty is the Poniente region of west and southwestern Juárez, an area where Robles did in-depth interviews in 2002–2003.

Abusers threaten women with femicide—committing murder and dumping the body in the desert periphery surrounding the city, with few consequences from law enforcement. As a woman told Robles in the 2002–2003 interviews, "Once when we were fighting, we went out and he shouted at me that one day he will come and throw me where they kill all the women." The lack of state accountability for murders of women gives abusers additional leverage to threaten and intimidate their victims.

Domestic Violence: Underreported Crimes

With respect to domestic violence, there are inherent challenges to documenting spatial insecurity, because the data only emerge when survivors of domestic violence report crimes against them or seek shelter, for example, in homeless or battered women's shelters; and victims rarely report crimes to law enforcement institutions they do not trust. In Staudt's survey of a representative sample of 404 women in Ciudad Juárez, 2004–2005, 75 percent of respondents said they did not trust the police; 80 percent said they would not call the police if physically abused (Staudt 2008: Ch. 3). In workshops conducted in connection with the research, one woman said (translated): "Public officials usually use their power to rob, trick, ridicule, and even beat the community. And although it sounds bad, they even rape and kill" (ibid: 60).

In both cities, the police departments organize themselves into regional command centers, serving different areas and spaces of the cities. Densely settled Ciudad Juárez settlements are organized into neighborhoods called *colonias*, each with their own names and identities. The low-density, sprawling city of El Paso, built around the southern-most segment of the Rocky Mountains, categorizes space in the city by geographic and directional labels (west, northeast, and so on). In Ciudad Juárez, the number of *colonias* that police serve ranges from 61 to 225, as the subsequent map shows. Population density is especially high in the impoverished western and southwestern spaces of the city, settled on the Juárez Mountains, where many femicide victims' bodies were dumped.

Robles secured month-by-month data from the municipal police to compare 2003 and 2008 and found increased report-filing rates. For August, a hot, high-report month, 71 complaints in 2003 increased seven-fold to 497 complaints in 2008. Still, the total number of annual reports is a mere fifth of reports in El Paso, a city twice the size of Ciudad Juárez, despite similar prevalence rates of approximately 1 in 4 reported in both countries (Staudt 2008: Ch. 2). Why are report rates so low? Besides people's lack of trust in the police and police response, victims are ashamed and fear their abusers, given the threats to harm them more. As a woman told Robles in her 2002–2003 interviews, "He clearly told me that the day he knows I told someone else, or complain of the beating, I will be beaten even worse." This woman spoke with a counselor and then went to a doctor who warned, "You could not do anything to him because the marks were from his belt." Afterward, the abuser escalated his attacks and then threatened to strike her with a hammer; she called the police, and they locked him up temporarily. One woman that Robles interviewed in 2002–2003 was knifed in the stomach when she was pregnant; in another case, her husband shot at her, but, fortunately, missed. Again, the phrase domestic violence mutes the seriousness of attempted murder. Mexico's criminal codes on the severity of crime shape police responses. As Amnesty reports, corroborated by our local interviews, "[T]he severity of the offence depends on the assessment of the lasting impact of physical injuries. Cases where the injuries will heal within 15 days are considered minor offences" (2008: 24).

Data from Police Departments

Below we report data from the city police departments on the number of domestic violence calls, incidents, and arrests. Despite shared urban space at the border, police departments in the two sovereign countries report cases filed and prioritize data collection differently, making comparisons problematic. We once again call readers' attention to the highly variant report rates of domestic violence— approximately 30,000 annually in El Paso, a city only half the size of Ciudad Juarez, which itself reports an all-time high rate of just over 6,000 complaints. As discussed earlier, we interpret this in the context of people's low trust and low report rates to police departments in Mexico generally, along with the belated attention and low priority that police have given to violence against women in Ciudad Juárez. Monárrez and Bejarano address the number of murders of women in the Paso del Norte region that skyrocketed to 571 (1993–2008) in Ciudad Juárez and to 21 in nearby Las Cruces, New Mexico. Earlier, we reported 32 El Paso women murdered from 1998–2006 (www.tcfv.org). Despite the inherent problems of reported versus actual domestic violence rates, we work with the data we have. Of course, in this chapter, our focus is the everyday terror of women living in homes with domestic violence, a pattern some can exit and escape from while others cannot. Domestic violence sometimes leads to murder, and the term "domestic violence" mutes the horror of attempted murder as respondents reported in Robles' interviews and in the Amnesty interviews associated with legal cases.

In Ciudad Juárez, data collection was once nonexistent to low priority. In a large national survey sponsored by the National Women's Institute (INMUJERES, Instituto Nacional de las Mujeres), Mexico's Census Bureau (INEGI, Instituto Nacional e Estadística Geografía e Informática), and the United Nations UNIFEM, researchers disaggregated data geographically only up to the state level (published in 2004, cited in Staudt 2008: Ch. 2). They defined and identified a range of domestic violence, from verbal and psychological to physical and sexual assault. Taking *all* types of domestic violence, almost half of women reported some type of violence in their lifetimes, and rural rates of violence exceeded urban rates. The lack of data disaggregated to the city level in part prompted the 2004–2005 data collection in Ciudad Juárez. In the representative sample of 404 women, aged 15–39, 27 percent reported physical violence at the hands of partners during their lifetimes (Staudt 2008: Ch. 3). Had all women reported the crimes, the official statistics would be much higher. But in Juárez, just like El Paso, the crime is underreported. However, now more survivors are reporting crimes.

Ciudad Juárez: Incidence of Domestic Violence

The Municipal Secretariat of Public Security in Ciudad Juárez reported just 6,347 complaints, resulting in 1,441 arrests, in 2008. During the same year, Casa Amiga, the nonprofit antiviolence counseling center, received 2,129 cases of domestic violence—a number larger than the number of arrests.

In Staudt's 2004–2005 survey, women expressed widespread awareness of domestic violence as a crime and reluctance to excuse abusers because of drinking or cynicism about abusers' promises to change. Of all the women interviewed in the survey, 27 percent reported that they had experienced physical violence in their lives. As for the causes of such violence, the most common remark women made was that some men did not respect or value women. Women also referred to poverty, drug and alcohol use, flaws in government and police, and lack of solidarity with neighbors as other causes (2008: Ch. 3). Women responded to violence with various strategies, ranging from submission to fighting back, but few said they would call the police. Women expressed widespread mistrust of the police.

Certain demographic characteristics were common to those women who had experience with violence in the 2004–2005 surveys: household incomes of less than US$100 weekly, migration experiences, and education levels of *primaria* (6th grade) or less. As such, these characteristics matched with the census for the city. One factor emerged as distinctive for women who had experienced violence compared to those who had not: victim-survivors experienced extremely high levels of psychological and verbal abuse, diminishing their sense of self-value and self-worth and possibly the wherewithal to exit dangerous relationships (Staudt 2008: Ch. 3).

Below, we provide a map of Ciudad Juárez and its six regional police stations. The map contains the total number of *colonias* that each station covers, the number of domestic violence complaints, and the number of arrests.

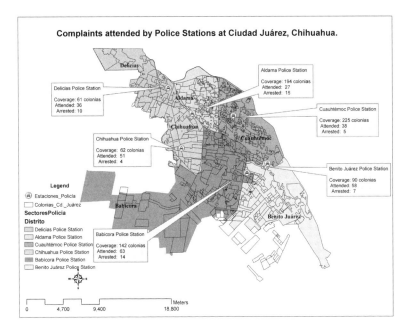

Map 4.1   Complaints attended by police in Ciudad Juárez, Chihuahua

Given the underreporting problem, and the widely varying numbers of *colonias* and people served, we cannot provide definitive
representations of the report-arrest figures. However, we note that
the Benito Juárez station, a less impoverished area, has the second-
highest number of complaints, yet one of the two lowest complaint-
to-arrest ratios, with 1 in 8 arrested (7 arrests of 58 complaints),
second only to Chihuahua station with 1 in 12 arrested. Research
on police response in Ciudad Juárez is in an early stage, one that will
hopefully instigate more detailed analysis.

El Paso: Incidence of Domestic Violence

For El Paso, we made a formal request to the El Paso Police Department for the latest data available (2007) that documented *incidence*
of domestic violence, of the approximately 30,000 calls to the police
at police district and subdistrict levels. From many studies in the
United States, we know that one in four women have experienced
physical violence at the hands of their partner at one time or another
in their lives (Staudt 2008: Ch. 2). This figure is similar to what
women reported in the survey in Ciudad Juárez.

When a potential victim calls Emergency Response (911), conversations are taped, a police officer or officers are dispatched to
the scene, and the officers determine whether domestic violence has
occurred and/or whether to arrest the aggressor. Approximately
6,000 investigations occur along with 3,000 arrests (Romero and
Yellen 2004: 27). The District Attorney's office provides a capable
staff of seven prosecuting attorneys who specialize in family violence and are committed to justice. Data are tabulated in the police
department's database, along with other crime data reported to the
state and Federal Bureau of Investigation. Domestic violence occurs
in households, between any household members, such as parent and
child or siblings, but the most common incidence is between intimate
partners. According to El Paso's Center against Family Violence
Battering Intervention and Prevention Program, (a court-ordered,
26-week course that abusers may take in lieu of jail sentences),
90 percent of the perpetrators are male and 10 percent female (Staudt
2008: Ch. 5). On the El Paso Police Department Web site, the mug
shots of those charged with domestic violence are posted for two
weeks—a type of public humiliation and warning—and approximately
90 percent of those pictured are men (http://www.elpasotexas.gov/
pdimug/default.asp?charge=Assault).

As stated above, each year, approximately 30,000 calls are made to
Emergency Response that are classified as domestic violence, but the
police classify less than half as actual incidents. In 2007, the El Paso
Police Department recorded 11,670 incidents.

Although U.S. research routinely shows that domestic violence
cuts across class and income lines, we anticipated that the incidence
of such crime would be higher in lower income neighborhoods due
to conflict that might emerge over money and scarce resources. Yet
we also expected that members of households with mixed citizenship
and immigration statuses—citizens, legal permanent residents, and
undocumented people—would be less likely to call the police for
assistance. Although the 1995 Violence against Women Act (VAWA)
provides a process for application for a special visa for immigrants
who report domestic violence (*if* married to a U.S. citizen or a Legal
Permanent Resident), many immigrants are wary of reporting crimes
that may result in the deportation of family members. Noncitizen
status likely overlaps with low-income status, thus potentially con-
founding our expected relationships. El Paso is one of the five poorest
big cities in the United States measured in household income terms.
The median income reported in the 2000 Census (1999 figures) was
US$32,124.

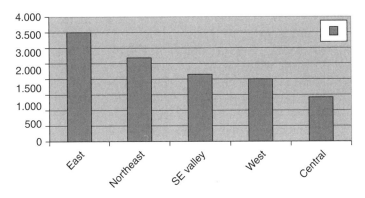

Figure 4.1 El Paso Police District domestic violence incidents, 2007
Source: Staudt's Reconstruction of Domestic Violence Incidence Data 2007, provided by the
El Paso Police Department in 2008.

On the City of El Paso Web site, one can find a map of the El Paso
Police Department's regional district stations, each of which has been
divided into subdistricts. Domestic violence incidence totals have
been compiled at both district and subdistrict levels. The boundaries
of the two spatial units do not mesh with census track boundaries.

Contrary to our expectations, when analyzing the incidence data,
we found domestic violence to be widespread across the city, not concentrated in poorer areas. El Paso's east side is a fast-growing region
north of the Interstate Highway 10, served by the Police Department's Pebble Hills Regional Command Center. El Paso's northeast
side hugs the eastern side of the mountain range and is home to U.S.
military bases. The southeast valley region, served by the Mission
Valley Regional Command Center, is a lower-income region south of
the Interstate Highway 10 and north of the international border with
Mexico. The west side, west of the Franklin Mountains, is a slightly
higher-income area with housing stock of somewhat higher value.
The central area, home to lower-income residents, includes older
housing stock, much of it in rental rather than ownership arrangements with residents. As Figure 4.1 shows below, some regions had
a far higher incidence of domestic violence than others. In the fast-
growing east side, 3,461 domestic violence incidences were reported,
compared with 1,431 in the central area.

The "Dangerous Dozen"

Each police district is organized into subdistricts, characterized by
different levels of domestic violence incidents. Although census track

boundaries do not mesh with subdistricts, we attempted to make a rough, imperfect match with the top three among what we call the "dangerous dozen" subdistricts and their spatial locations. The top three among the dangerous dozen display a wide range of median household incomes. The most dangerous subdistrict, on the east side, had a median per capita income of US$34,143 (higher than the city median figure); the second subdistrict on the list, in the southeast valley, had a median income of US$26,994; and the third subdistrict on the list, in the northeast, had an extremely low relative median income of US$12,837. The spatial distribution of the "dangerous dozen" includes 5 in the northeast, 4 each in the east and southeast, 2 in the west, and none in the central area (the last two categories had several regions recording 326 and 325 incidents, respectively).

Although the aggregate data do not reveal the exact household income where domestic violence incidents occurred, these data do not show a consistent relationship between neighborhood poverty and reported domestic violence. Rather, data show violence-based insecurity across spatial regions of the city, including middle- and upper-income neighborhoods. Once again, the limitations of these data include the general underreporting of actual domestic violence and the possible reluctance of noncitizens to expose conflict to the authorities due to concerns about vulnerability to deportation. It must also be remembered that in the United States, many live beyond their actual income means, given the easy access to credit and mortgages to purchase homes. The U.S. economic recession (2008–2009) has made obvious how deep indebtedness produces financial insecurity amid downturn, layoffs, and unemployment.

III. Closing Reflections on Border Domestic Violence, Transnational Activism, and the Persistent Exclusion of Violence Against Women as a Border Security Problem

In this chapter, we document the pervasive problem of domestic violence against women in the Paso del Norte Metropolitan border region, a magnet that likely increases the common and all-too-normalized violence against women worldwide. Through surveys, in-depth interviews, and data from police departments, we illustrate the potential terror of everyday life for approximately one-quarter of women in the region. In this political laboratory of a globalizing metropolitan region, national border security priorities are totally disconnected from human security to live free of violence. Instead, local law enforcement selectively addresses such crime and insecurity. In Ciudad Juárez, we show the "absent state," with untrustworthy local police and prosecutors on crimes that range from domestic violence to attempted murder. Yet a glimmer of hope emerges with the vast increase in victim-survivor reports. In El Paso, with its far higher call and incidence numbers, there is responsiveness and shelter, yet a grimly persistent problem of violence against women.

The maps and data offer a preliminary examination of the spatial distribution of reported incidents of domestic violence in the single Paso del Norte region. Crimes reported do not reflect actual crimes committed, given the problem of underreporting domestic violence generally and of the culture of nonreporting in Ciudad Juárez, a city with the reputation of widespread police and prosecutor impunity. Our analysis also reveals the difficulty in analyzing spatial characteristics of a common metropolitan region at the binational border, given the "methodological nationalism" that Sassen discusses (see preface), not only in the definitions and indicators for various phenomena for data collected in the censuses of both Mexico and the United States, but also for police departments and the borders and boundaries they utilize to control space and collect data therein.

Despite the size and scope of this problem, dominant hegemonic ideologies in the region make violence against women a local law enforcement issue rather than one of national or binational security. Yet law enforcement, one of the most masculinist of government agencies in many countries, is part of the hegemony. We remind readers that national U.S. border security policies focusing on drugs, terror, and immigration provide little attention to everyday public insecurity, such as violence against women or immigrant crossers who flee violence and poverty. On one side of the border, patriarchal hegemonies render law enforcement officials near useless in addressing the problem. On the other side of the border, patriarchy is tempered in law enforcement institutions, given feminist and human rights pressure over decades to treat violence against women seriously. The well-funded police, emergency response, and prosecuting attorney offices treat domestic violence as a crime *if* victim-survivors call and report incidents. And El Paso's nonprofit community provides meager but welcome shelter from batterers. El Paso "contains" the high rates of murder exemplified in Juárez, but women still experience the grim reality of everyday violence. As a phrase and label for crime, the term "domestic violence" hardly addresses the sheer terror of repeated beatings and attempted murder, especially with law enforcement institutions that do not regard the crimes as serious priorities.

Over nearly a decade, feminist and human rights activists have allied together in solidarity to denounce violence against women and press authorities to prevent murder and identify the killers (Staudt 2008: Ch. 4), whether strangers or intimate partners. Neighborhood organizations like OPI in Ciudad Juárez offer counseling and outreach about family violence. With femicide, transnational activists have utilized dramatic strategies and tactics to call attention to the crimes, especially infamous in Ciudad Juárez.

While activists have spread awareness and prompted government promises and reports, dominant hegemonic forces still privilege the limited state and free-market forces rather than the large pool of surplus labor, which is often viewed as disposable labor—people who work at precarious labor, who are almost totally responsible for their own safety. The term "disposable" might be viewed in literal and figurative terms, as the victims and survivors of misogynist crimes and abusive partners have little value and priority for some law enforcement institutions. All too often, murderers threaten, hurt, and kill women, the literal victims and terrorized survivors in this global metropolitan border region. Ironically, assaults and murders occur underneath a supranational security state apparatus that supposedly protects residents from crime, drugs, and terror. We look forward to the day when national and human security needs mesh better in this border metropolitan region.

Acknowledgment: Thanks to Julia E. Monárrez for her comments on this chapter.

REFERENCE LIST

Alvarado, Arturo, ed. 2008. *La Reforma de la Justicia en México*, pp. 423–468. México, D. F.: El Colegio de México.

Amnesty International. 2003. *Intolerable Killings: Ten Years of Abductions and Murders of Women in Ciudad Juárez.* New York: Amnesty International.

———. 2008. *Women's Struggle for Justice and Safety: Violence in the Family in Mexico.* New York: Amnesty International.

Congressional Quarterly. 2009. *City Criminal Rankings 2009–2010.* http://os.cqpress.citycrime/2009/CityCrime2009.html

Cornelius, Wayne and David Shirk, eds. 2007. *Reforming the Administration of Justice in Mexico.* Notre Dame, IN: Notre Dame University Press.

Enloe, Cynthia. 2007. *Globalization & Militarism: Feminists Make the Link.* Lanham, MD: Rowman & Littlefield.

Fernández-Kelly, María Patricia. 1983. *For We are Sold, I and My People: Women and Industry in Mexico's Frontier.* Albany: SUNY Press.

Gramsci, Antonio. 1971. *Selections from the Prison Notebooks.* NY: International Publishers.

Giddens, Anthony. 2000. *Un mundo desbocado. Los efectos de la globalización en nuestras vidas.* México. Editorial Taurus, 2000.

INMUJERES et al. 2004. *Encuesta nacional sobre la dinámica de las relaciones en los hogares 2003.* Mexico DF: INMUJERES http://cedoc. inmujeres.gob.mx/php_general/muestra_docto.php?ID100411

Kopinak, Kathryn, ed. 2004. *The Social Costs of Industrial Growth in Northern Mexico.* La Jolla: Univeristy of California at San Diego Center for U.S.-Mexican Studies; Boulder: Lynne Rienner Press.

López-González, Gloria. 2005. *Erotic Journeys: Mexican Immigrants and their Sex Lives.* Berkeley: University of California Berkeley Press.

Monárrez Fragoso, Julia E. and César M. Fuentes. 2004. "Feminicidio y marginalidad urbana en Ciudad Juárez en la década de los noventa." In *Violencia Contra las Mujeres en Contextos Urbanos y Rurales.* Marta Torres Falcón, ed., pp. 43–70. Mexico City: El Colegio de México.

Payan, Tony. 2006. *The Three U.S.-Mexico Border Wars: Drugs, Immigration, and Homeland Security.* NY: Praeger.

Romero, Manuela and Tracy Yellen. 2004. *El Paso Portraits: Women's Lives, Potential & Opportunities: A Report on the Status of Women in El Paso, Texas.* El Paso: YWCA/UTEP Center for Civic Engagement.

Ruiz Marrujo. Olivia. 2009. "Women, Migration, and Sexual Violence: Lessons from Mexico's Borders." In *Human Rights Along The U.S.-Mexico Border: Gendered Violence And Insecurity.* Staudt et al., ed., pp. 31–47.

Sassen, Saskia. 2001. *The Global City: New York, London, Tokyo.* Princeton, NJ: Princeton University Press.

Staudt, Kathleen. 2008. *Violence and Activism at the Border: Gender, Fear and Everyday Life in Ciudad Juárez.* Austin: University of Texas Press.

Staudt, Kathleen, Tony Payan, and Z. Anthony Kruszewski, eds. 2009. *Human Rights along the U.S.-Mexico Border: Gendered Violence and Insecurity.* Tucson: University of Arizona Press.

Staudt, Kathleen and Irasema Coronado. 2002. *Fronteras no Más: Toward Social Justice at the U.S.-Mexico Border.* NY: Palgrave USA.

Staudt, Kathleen and Beatriz Vera. 2006. "Mujeres, políticas públicas y políticas: Los caminos globales de Ciudad Juárez, Chihuahua-El Paso, Texas." *Región y sociedad* 18(37), pp. 127–172.

Texas Council on Family Violence. Accessed 12/08. www.tcfv.org

Weldon, S. Laurel. 2002. *Protest, Policy, and the Problem of Violence against Women: A Cross-National Comparison.* Pittsburgh: University of Pittsburgh Press.

SECTION II

GLOBALIZED PRODUCTION, URBAN SPACE, AND PUBLIC SERVICES

CHAPTER 5

GLOBALIZATION AND ITS EFFECTS ON THE URBAN SOCIO-SPATIAL STRUCTURE OF A TRANSFRONTIER METROPOLIS: EL PASO, TX-CIUDAD JUÁREZ, CHIH.-SUNLAND-PARK, NM

César M. Fuentes and Sergio Peña

INTRODUCTION

The expansion of export processing zones, such as those located at international borders, as a result of globalization process, has produced a change in the development of economic activities with urban socio-spatial implications on both sides of the U.S.-Mexico border cities. It has been argued that the rapid urbanization of the U.S.-Mexican border cities has generated a number of serious problems on the Mexican side of the border, including lack of drinking water, inadequate water sanitation services, substandard housing, ineffective waste management, etc. (Canales, 1999). Besides, urban development has created enormous pressure on the transborderland markets (Fuentes and Cervera, 2006).

The main argument put forward in the chapter is that the increasing delocalization and the deepening commodification of real estate property seem to portend a significant impact on the transborder, urban socio-spatial structure. On the one hand, since the beginning of the industrialization process, the promotion of the Mexican border city as regional industrial park by developers contributed to the delocalization of real estate property; it became more deeply commodified (i.e., further separated from its social function) and valued more for its performance as a financial asset (Beauregard and Haila, 2000). In this context, local corporations, such as the Bermudez Group, played an important role as industrial promoters, property developers, real estate investors, and construction contractors operating transnationally. The ownership of urban real estate, particularly industrial properties, becomes increasingly nonlocal and international. The increasing delocalization of activities produces a global portfolio effect that inflates the value of international quality properties in the local real estate market (Beauregard and Haila, 2000). This situation influences the behavior of local industrial park developers to concentrate on large extensions of land with the expectation to sell at a higher price, thus affecting values for other land uses such as residential, commercial, and services; this process has been called the commodification of real estate property (ibid). Besides, the success of the Mexican industrial projects encourages the presence of economic and political groups interested in promoting industrial growth on both sides of the border (Llera, 2005). For example, in Sunland Park, New Mexico, local investors have targeted land development toward the boundary line between the states of Chihuahua and New Mexico to attract urban and industrial activities (Santa Teresa, NM and San Jerónimo, Chih.). As a result, developers concentrated their control over large amounts and strategic pieces of land to make quick profits on this project. Additionally, the availability of many job positions as a result of the location of export assembly plants (maquiladoras) attracts immigrants to the city, incrementing the demand of land and placing additional pressure on the local land market.

On the other hand, the industrialization process has led to an even stronger social and economic polarization effect similar to the ones taking place at global cities per se. Sassen (1984; 1991; 1998) also argues that this globalizing process generates inequality in the profit-making capabilities of different economic sectors, engendering massive distortions in the operation of various markets, from housing to labor. In Ciudad Juárez, the fastest growing manufacturing industries are characterized by a larger-than-average concentration of low-wage jobs as well as a few high-income jobs. The low-wage groups dominate in occupations like line production workers, technical and administrative staff; the higher-income groups are characterized by managerial activities.

These two processes have been translated into new forms of urbanization, forcing us to consider the economic transformations that these cities experience in their urban sociospatial structure. In the Mexican city, the exclusion of wide segments of the population from the land market has displaced poor residents to the distant periphery and the surrounding hillsides with the consequent consolidation into a shantytown pattern or squatter settlements. In spatial terms, this process is generating a dual city. The parts of the population with middle and high income—related to managerial or administrative activities in the maquiladora industry—live in the flat, northeast part of the city where public services are readily available. Whereas the part of the population with low income—most of them employed in low-skill activities in the maquiladora industry—lives in the hilly, west part of the city in areas with low levels of public infrastructure. During the consolidation of the maquiladora industry program, the urban elite excluded the masses of poor residents from its urban projects. Even in the United States, perhaps the most well-developed land market, this polarizing process occurs to a lesser degree; some residents have been displaced to substandard urban settlements called *colonias* as a result of poverty, migration, and lack of affordable housing (Ward, 1999).

In this study, we take an urban sociology perspective to examine the effects of globalization on urban sociospatial structures resulting mainly from the land market imperfections of transfrontier metropolises: El Paso, Tx.; Ciudad Juárez, Chih; and Sunland-Park, NM. The rest of the chapter is divided into five sections. The first section presents a discussion on globalization and urban form. Then, we move into explaining the polarization process in the area of study, with a discussion of how real estate property has been commoditized through the dynamics of globalization. The following section presents empirical evidence of the sociospatial impacts relying in census data and geographic information systems. The chapter ends with conclusions where we emphasize the lack of institutional tools by local governments to steer the development process in such a way that the polarization effects are mitigated.

I. GLOBALIZATION AND URBAN FORM

Numerous theorists on globalization and its effects on urban sociospatial structure have focused primarily on global cities (Marcuse, 1989; Mollenkopf and Castells, 1991; Sassen, 1991; Fainstein, Gordon, and Harloe, 1992). Sassen (1991) argued for the existence of new types of global cities that concentrate worldwide corporate and financial control functions. The major changes in the reorganization of the economic activity—products of the globalization process over the last fifteen years—have been the emergence of an uneasy feeling of general economic insecurity and new forms of employment-centered poverty. Furthermore, Sassen identifies three processes: (1) the growing inequality in the profit-making capacities of different economic sectors and in the earning capacities of different types of workers; (2) the polarization tendencies embedded in the organization of service industries and the casualization of the employment relation (e.g., housework); and (3) the production of urban marginality, particularly as a result of new structural processes of economic growth and market forces rather than those produced through public policies of abandonment.

Friedmann (1986) also argues that polarization can occur at three levels or scales. The first level is global and corresponds to the widening of the wealth, income, and power between peripheral economies and a few rich countries; in this sense, polarization is between central and peripheral countries. The second level of polarization is delimited at the interior of the countries, regardless of whether or not regions are able to hook themselves to the globalization process. The third level of polarization can be found in the interior of regions, among those individuals or laborers that are articulated to globalization and those that are not. This last level of polarization can be seen in three dimensions. First, there is a widening gap of income between elites and the group of employees with lower levels of income and skills. Second, polarization is caused by the migratory movements of rural population. Third, this polarization can also present structural tendencies to changes in employment as a result of the tertiarization of the economy, considering the last as the base for the presence of social polarization in developed countries.

The structural changes in the economic activities of developed countries, combined with a shift in location of production process, have transformed the characteristics of global cities' employment base. The most important changes have been the declining importance of the manufacturing sector and the increasing importance of the service sector. The new urban economic core of financial and service activities comes to replace the older, typically more manufacturing oriented core of services and production (Sassen, 1998).

The growth of services, in terms of both jobs and firm inputs, needs to be "unbundled" in order to capture the impact on issues regarding inequality and new forms of employment-centered poverty. In the United States, service industries have generated a significant share of all new highly skilled jobs created over the last fifteen years. Most of the other jobs created in the service sector fall at the other extreme (Sassen, 2007).

The declining welfare state, the reduction of subsidies for social housing, and greater reliance on market forces have led to higher prices for new dwellings. Lower income households have then seen reduced access to new dwellings. The choice for lower income households diminishes even further, relegating them to an ever-shrinking number of neighborhoods where they still can afford to pay for their housing (Marcuse and Van Kempen, 2000). This situation has in turn led to segregation.

Meanwhile, a low-income neighborhood desirable for its location or character may be invaded by higher income households, because they are the ones that can afford to pay for dwellings in those areas—a process known as gentrification. Gentrification is by the same token likely to increase displacement of the poor from gentrified areas. Areas of gentrification generally consist of older buildings, left vacant by poorer households after a process of displacement and rising prices. Gentrified neighborhoods are not necessarily located in older cities; their essential characteristics can be found in some suburbs and their social characteristics are exclusionary enclaves.

These processes, described above, predict an increasingly divided city, including the dual city (Mollenkopf and Castells, 1991), the quartered city (Marcuse, 1989), and the divided city (Fainstein, Gordon, and Harloe, 1992). According to Mollenkopf and Castells (1991), the main characteristic of a dual city is an increase in levels of inequality. As the manufacturing sector declines, information technologies advance and investment strategies seek to create growth machines through high-tech and financial industries, major urban areas undergo simultaneous development and decay.

The service industries that have driven large urban economies since the 1980s show greater dispersion or inequality in occupations and earnings, a proliferation of jobs in the lower-paying echelons, and weak or absent unions. Growth occurs at the high-end of the income spectrum, while the middle declines. In theory, a 10 percent increase at the top would be worth more in dollars than a combined 10 percent drop in the middle and ten percent increase in the lower level. Furthermore, the total net gain could be reinvested in public structures and services, thereby increasing the quality of life in the city overall. Even if the poorest residents are carrying most of the financial burden, these improvements would benefit them anyway. This theory derives from premodern notions of inequality: the rich own land and move money throughout the formal economic system, while the poor, independently and outside of these processes, scratch out a living any way they can through unregulated, often illegal activities of the informal economy. The dual city manifests the coexistence of a professional sector with high income and a growing urban subculture. For Marcuse (1989) the concept of quartered city may be intended in a double way: either as neighborhoods or as "quarters," pieces of the city. The city therefore is divided into islands of wealth, separated from other urban conditions of poorness.

Another important impact of globalization on the urban form is the changes in real estate dynamics—the delocalization and deepening commodification of real estate property (Beauregard and Haila, 2000). Numerous theorists (Sassen, 1991; Logan, 1993; Savitch, 1995) have commented on delocalization. They point to the rise to global prominence of property developers, real estate investors, and construction contractors that operate transnationally (Fainstein, 1994). The ownership of urban real estate, particularly prime commercial properties, has become increasing nonlocal and international. Simultaneously, real estate has become more deeply commodified (that is, further separated from its social function) and valued more and more for its performance as a financial asset (Haila, 1991; Lindahl, 1995).

> Opportunities for profit making through financial maneuverings expanded relative to those related in the production of goods and services. Developers built, investors bought, and financial institutions made loans because they expected a rapid appreciation in value. The income-generation potential of the property became disconnected from the investment decision. Real estate property thus became more like a stock or a municipal bond than like a business whose income stream mainly determined its profitability
>
> Beauregard and Haila, 2000: 31–32.

The increasing delocalization and deepening commodification produce a global portfolio effect that inflates the value of international-quality properties in the local real estate market. The price of local real estate is influenced by price levels in other markets (ibid).

Although globalization is a process that has a broad impact, there are important questions specifically concerning intracity spatial effects of this process. Globalization is not automatically translated into spatial patterns, even in the case of a growing social polarization. Symbiosis between groups might or might not lead to urban areas that include neighborhoods where people with different incomes, ethnicities, skills, and education live together. It might also very well lead to different consequences for different groups, leading some to form enclaves and others to be confined to ghettos (Marcuse and Van Kempen, 2000).

II. GLOBALIZATION AND THE POLARIZATION PROCESS IN THE U.S.-MEXICO BORDER CITIES

The Mexican side of the border plays an important role among the export processing zones not only for the availability of cheap labor, but also the location with respect to the U.S. market, which provides additional advantage, such as lower transportation costs. As a result, the region has been receiving an important amount of foreign direct investment in the form of export assembly plants (maquiladora program). Mexican border cities had experienced a tremendous expansion in the number of maquiladoras plants and workers over the last four decades (Fuentes, 2001).

Since then, the urban economy of Ciudad Juárez begun its transformation of service oriented toward manufacturing. Given the functions assigned to the city in the transnational urban hierarchy as a manufacturing center, the city experienced an inverse process to that occurring in global cities in terms of the declining importance of manufacturing and the increasing significance of services. The proportion of the economically active population employed in the tertiary sector went from 53 percent in 1970 to 23 percent in 2000, while the proportion in the secondary sector passed from 27 percent in 1970 to 55 percent in 2000. Table 5.1 shows that since

Table 5.1 Participation of the economically active population in Ciudad Juárez, Chihuahua, by sectors and percentage of change in 1970 and 2000

Sectors	1970	%	2000	%	% Change
Primary	9,342	8.7	2,742	0.6	−92.3
Agriculture	9,342	8.7	2,742	0.6	−92.3
Secondary	28,888	26.7	254,882	55.2	106.7
Mining	403	0.3	131	0.0	0
Manufacturing	19,215	17.7	222,042	48.1	171.7
Construction	8,851	8.2	30,880	6.7	−18.2
Electricity	419	0.4	1,829	0.4	0
Tertiary	57,305	53.0	105,643	22.9	−56.8
Commerce	19,149	17.8	68,001	14.7	−17.41
Communications and transportation	4,532	4.2	14,869	3.2	−23.8
Services	33,624	31.1	45,073	9.7	−68.8
Government	7,240	6.7	10,151	2.2	−62.6
Total	108,070	100.0	461,422	100.0	

Source: Own elaboration based on U.S. Census and Mexican Population and Housing Census (Inegi), 1970 and 2000.

1970, the service sector began its decline and the manufacturing sector increased its importance. In 1970, the economic base of the city specialized in the tertiary sector (commerce [17.8%] and services [31.1%] of the economically active population, respectively), the secondary sector represented 26.7 percent (the manufacturing sector only represented 17.7%), and the government employment represented 6.7 percent. Thirty years later, in 2000, the manufacturing sector represented 46.3 percent of the economic active population, meanwhile commerce and service represented 14.6 percent and 26.6 percent respectively, and government employment reduced to 2.2 percent of the total employment. During the 1970–2000 period, manufacturing employment grew 106.7 percent, while commerce (−17.4%), services (−68.8%), and government (−62.6%) had negative growth rates. These results show two important findings: (1) the importance of the maquiladora employment can be measured by the fact that in 2000 nearly 45 percent of the urban employment was related to maquiladora industry, i.e., related in someway to global activities; and (2) the reduction of the commerce, service, and government employment during the period that reflects the shrinking state.

At the same time, the location of maquiladora industry in Ciudad Juárez has been fundamental to the generation of employment in neighboring El Paso. It has been estimated that 20 percent to 37 percent of the new jobs created in El Paso are related to the maquiladora industry in Ciudad Juárez (Várgas, 2001). Both cities have been considered a binational production center (Hanson, 1996). In this context, Herzog (1991) suggest the term "transfrontier metropolis"[1] may be the most appropriate way to describe US-Mexico border areas. In this sense, El Paso,Tx, Ciudad Juárez, Chih, and Sunland Park, NM can be considered as transfrontier metropolises[2] as well.

The economies of El Paso and Ciudad Juárez have become highly integrated during the last three decades However, they have different functions in the transnational urban hierarchy; the Mexican side produces the final step of the manufacturing process (i.e., assembly), and the U.S. side provides specialized services, raw material, and components. As a result, the economic base of El Paso experienced a declining importance of the manufacturing sector, primarily of textile, and the increasing importance of the service sector, typical of developed countries.

The employment data for El Paso from 1970 to 2006 supports what we have already argued, that the apparel manufacturing industry

Table 5.2 Employment in El Paso by sector (1970, 2001, 2006)

Sector	1970	%	2001	%	2006	%
Agricultural Services	353	0.2	709	0.2	791	0.2
Mining	172	0.1	670	0.2	423	0.1
Utilities	0	0.0	1395	0.4	1166	0.3
Construction	7207	4.8	18351	5.6	20391	5.7
Manufacturing	23896	16.0	36432	11.2	23750	6.6
Wholesale trade	7385	4.9	11646	3.6	12762	3.5
Retail trade	22883	15.3	39232	12.0	43131	12.0
Transportation and warehousing	8881	6.0	14160	4.3	17954	5.0
Information	0	0.0	5374	1.6	5307	1.5
Services	23322	15.6	117788	36.2	156453	43.6
Finance and insurance	8263	5.5	9554	2.9	11379	3.2
Government and government enterprises	44926	30.1	68661	21.1	75308	21.0
Federal civilian	8882	6.0	8478	2.6	9707	2.7
Military	20771	13.9	11979	3.6	14671	4.0
State and local	15273	10.2	48204	14.8	50830	14.2
Local government	0	0.0	40459	12.4	42906	12.0
Total	149223	100.0	325114	100.0	358334	100.0

Source: Data from the BEA Regional Economic Information System (REIS) CA 25.

declined while some other sectors related to supply inputs and services to the maquiladora industry have grown, such as transportation and warehousing. Furthermore, some industries that supply inputs to the maquiladora sector, such as electrical and electronic equipment, rubber, and plastics have had a robust growth. Between 1970 and 2006, the employment sectors that grew more rapidly were transportation and warehousing (102%), construction (182%), and services (570%). In contrast, the manufacturing sector had a negative growth (−0.6%). Table 5.2 shows that in 1970 the main employers were manufacturing (16%), services (15%), retail trade (15%), military (13%), state and local employment (10%), and government (30%). In 2006, the manufacturing and military reduced their participation in the total employment from 16 percent to 6.6 percent and from 13.9 percent to 4.0 percent. In contrast, the service employment increased its participation in the total employment from 15.6 percent to 43.6 percent.

Parallel to changes in the urban economy of both cities, polarization is evident in terms of the occupations that the maquiladora industry incorporated. Given the fact that the decentralization of the industrial operations from developed countries to less developed countries was driven by reduction in the production costs through low wages, most of the positions created with the export assembly plants (maquiladora industry) are low-wage occupations.

According to the Mexican Census Bureau (known as INEGI for its Spanish acronym) statistics on the maquiladora industry (2007) show an overwhelming concentration of workers occupations is in the production line (75%) followed by technical (14%), administrative (9%), and managerial (2%) occupations. The new structure of the economic activity creates changes in the organization of the labor reflected in the supply of employment and a polarization in the occupational distribution of workers, high percentage of low-skill workers and low percentage of high-skill labor generating social polarization.

At the same time, this process not only polarizes occupations but also deepens income distribution inequalities (economic polarization). Given the high concentration of production workers, most of them have weekly wages[3] ranging from 59 to 71 US$. Additionally, this activity reinforces gender differences in terms of income inequalities; women in the same occupation have lower wages than men. In contrast, other occupation holders, such as administrative staff, earn almost 7 times more than production workers (see Table 5.3).

In summary, in this section we have shown that the industrialization process has exacerbated the polarization resulting from globalization based on occupations and earnings. In the following section, we discuss how globalization has affected the real estate dynamics of the region in a context of rapid industrialization process.

Table 5.3 Weekly income by occupation and gender of maquiladora workers (2000–2006) (U.S. dollars)

Year	Total	Production Women	Workers Men	Technical Total	Administrative Total
2000	59.06	57.45	60.86	172.84	352.50
2001	65.20	62.19	66.47	180.05	402.24
2002	69.30	69.40	73.28	184.09	442.08
2003	63.45	69.18	75.66	180.71	468.66
2004	64.24	74.02	80.00	193.11	490.91
2005	69.20	76.50	83.00	205.39	498.79
2006	71.93	79.02	87.30	208.77	519.59

Source: Estadísticas de la Industria Maquiladora, INEGI, 2007.

III. Globalization, Delocalization, and Commodification of Real Estate Property of a Transfrontier Metropolis: El Paso, Tx; Ciudad Juárez, Chih.; and Sunland Park, NM

During the globalization process, export processing zones, such as the Mexican border cities, played the role of being places for manufacturing production. As a result, the region received the highest percentages of FDI in the manufacturing sector in Mexico, and part of this investment went into real estate properties.[4] This marked the beginning of the delocalization of real estate properties and its commodification along with the impact on the urban sociospatial structure. In this context, real estate has become more deeply commodified (that is further separated from its social function) and valued more and more for its performance as a financial asset (Beauregard and Haila, 2000). In this process, local property developers, such as Bermudez International Group,[5] played an important role as industrial promoters, property developers, real estate investors, and constructions contractors operating transnationally. In this sense, industrial park developers have contributed to property delocalization. In Ciudad Juárez, 30 percent of the industrial plants are owned by companies headquartered outside the city; the rest are leased.

Furthermore, based on historical data, an area of about 183 square feet (17 square meters) is required to accommodate each additional job in the city. In Ciudad Juárez, the market size for industrial facilities is estimated at about 43 million square feet (4 million square meters) of space, making this city one of the largest markets of industrial facilities in the country (AMPI, 2000). The demand for industrial space has a strong influence on the behavior of transborder industrial park developers, therefore impacting the land market in different ways that are discussed below.

First, the increasing delocalization of real estate property produces a global portfolio effect that inflates the value of international-quality properties in the local real estate market (Beauregard and Haila, 2000). According to Bermúdez Industrial Parks, the price for industrially developed land varies from city to city. For example, the price of land for border cities, such as Ciudad Juárez and Tijuana, varies from US$4.50 to US$5.50 per square foot and for nonborder cites such as Torreón and Hermosillo the price of land varies from US$1.00 to US$1.50. In Ciudad Juárez, price of facilities leased for maquiladora production ranges from US$5.00 to US$5.75 per square foot per year for new construction and US$3.50 to US$4.50 per square foot

Table 5.4 Land use change in Ciudad Juárez, Chihuahua (1995 and 2001)

Land Use	1995 Surface (hectares)	Percent	2001 Surface (hectares)	Percent	Percent of Change
Residential	8,416	44.8	9,992	45	18.72
Industrial	1,209	6.4	1,844	8.3	52.52
Commercial	1,075	5.7	1,638	7.4	52.37
Mixed Use	617	3.2	503	2.2	−18.47
Open Spaces	446	2.3	605	2.7	35.65
Roads	4,785	25.5	5,040	22.7	5.32
Vacant Land	2,219	11.8	2,500	11.3	12.66
Total	18,767	100	22,122	100	17.87

Source: Peña and Fuentes 2007.

per year for existing building. Currently, there are 21 industrial parks. Table 5.4 shows that industrial land use grew at a rate of 52.5 percent during the 1995–2001 period. The data indicate that land conversion can be substantial. From 1995 to 2001, industrial land use increased at a rate of 105 hectares per annum, equivalent to approximately 259 acres (Peña and Fuentes, 2007).

Second, the attractive business climate and increasing demand for urban land—resulting from the presence of local industrial park developers, who concentrate large extensions of land with the expectation to sell the land a higher price—affect local land values. The acquisition of urban land by private industrial promoters and alliances with traditional, wealthy landholders are old practices given their linkage to international investors and the profits that they expect to make following the urban boom produced by the maquiladora industry. The largest developers in the area are Intermex, Prologis (Formerly Security Capital), Cambridge, and Bermudez. The Bermúdez Group owns and operates four industrial parks named Bermúdez, Río Bravo, Panamericano, and Los Aztecas; its current portfolio amounts to 3.5 million square feet of industrial space. The concentration of 78,777 acres of land by five groups of land investors (the Villegas, Bermúdez, Quevedo, Vallina, and Zaragoza families) has subordinated local governments to the economic interest of landholders (Guillén and Rodríguez, 1995). The most important beneficiaries of this process have been former politicians, industrial developers who have taken advantage of the economic power or political position to amass urban land (Llera, 2005).

Third, the local land market has been impacted by the location of the maquiladora industry, which requires a large amount of industrial land, fueling the demand for residential land. This demand has been influenced mainly by large-scale migration flows to the region, motivated by the perception of work opportunities. As a result, the city's population growth rates have been higher during the 1960–2005 period. From 1960 to 1970, the population almost doubled from 276,995 to 424,135, but the size of the urban area grew threefold. The urban area increased from 4,680 acres (1,894 hectares) in 1960 to 13,857 acres (5,608 hectares) in 1970, having an annual growth rate of 10.8 percent (Fuentes, 2001). The city population increased from 567,365 inhabitants in 1980 to 798,499 inhabitants in 1990. The urban land reached 23,215 acres (9,395 hectares) in 1990. In 2000, the population reached 1,217,818 and the total urban area occupied 53,304 acres (21,572 hectares) of land. In 2005, the city reached the 1-million-inhabitant mark and overshot it. (Fuentes and Cervera, 2006).

In 1920, the population of El Paso (77,560) was larger than Ciudad Juarez (43,138). The population in El Paso has grown at a slower pace during the same period; it almost doubled from 276,687 in 1970 to 740,648 in 2005.

At the same time, the rapid population growth increased the residential land demand. Residential uses and roads are intrinsically linked and account for almost three quarters of the urban land of Ciudad Juárez. From 1995 to 2001, the annual growth rate of residential land was 3.4 percent. In absolute terms, during the same period, residential land use increased by 3,894 acres (1,576 hectares), industrial use by 1,569 acres (635 hectares), and commerce and service by 1,391 acres (563 hectares) (Peña and Fuentes, 2007).

El Paso and Ciudad Juárez urban areas currently extend for 134,029 acres (209 square miles or approximately 541 square kilometers). El Paso accounts for 59.5 percent of the developed land but only 34.4 percent of the population living in El Paso, as a result El Paso has a population density of .799 persons per acre; meanwhile, Ciudad Juárez's population density is 22.4 persons per acre. The urban boundary of Ciudad Juárez in the last decade (1990–2000) has increased its size 1.5 times, whereas the urban boundary of El Paso in the same decade grew by a factor of .855, almost half the rate of Ciudad Juárez (City of El Paso, 1999).

Fourth, the success of the Mexican border industrial program encouraged the presence of land developers interested in promoting industrial activities on the U.S. side of the border, impacting the transborder land market.[6] For example, in Sunland Park, local investors have targeted land development toward the boundary line between the state of Chihuahua and the state of New Mexico acting on the plan to develop an industrial city on the Mexican side. The availability of vacant land and the presence of land investors with large properties have encouraged the adoption of more ambitious strategies to extract profit from land development. This situation also encourages the concentration of land on the U.S. side of the border. The two main developers of San Jerónimo, Chih, and Santa Teresa, NM, are respectively Eloy Vallina and Bill Sanders. On the Mexican side, Vallina's family owns about 49,420 acres (20,000 hectares) of land in San Jerónimo (Llera, 2005), almost the same size of the current urban area of Ciudad Juárez. In Santa Teresa, New Mexico, Bill Sanders bought 21,000 acres of land and announced his binational development project (Nathan, 2008). Eloy Vallina is a member of Sanders' development group for Santa Teresa. Indeed, since the 1990s, a highway has been built linking the west part of Ciudad Juárez, Chihuahua, to Santa Teresa, New Mexico, where all that transborder development is set to take place.

In 2003, the perception of business opportunities in the northwest part of Ciudad Juárez, as a result of the plan to develop a new industrial city, generated a conflict between the Zaragoza Family[7] and poor residents of the once-squatter settlement known as Lomas de Poleo; the residents were evicted of their homes and lands as a result of land dispute.[8]

Rich families such as Vallina, Zaragoza, and Bermúdez influenced the city's urban growth toward the western outskirts, which included Lomas de Poleo. In 2004, the Juarez City Council approved to expand the city limits to San Jerónimo, in other words, open to the 49,420 acres of land that Vallina owns. This situation generated opposition from many groups who disapproved of the initiative, because the development is so dependent on massive infrastructure and the city will continue its expansive urban land pattern with wide areas devoid of public services. However, the control of rich entrepreneurs (Bermúdez, Vallina, and Zaragoza) over the City Council[9] allowed the project to be approved. As a result, in 2007, as a part of the infrastructure investments, another road opened in northwest Juárez, called the Camino Real. So far, it has cost almost a million U.S. dollars; it will connect downtown Juárez to Santa Teresa, New Mexico.

The main arguments used for the developers to approve the San Jerónimo project were the increase in revenues of the local government product of property tax, the attraction of new investments, decrease of land prices, etc. However, expectation about future development in San Jeronimo and Santa Teresa has led to fevered land speculation in Juárez; as a matter of fact, a tiny lot not far from Lomas de Poleo has lately increased to 26 times its original price (Nathan, 2008). Besides, in 2009, the Vallina family as a reaction to the increase in land values went to the Court seeking an injunction relief to avoid paying property taxes assessed based on the new value of land. In brief, neither tax revenue increased nor access to land for residential use has increased and prices continue to be high.

It is important to emphasize that the different urban structures of El Paso and Ciudad Juárez are the result of institutional frameworks that controlled the urban process. The Ciudad Juárez model is closer to the typical speculative model that privatizes benefits and socializes costs. Politically connected Mexican developers steer the development process by channeling capital facilities investment to their lots capturing quick profit, unlike in the United States, where speculation is minimized due to the property tax structure and other legal tools (Llera, 2005). Local governments in Mexico, unlike their counterparts in the United States, have very little power to control land development and speculation due to the fact that the eminent domain power rests at the state level and not at the local level. Eminent domain, particularly the takings or expropriation clause, is an important tool of local governments to control and steer the urban development process (Peña, 2002). The following section discusses the urban sociospatial impacts of globalization in the region.

IV. The Effects of Globalization on the Urban Socio-Spatial Structure of a Transfrontier Metropolis: El Paso, Ciudad Juárez, and Sunland Park

The effects of globalization on the real estate market through the investment of multinational companies that inflate the land value, the concentration of land for developers, the rapid industrialization process that increase the demand for industrial and residential land, have interacted and reconfigured the urban socialspatial structure of the transfrontier metropolis: El Paso, Tx, Ciudad Juárez, Chih, and Sunland Park, NM. In this section, we discussed some of these impacts.

The interaction of all the factors mentioned above have created a highly restrictive and exclusionary land market forcing many residents to locate around the peripheral areas, especially, to the southwest. Migrants increased the demand for housing, often resulting in a competition among households, especially lower income household, generating pressures throughout the housing market (Marcuse and Van Kempen, 2000). The low-income households cannot afford a house near the well-served areas and the only choice is the peripheral areas, where the land is cheaper as a result of the lack of infrastructure or city amenities.

In the last two decades, people have tended to locate on the southeast side of the city; the growth in the southeast side of the city has been due to affordable housing programs since the 1990s targeting mainly the working-class population employed in the maquiladora industry. The northwest side of the city developed as a result of squatter practices. In developing countries, migrants establish their residential units either in the periphery or areas prone to hazards (e.g., flooding) given the low cost of the land or high cost to urbanize. As a result of the lack of infrastructure, a sociospatial segregation pattern of a wide sector of the population emerges (Marcuse and Van Kempen, 2000).

The spatial distribution of the population in El Paso shows that the majority of the population is located in the west and east side of the city; the central area—as is true in other cities in the United States—is going through a depopulation stage. The west and east sides of El Paso have experienced faster rate of population growth—particularly, the east side of El Paso, where the majority of new subdivisions are located. The characteristics of the population of the east and west side of El Paso are also different; the west can be characterized on average as a white-collar population, whereas the east is more of a blue collar.

The dependency ratio[10] is an indicator that is used to compare the urban structure of the two cities and to be able to visualize where the highest concentration of poverty is located. Dependency ratio is an indicator of poverty in the sense that it shows how many persons each worker supports in an economy; thus, the higher the ratio the lower the rate of savings of the household and fewer resources invested in the worker's family human capital and other nonessential goods, such as those in the categories of leisure, health, etc. Map 5.1 shows that in Ciudad Juárez the largest dependency ratios are found toward the periphery of the city; again, the farther from the center the higher the dependency ratios. This reflects the migration of poorer populations to the periphery as discussed previously. Pick et al. (2000) used the same indicator with data from the 1990 population census, and they found similar sociospatial distribution of the indicator; the only difference was that the process in 2000 was widening; before it was more concentrated in the northwest, while today the southwest has been added. In El Paso, the highest dependency ratios are concentrated

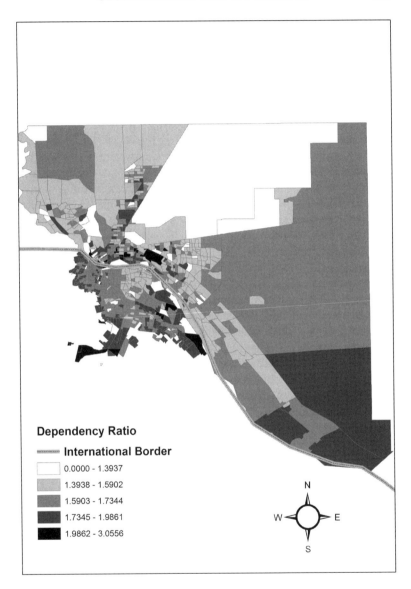

Map 5.1   Dependency ratio for El Paso-Ciudad Juárez

in the lower valley (southeast) and central sections of the city. It is
not surprising that the recent migrants to the United States bring
with them dependency ratio characteristics from Mexico. Since these
migrants tend to have lower-middle to lower level incomes in Mexico,

it is not surprising that their dependency ratios are higher than the U.S. average (Pick et al., 2000).

The spatial distribution of population employed in the manufacturing sector on the urban structure of both cities reflect the different functions of each side of the border (see Map 5.2). Ciudad Juárez clearly has a functional specialization whose population is employed in the manufacturing of goods produced mainly by the maquiladora sector. On the other hand, El Paso is more specialized in services; trade logistics has been one of the fastest growing sectors in the city. In this sense, the region shows a duality in the distribution of population employed in the manufacturing sector. In other words, the foreign direct investment in the form of manufacturing investment has restructured the region in a dual yet economically functional structural pattern.

At the intra urban level, the location of population employed in the manufacturing sector became concentrated in some parts of the city. On the Mexican side of the border, the population with this characteristic is located mainly in the peripheral areas. This is, in part, as a result of the maquiladora workers not being able to afford a house or a plot of land in the well-served central areas given the low wages and the only alternative is the periphery with low levels of public services and lower cost of land (see Map 5.3). A characteristic of the maquiladora industry is the intensity in the use of a labor force in the production process, as shown earlier. In 2006, the production workers represented 77.1 percent of the maquiladora employees. In this sense, some analysts argue that globalization leads to an increasing polarized society, which can be seen in an increasing number of workers in low positions and few highly skilled workers in high positions with different level of incomes (Sassen, 1991). On the U.S. side of the border, manufacturing employment in El Paso clearly is less prominent than in Ciudad Juárez given its function as a service center for the maquiladora industry.

Hernández (2002) found similar results for the case of Tijuana in 1990; his findings showed that population related with service activities live in the west part of the city (where services are readily available), and the people employed in the manufacturing sector live in the east part of the city (where there are low levels of public services). Rabelo (2006) suggested that the industrialization process in Tijuana has created a dual city as well.

The spatial distribution of people employed in the secondary sector also reflects a connection between the maquiladora industry and the transborder housing market. A common practice among

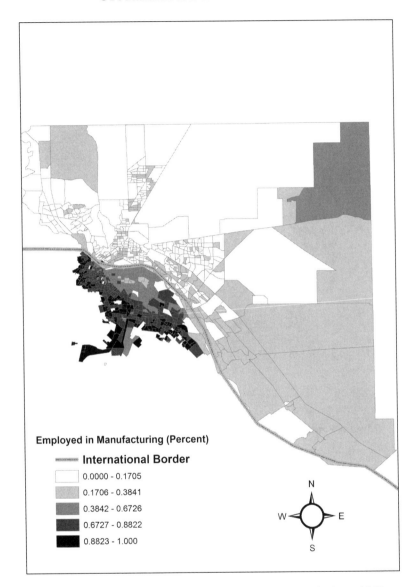

Map 5.2 Population (15–64) employed in manufacturing in the Paso del Norte Region

managerial personnel in high-level positions is to establish their place of residence on the U.S. side of the border, taking advantage of the amenities that the city provides. Meanwhile the production workers find housing units on the Mexican side of the border, given their

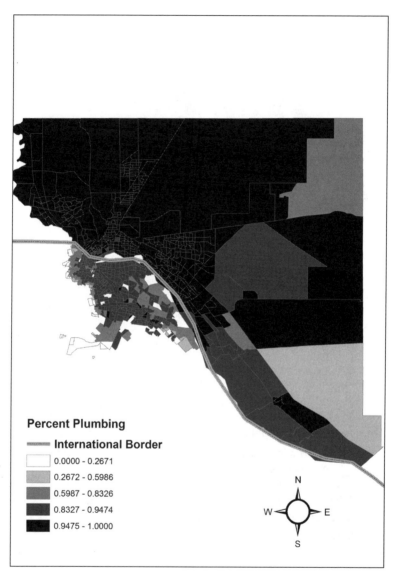

Map 5.3 Public service access (Indoor Plumbing) in the Paso del Norte Region

income possibilities. In this sense, the maquiladora industry contributes to a residential segregation between employees with different
occupations living in different countries.

Access to public services is not only an indicator of governmental
capacity to deliver services, but it is also an indicator of sociospatial

segregation. Access to indoor plumbing is used because it is an indicator that is comparable and available in both censuses. In the case of Ciudad Juárez, the probability of coverage diminishes as we move outward. (see Map 5.3). The capacity of the local government has lagged behind the demand in many instances although in recent years the coverage has improved substantially (Peña, 2005). Poor households have very limited choices to establish their residences where services are readily available, and wealthier households have the ability to locate in those neighborhoods where services are readily available.

The sociospatial segregation[11] is particularly compelling because of the extreme nature of the physical segregation (poor households are being resettled at a great distance from the well-served areas) as well as the clarity of the three sets of variables influencing the resettlement sites: distortions of the land market, institutional mechanisms (low application of the urban planning legislation), and the socioeconomic pressure that emerged since the implementation of the maquiladora program (Fuentes and Cervera, 2006). Government capacity is clear in El Paso, where the coverage is close to 100 percent with the exception of some areas in the southeast side of the city, known as the lower valley, where some *colonias* (Ward, 1999) emerged.

In this urban context, since 1995, the Municipal Institute of Planning and Research (IMIP) was created with the mission to provide the plans for urban projects that the city needs for its sustainable development. However, it has limited capacity and lacks any normativeness or ability to enforce the law.

CONCLUSIONS

In this chapter, we have shown that the U.S.-Mexico border cites have been integrated to the globalization process through the maquiladora program. However, foreign direct investment has not only had an impact on manufacturing sector in Mexico, but also has had a significant influence on land markets because parts of these investments were in real estate properties. Often studies focus on the labor, output, wages, labor conditions, etc., but few focus on land and the urban structure being produced by global forces. In this chapter, we show that the delocalization of real estate property and the deepening commodification would seem to portend a significant impact on the transborder, urban sociospatial structure.

In this chapter, we have address some of the issues Sassen (2007) called for the need to "unbundle" and analyze the local impacts of globalization. We have contributed to show that globalization, through the decentralization of production, is a double-edged sword. On the one hand, it generates employment opportunities that are needed in the developing world. On the other hand, it is a powerful force that distorts local land markets. When these dialectic forces of globalization are combined with the limited capacity of local governments to steer and row the urban development process, the results are what we have shown—a city that is highly segregated physically and poorly integrated socially.

Finally, the transborder region on the U.S.-Mexico border is a quintessential example of the "spaces of flows" that Castells (2000) references: a space that is important for its relative position in time-space. The comparative advantages of the border region (low labor and location) that characterized the spaces of flows have been exploited to the maximum. However, very little attention has been given to the region as a place. A central focus of urban politics of place has to do with how to revert the spatial segregation produced by globalization forces. An important task to undo some of these impacts is to retool local governments, particularly in Mexico, with the capacity to govern the urban process. Local municipalities in Mexico lacked of eminent domain since this rests on the governors—to be able to control growth in the way their counterparts in the United States do. It is important to add that localities such as Ciudad Juárez have created institutions such as the Municipal Planning Institute (IMIP), which has only advisory capacity and lacks any normativeness or ability to implement projects.

NOTES

1. Transfrontier urban zones are specialized regions created by transnational economic and social forces (Herzog, 1991).
2. For purposes of this study, the transfrontier metropolis of El Paso, Tx, Ciudad Juárez, Chih, and Sunland Park, NM, encompasses urban land development in three different cities from two countries and three states.
3. The wages here include fringe benefits and data provided by Martha Miker in Chapter 6 does not include fringe benefits; thus, this accounts for the difference in the information.
4. Changes in Mexican Property Law in 1993 and 1998 made it possible for foreign ownership of land in Mexico within 100 kilometers of the border and 50 km of the coastline as long as the land is purchased by a Mexican company (a subsidiary of a multinational company).
5. Bermudez International Group is advertised as the leading edge of Mexico's industrialization process. The founder of the company was the prime mover and architect of Mexico's maquila/twin plant industry.

6. The transborder land market is made up of developed and unde-
veloped land as well as buildings encompassed within the city limits of contiguous cities located on both sides of the U.S.-Mexico
border.

7. In late 1990s, the Zaragoza family realized Lomas de Poleo was
getting valuable. Real estate interests on both sides of the border
were hatching grand plans for a new international port of entry and
NAFTA binational community. It would straddle the international
line at Santa Teresa, New Mexico, and include extensive manufacturing parks, as well as passage for cargo trucks and lots of brand new
housing and stores (Nathan, 2008).

8. Over the past 30 years, hundreds of families have settled on the mesa,
but now only about 300 families remain. Despite a 1992 court rul-
ing that denied the Zaragoza family the right to claim ownership of
the land, and a current injunction prohibiting eviction, the Zaragoza
family continues to claim ownership of the land and uses intimidation
and harassment tactics to force people to leave. Now the Zaragoza
family has once again invaded the mesa, but this time with 18 wheel-
ers full of cement and barbed wire, earth-moving equipment, and a
group of vigilantes. They have already encircled the community with
cement post, barbed wire, huge steel gates, and 3 metal watchtowers
strategically placed to keep the entire community in fear.

9. In Ciudad Juarez, local urban politics cannot be understood without considering the competition between the two most important
national parties, PRI and PAN, to gain control over the local government. Control over the local government is important for local land
investors who wish to influence the elaboration of local policies and
encourage urban expansion toward their properties (Llera, 2005).

10. Dependency ratio was calculated as follow: total population / population age 15 to 64.

11. An operational definition of sociospatial segregation is unequal access
to either public networks of services or private networks of the market
place (Fuentes and Cervera, 2006).

REFERENCE LIST

Asociación Mexicana de Parques Industriales (AMPI). 2000.

Beauregard, R. and A. Haila. (2000). "The Unavoidable Continuities of the
City," in P. Marcuse and Van Kempen R. (eds), *Globalizing Cities; A New
Spatial Order*. Oxford: Blackwell.

Canales, A. (1999). "Industrialization, Urbanization and Population Growth
on the Border," *Borderlines*, 7(7).

Castells, M. (2000). *The Rise of the Network Society*. Oxford: Blackwell.

Fainstein, S., Gordon I. and Harloe, M. (1992). *Divided Cities; New York &
London in the Contemporary World*. Oxford: Blackwell.

Friedmann, J. (1986). "The World City Hypothesis," *Development and Change*, 17, pp. 69–83.

Fuentes, C. (2001). "El manejo del suelo urbano en las ciudades fronterizas mexicanas" *Comercio Exterior*, 51(3), pp. 185–196.

Fuentes, C. and Cervera, L. (2006). "Land Markets and its Effects on the Spatial Segregation" *Estudios Fronterizos*, 7(13), pp. 43–62.

Guillén, T., and Rodríguez L. (1995). "Planeación y control urbanos: El Caso del Lote Bravo," in Guillen, T. (eds.), *Municipios en transición: Actores sociales y nuevas politicas de gobierno*, México, Fundación Friedrich Ebert.

Haila, A. (1991). "Four Types of Investment and Land Property," *International Journal of Urban and Regional Research*, 15(3), pp. 343–365.

Hanson, H. G. (1996). "Economic Integration, Intraindustry Trade and Frontier Regions," *European Economic Review*, 40, pp. 941–949.

Hernández, E. (2002). "Polarización económica en Tijuana," *Paradigmas*, año 10 num. 39.

Herzog, L. (1991). "Cross-national urban structure in the era of global cities: the U.S-Mexico transfrontier metropolis", *Urban Studies*, 28(4), pp. 519–533.

Lindahl, D. P. (1995). "Change in Commercial Real Estate Finance and the Transformation of Regional Economics," Paper presented at the meeting of the Association of American Geographers, Chicago.

Logan, J. (1993). "Cycles and Trends in the Globalization of Real Estate." In P. L. Knox (ed.), *The Restless Urban Landscape*, Englewood Cliffs, NJ: Prentice Hall, pp. 35–54.

Llera, F. (2005). "El Paso del Norte Region: Who Governs the Urban Planning Process?" In Fuentes and Peña (Editors). *Planeación Binacional y Cooperación Transfronteriza en al Frontera Mexico-Estados Unidos*, COLEF-UACJ.

Nathan, D. (2008). "Making a Killing: Land Deals and Girl Deaths on the U.S.-Mexico Border," Newspaper Tree El Paso.

Marcuse, P. (1989). "Dual City: A Muddy Metaphor for a Quartered City." *Journal of Urban and Regional Research*, 13(4), pp. 697–708.

Mollenkopf and Castelles M. (1991). *Dual City: Restructuring New York*. New York: Russell Sage Foundation.

Marcuse, P. and Van Kempen, R. (2000). "Introduction" in Marcuse P. and Van Kempen R. (editors) Globalizing Cities: A New Spatial Order, Blackwell Publishing.

Peña, S. (2002). "Land Use Planning on the USA-Mexico Border: A Comparison of the Legal Framework," *Journal of Borderlands Studies*, 17(1), pp. 1–19.

———. (2005). "Recent Developments in Urban Marginality Along Mexico's Northern Border," *Habitat International Journal*, 29(2), pp. 285–301.

Peña S. and Fuentes, C. (2007). "Land Use Changes in Ciudad Juárez, Chihuahua: A System of Dynamic Model," *Estudios Fronterizos*, 7(13), pp. 43–62.

Pick, J. et al. (2000). "Spatial Measurament of Binationality in the Twin Cities of Ciudad Juárez, Mexico and El Paso, Texas, USA." Proceedings of American Statistical Association, Statistical Graphics Section.

Rabelo, J. (2006). "Segregación Socioespacial y Concentración del Ingreso en Tijuana, Baja California," Doctoral Dissertation, Universidad Autónoma de Baja California.

Sassen, S. (1991). *The Global City: New York, London, Tokyo*. Princeton, NJ: Princeton University Press.

———. (1998). *Globalization and Its Discontents: Essays on the New Mobility of People and Money*. New York: The New Press.

———. (2007). Ed. Deciphering the Global: Its Scales, Spaces, and Subjects. New York: Routledge.

Savitch, H. V. (1995). The Emergence of Global Cities. *Urban Affairs Review*, 31(1), pp. 137–142.

Várgas. L. (2001). "Maquiladoras: Impact on the Texas Border Cities," *Business Frontier*, Federal Reserve Bank of Dallas, Branch El Paso, pp. 25–29.

Ward, P. M. (1999). *Colonias and Public Policy in Texas and Mexico: Urbanization by Stealth*. University of Texas Press.

CHAPTER 6

WORLD-CLASS AUTOMOTIVE HARNESSES AND THE PRECARIOUSNESS OF EMPLOYMENT IN JUÁREZ

Martha Miker Palafox

This chapter[1] analyzes the impacts of globalization on the process of automotive harness production, the regional industrial concentration, and labor relations in one of the most important cities of Mexico's northern border—Ciudad Juárez—which has been called "the valley of harnesses." Harness manufacturing is a highly skilled and complex industry. Alejandro Lugo defines a harness: "A harness forms part of a system of energy distribution, signals and lights, which controls and conducts the electric functioning of an automobile" (2008: 132). Automobile assembly industries, established during and after the peso devaluation of 1983, which reduced labor costs, were "running away from strong labor unions in the American Midwest" (ibid: 74).

The chapter will identify the main features of precarious employment and automotive harness production in Ciudad Juárez. It also characterizes the cluster of megaglobal manufacturing leaders in harness production, located in Juárez, and the process of integration and complexity in the global economy. My approach to the study involves comparative analysis. I compare four *maquiladora* plants belonging to global corporate leaders in the manufacture of automotive harnesses, focusing particularly on the problems of job insecurity. This insecurity results from the corporate strategies and the local policies that legitimize new, disciplined labor standards that operate partly outside the labor laws, among other things. I also analyze jobs and management control systems as they relate to harness production.

Theoretical Perspectives

Initially, the analysis of autoparts plants (export-assembly factories, called *maquiladoras*) occurred from the perspective of the New International Division of Labor (NIDL) (Fröbel et al., 1980). NIDL analysts argue that since World War II, a new capitalist economy emerged based on mass migration of capital in industrialized societies toward the Third World (now known as countries of the south). This influx of capital was stimulated by both the deterioration of industrialized society recovery and the existence of a cheap labor force abundant in the periphery.

The NIDL theory was a limited response to global economic processes, providing more complexity than in the past. But in any case, the open, remaining questions include the following. What theory best explains the current situation? And more so, to what extent is it appropriate to continue talking in terms of international division of labor? Shaiken (2003: 20) notes that in Mexico, like many developing countries, globalization is particularly advanced in the automotive industry.

In the current debate around the global production of automotive harnesses, industrial relations, and regional industrial concentrations, we can identify three groups, with three different positions: The *first* studies that analyzed the establishment of the auto assembly industry made reference to the modernization of the *maquiladora* industry with emergent new models of production. Studies of the automotive *maquiladora* industry were carried out with great particularity. One can say that it has undergone significant changes, such as the increased use of automated technologies, the incorporation of flexible schedules in the organization of production, and the wide dissemination of the "Just in Time" systems (JIT) and Total Quality Control (TQC) (Gereffi, 1996; Wilson, 1992; Koido, 1992; González-Aréchiga and Ramírez, 1990; Pelayo, 1992).

In the case of flexible production techniques associated with the assembly of autoparts (Wilson, 1992, 1989; Shaiken and Brown, 1991), the adoption of quality improvement and production is also a priority practice of transnational firms (mainly automotive and electronic). Some authors of the period note that changes in export-processing industries were generally seen as caricatures of post-Fordism (Wilson, 1992; Shaiken and Brown, 1991). For others, these changes have resulted in an enrichment of tasks, complexity of processes, and development of potential suppliers (Carrillo and Ramírez, 1993; González Aréchiga and Ramírez, 1990).

More recently, de la Garza (1998) said that the focal point of transformation was not technology but forms of work organization and labor relations. He therefore ruled out the convergence toward an optimal solution that would be the "one best way" for all companies, as expressed by Freyssenet et al. (1998). One can also take into account changes in the processes of hybridization that are the source of innovative solutions (Boyer et al., 1998). It is relevant to analyze socioproductive settings and reflect on their different dimensions in the harnesses *maquiladora* industry in Juárez.

A *second* group of studies relates to industrial relations and labor conditions which have been introduced in such *maquiladora* plants and which, since their arrival in Ciudad Juárez, have benefited from trade unions and industrial relations related to their interests, especially with wide powers of decision in the process of production. This translates into a high contractual, numerical, and functional flexibility, where unions have served little to protect workers, and representatives of the state are complicit by their silence and their lack of enforcement of legislation (Kopinak, 1996; De la O, 2002; Quintero, 2002).

A *third* group of studies focuses on global production systems and value chains (Gereffi and Korzeniewicz, 1994; Gereffi et al., 2001; Carrillo et al., 2001). These authors examine global value chains and production systems, including relationships among diverse actors along production lines and differences in the structure of and relationships between companies (Barrientos, 2007; Gereffi, 1999; Sturgeon, 2000).

The major contribution of this Global Commodity Chain approach is to capture organizational changes in production and global trade. This analytical perspective outlines all the inputs required for a product, from conception to the intermediate stages of production, and ultimately to consumers. The commodity approach enhances the analysis of linkages and coordination between economic agents and places. In this approach, authors explicitly incorporate international dimensions in their analysis, reflecting their primary concern with the emergence of manufacturing systems that are dispersed and integrated on a global scale.[2]

My research can be included in this third group of studies. And from this perspective, the following question is posed: "Under what kind of relationships and working conditions are world-class harnesses produced in Juárez?" Ciudad Juárez is an important part of the new transnational economy (Sassen, 1998) and denationalized space, with productivity process interdependence, marginalization and exclusion (Harvey, 1996; Castells, 1999). I formulate three assumptions in this chapter:

(i) Ciudad Juárez, one of the locales of global economic dynamics, is in the process of economically restructuring global localizations, which has generated a large growth in the demand for low-wage workes and jobs that offer few advancement possibilities. Just as in other global cities, in Ciudad Juárez, women and recent inmigrants emerge as the labor supply that facilitates the imposition of low wages and few benefits, even when there is high demand and these jobs are in high-growth sectors (Sassen, 2006: 180).

(ii) The concentration of harness plants in a locale has allowed greater vertical integration of production process complexity of the corporate world's largest automotive harnesses, which are regulated mainly through global private institutions, such as the International Organization for Standardization (ISO) (www. iso.org), in denationalized space or what Sassen refers to as the relative absence of the state (2007: 92).

(iii) As with Kopinak (1996), every harness *maquiladora* has employed innovative technologies and labor practices associated with flexible production strategies, including the espousal of "just-in-time" inventory management goals.

METHODS AND CHAPTER OUTLINE

For this chapter, my empirical analysis is based on the processing, systematization, and analysis of semistructured interviews, participant observation, and information from various studies and corporations, such as their web pages—considered part of my fieldwork for the dissertation. Initially, 35 interviews were conducted with direct production workers and officials of the plant. The second approach involved participant observation in four *maquiladora* plants in periods ranging between three and six months of observation during 2005 and 2006. And third, I examine statistical and historical information on the corporations and plants: Real Corp/Real, Arreos American Corp/Arreos American, Nipona Corp/Nipona, and Sushicon Corp/Sushicon.[3]

The chapter contains three sections. In the first section, I describe the production process of automotive harnesses. In the second section, I characterize the harness production industry in Ciudad Juárez through the number of plants, the volume and type of employment they have generated in the city, along with the practices, methods, and standards associated with systems of quality management that comply with ISO world-class production. I also include indicators such as sales and manufacturing location in four companies: Arreos American Corp, Real Corporation, Sushicon Corp, and Nipona Corp. And in the third section, I outline the conditions of employment, focusing on failure, instability, and insecurity, according to Guerra's concepts (1994), drawing on the jobs and the reflections from industrial workers in the region.

I. Automotive Harness Production

Automotive harnesses are the "nervous systems" of cars: harnesses convey information between electronic or electrical parts. The configuration of the automobile harness vehicle model changes for different options offered by the car such as airbags, power windows and doors, power seats, cruise control, or automatic suspension of automatic handling. These features cause many changes in product specification. In addition, there are three more factors to understand the further diversification of automotive harness production. First, there is a vast increase in the number of electronics parts in vehicles,[4] which has made harness systems larger and more complex. One passenger car needs an average of 800 wires second; an increase in the diversification of cars in recent decades has required a greater number of automotive harness types; and third, each car has nearly twenty different harnesses on average. By combining the first and second factor, each car can include a vast number of different subharnesses. Increasing diversity within the sector of automotive harnesses makes it extremely difficult to standardize the production process. The wide variety of products often requires changes in production lines. This results in a labor-intensive harness production process (Koido, 1992: 349). In the case of automobile harnesses, the introduction of new, flexible machines is very difficult because of the exceptional diversity of the product. Therefore, only in the early stages of harness production, such as cutting and pressing, has this type of machine technology been introduced. However, the substitution of fiber optics for automotive harnesses can completely transform the process of production of communication networks in cars of the future, but this could be done only through a very lengthy process to complete the implementation of this technology (Koido, 1992: 349). Short of that, giant corporations have chosen to carry out technological advances by reducing the thickness of cable (0.13mm2) impact on the weight of the vehicle.

Besides the technical difficulties in dealing with the wide variety of harnesses in ever-more sophisticated vehicles, another factor in the production of automotive harnesses is that it is labor-intensive. In fact, automotive harnesses are made for each structure of every car's electronic system, not only for its diversity but also by the constant changes of design and flows from them. In particular, the acceleration of the product cycle, or in other words, the introduction of new products, has encouraged the rapid changes in the design to assemble harnesses. By changing the model of the car each year, the designs of harness assembly lead to changes in the process of producing them. Furthermore, even small changes in certain electronic components can induce changes in the design of automotive harnesses even in "standard" cars. Uncertainty in harness design makes the standardization of production processes and automation extremely difficult (Koido, 1992: 350). Because of these characteristics, the production of harnesses forms a bottleneck in the automation of production in the automotive industry. However, the production process is not homogeneous but consists of heterogeneous processes with varying degrees of intensity and automatization (Koido, 1992: 350).

The harness industry's technological trajectory is divided into three groups: the first by a simple harness (1900–1973); the second is characterized by its rejuvenation—this is caused by a process of convergence between the automotive and electronics industries (1974–1993); and the last, the third generation in contrast to the second generation, in which a harness system is no longer independent, but an integrated system of physical and functional parts of the car from 1994 to the date the harness is integrated within a modular system (Lara, 2003: 116). Industrial plant complexities have vertically integrated their production in Ciudad Juárez (Carrillo and Miker, 2009) as presented in the following section.

Structure of Production

The production of automotive harnesses involves a complex division of labor, because the process transforms thousands of wires, cables in many types of integrated systems, or different harnesses. The process for the production of automotive harnesses consists of five different stages and can generally occur in the same industrial area.

In Phase I, the electric wires are cut to specific lengths and have plastic covers on their tips that are uncovered or torn. The terminals are then pressed into the ends of these cables. Both processes can be made in a single machine or at high speeds on two different machines and processes for cutting and assembly. Wire cutting and pressing of terminals can be done in separate processes, using a cutting machine and a presser machine, manually controlled or a different level of technology machinery. This process is generally more automated; it has the highest technological level, concentration of most workers and male career paths within the plant, and the highest level of basic schooling.

In Phase II, which is called "joint," "directed,"or "routed," different wires are connected to each other. For this purpose, the plastic coating of the wire is torn at the ends. These points are connected manually then covered with tape. This phase is more labor intensive and is located at the same plant.

In Phase III, the wires to be connected and to be fitted with terminals—the smallest units of integrated cables—are assembled in these cells or production lines. This stage is fairly labor intensive and is performed at the same plant.

In Phase IV, subassembly wires are integrated into their final assembly. Because of the increase in electronic parts by automobiles, automotive harnesses have been getting larger and more complex.[5] In particular, the process of automotive harness assembly became more standardized and larger tasks became divided into simple connecting cables to the subassembly and organized by a division of labor in an assembly line, subassembly, mounted, routed, and curbed. Therefore, this process usually occurs in the main plant, despite being labor intensive.

In Phase V, the "armed harnesses" are completed, with their part number printed and installed in their peripheral parts. After this, the sets are checked visually by operators against the sample, and then electronically through the examination of the connections and wire conductivity stations for electrical tests, which have continuously progressed in their level of technology. Finally, the sets are packed in plastic and placed in boxes and shipped, mainly to car assembly plants in the United States.

In total, the production of automotive harnesses usually takes the form of pyramids of subcontractors (Ikeda, 1985 cited by Koido, 1992: 352). Due to processing-intensive work production, facing cost-reduction pressures from suppliers, producers of automotive harnesses are also required to seek lower labor costs geographically. The production of automotive harnesses tends to be decentralized and located in geographically peripheral areas around the platforms of plant owners who cater to the traditional and emerging markets. However, there is also a sexual division of labor among work areas, from the highest technological level (stage cut and presses) to lowest (subassembly and final assembly), though this is not the case with intermediate levels of technology (quality tests and resistance). The cutting and pressing tasks are dominated by men with more seniority, more education, and higher salaries than direct production workers. The final and subassembly processes are mostly dominated by young women with limited seniority and lower education and salary levels. Both men and women work in intermediate-level technology jobs, such as electromechanical tests; while they have higher levels of education, they do not necessarily have much seniority.

II. COMPLEX GLOBAL MANUFACTURING IN CIUDAD JUÁREZ

Over the past thirty years, the face of Ciudad Juárez in the larger metropolitan region with El Paso, Texas, has changed substantially due to the tremendous growth of the global economy. It is the engine of dynamism in the region.

The general characteristics of the harness *maquiladoras* in Juárez are as follows: First, these plants are large establishments, employing 24 percent of the total jobs generated by the global manufacturing industries in Juárez in 39 plants with an average of 1,415 employees per establishment; second, there is a high concentration of the world automotive leaders in these first-tier corporations. Of the 39 establishments that make up the branch of the harness sector, five companies own 32 plants and employ 43,626 workers, which accounts for 79 percent of this industry in the city; third, among their clients are several assemblers of American, Asian, and European cars, both light and heavy vehicles; fourth, since 1994, comprehensive technical centers have been created which design harness research, development, assembly, cutting, and shipping to the U.S. automotive industry, such as Delphi and Engineering and Design Centers in Juárez;[6] fifth, with competition, struggle for survival, and contraction of the U.S. market, firms have started to expand their corporate client base to other emerging markets like Asia and Europe (El Diario/Manufacturing Supplement, 27 May, 2008); and sixth, state regulations have been displaced in order to produce at world-class levels that comply with convergent norms based on private institutions (such as ISO's).

Also, production processes have become increasingly complex due to different methods and practices directly associated with the "Lean Production Model" that erases "national" differences in harness production. Juárez has become a leading global manufacturing site in this respect. Mexican-trained managers have instituted many aspects of the Lean Production Model, organizing workers into teams where "the maquila's symbolic practices around femininity highlight independence, assertiveness, and the capacity to make decisions" (Salzinger, 2003: 76).

In summary, the megaharness-manufacturing cluster in Juárez consists of "global players." These large corporations are competing in global markets and produce both harnesses and other systems and components for many businesses terminals (now denominated in various firms as electrical distribution systems). Let us take the case of the four most important companies in Ciudad Juárez, which concentrated tens of thousands of workers in this city and four of the five "global players" in the most important industry to manufacture harnesses worldwide: Nipona Corp, Arreos American Corp, Real Corporation, and Sushicon Corp.

Nipona Corporation

Nipona is a Japanese corporation that employs about 200,000 workers at 463 companies in 39 countries worldwide, with a capital of 3.191 billion yen. One of the main product groups of this corporation is the automotive area; it is divided into Nipona Electrical Wire Co. and Nipona Parts Co., manufacturers of wire harnesses and automotive electrical systems and modular production respectively. Nipona Parts Co. of Nipona North America, headquartered in Michigan, is highly internationalized. Sales outside Japan grew 200 percent between 1992 and 1997, and international employment was 178,916 employees in 2007: eight times higher than those who remained in Japan. In México, Nipona has 19 plants and 9 subsidiaries. In Ciudad Juárez, there are three companies: Autopartes y Arneses de México, S. A. (Nipona plant/Nipona), established in 1982, which has 8 plants in the state of Chihuahua, with Juárez employing 5,162 workers. On the other hand, Productos Eléctricos Diversificados, S.A., (PEDSA), has six plants in Ciudad Juárez with 10,802 employees. Nipona's third plant in the city is Autoelectrónica Juárez, established in 1985 within the EWD Nipona North America, with 2 plants and 5,401 employees.

Arreos America Corporation

Arreos America Corporation operates 156 manufacturing facilities in 34 countries with sales of US$22.3 billion dollars in 2007. It has regional offices in Paris, Tokyo, and Sao Paulo; the central offices are located in Warren, Ohio. Arreos American Corporation is composed of seven divisions under the concept of systems; however, these areas are called Division Systems and are responsible for analyzing the architecture of the electrical and electronic systems throughout a vehicle, electronic distribution and integration, and optimization of the design of complete systems. In 2008, the corporation employed approximately 169,500 employees worldwide, with Mexico being the largest recipient of employment: 68,000 employees in 50 plants. The company is currently the forty-ninth largest employer in Mexico,[7] with 48,000 employees in 48 plants. Juárez has 15 industrial plants of which 8 belong to the holding company Arreos American Corporation with 11,231 employees. This company manufactures various types of automotive harnesses for various clients including Ford, Harley, GM, Harrison, BOS Wagner, Panasonic, Ford, Subaru, Lear Corporation, Interior Packard, and Toyota.

Real Corporation

Real, involved in car seat assembly and the aviation industry, was acquired by Real in 1966. The annual net sale was US$16 billion dollars in 2007. The world-class products of the company are designed and manufactured by 90,000 employees at 215 locations in 34 countries in the Americas, Europe, Asia, and Africa. Real Corporation's headquarters are in Southfield, Michigan. The division with electrical harnesses automotive products had 102 plants and 45,538 jobs worldwide in 2005 (Ortiz, 2005: 27). For its part, Mexico had 34,702 jobs in its 2 divisions and 38 plants, which represented 32 percent and 12 percent of jobs and plants to the corporate world, respectively. Electric System Divisions, producer of automotive harnesses, has 15,070 employees and 19 plants representing 19 percent and 33 percent of the division worldwide, respectively. In Juárez, Real has more than 50 percent of it plants and employment at the national level (ibid: 30). For instance, the Electrical Systems Division is in charge of assembling electrical harnesses and electronics in maquiladoras. Begun with the purchase of United Technologies Corp (known as UTA) in 1999 (Carrillo and Hinojosa, 2001: 106), in 2007, Real managed the most assembly plants dedicated to automotive harnesses found in Ciudad Juárez.

Sushicon Corporation

Since 1996, the name Sushicon Electric Wiring System has been a Joint Venture with Osaka Yokkaich Sushicon Wiring Systems. With capital of 7,541 million yen, SEWS has 53,147 employees worldwide, with a presence in 30 countries; its sales reached 511,958 million yen in March 2007. Despite being a Japanese corporation, 90 percent of its production occurs in other countries. In 2005, Sushicon Corp was the third-largest producer of automotive harnesses worldwide, and its goal for 2010 is to have between 15 percent and 20 percent of the global market for automotive harnesses. The manufacture and sale of automotive harnesses, electrical components, and wire are Sushicon's primary business. Currently, the company is reorganizing and restructuring the production based on a model of global production.[8] At regional level during 2003, Sushicon moved all its manufacturing plants in the United States to Mexico, leaving only a Detroit-based research and design center for automotive harnesses. In Mexico, it has three businesses: Conductores Tecnológicos, Autosistemas de Torreón, and Sistemas de Arneses K&S Mexicana, S.A. de C.V. The main headquarters in Mexico are concentrated in Juárez, where some 48 percent of plants and 40 percent of employment exist nationwide.

III. Labor Flexibility and Precarious Employment

According to the Organización Internacional del Trabajo (OIT, 1998) [International Labor Organization], precarious employment is an "employment relationship where the lack of job security [is] one of the main elements of the employment contract." Rodgers (1989) identifies four criteria for determining whether a job is precarious: first, with a high risk of job loss; second, when there is little chance of the worker controlling the conditions of employment; third, when there is no protection or social security is not guaranteed; and, finally, where low incomes result in poverty. These criteria cover the dimensions of instability, lack of protection, insecurity, as well as social and economic weaknesses. Guerra proposed the concept of "precarious employment"; here, job instability and insecurity in labor are the most decisive factors in this type of concept (Guerra, 1994: 56). For the author, unstable employment is one where there is an indefinite employment contract: the employee either has no contract or has a fixed-term contract, fees (*contrato por honorarios*)—temporary or casual—while a job lacks safety net or backup coverage with social laws, such as occupational health. In my research, Guerra's concepts are affirmed (1994), meaning precarious jobs share certain characteristics: the perspective of uncertainty, the prospect of instability, and the prospect of failure.

Failure: Low Wages

Before the value of the Mexican Peso declined, from 10 pesos to the dollar to 14 pesos to the dollar, in response to the U.S. economic crisis of fall 2008, wages in the complex harness factories were relatively low. In the Sushicon Corp/Sushicon plants, the weekly wages of production operations in 2006 ranged from US$39 for the new operators to US$93 for the cutting machine's operators and pressing jobs. At Real, plant workers had daily wages ranging from US$5.60 to US$6.50 (Ortiz, 2005: 35), making the weekly wages for operators range from $28 (for operators in training) to $98 for the flexible plant operators. At Arreos Plant/Arreos Corporation, salaries are low in general. For operators recently admitted (in coaching and general), the payment is governed by the legal minimum wage for this area: In 2004–2005, this was 45.24–46.80 pesos respectively per day, plus benefits. (In 2004–2005, the US Dollar exchange rate was 10 pesos per US$1; in 2008, it is 14 pesos for US$1, lowering the costs of wages.) In the case of employees who have a permanent contract, after one to three months in the plants in Nipona/Nipona Corporation and Sushicon/Sushicon Corporation in the areas of assembly and final subassembly, wage increased about 10 percent (special operations and operators after 30 days) and for areas considered with a higher level of technology (like cut and press), the wages are then twofold. In general, one finds four levels of operational staff: Operator-in-coaching, general, universal, and flexible. The operators-in-coaching and general operator are involved in standard operations; the universal operator dominates all the stations in an area and flexible operators are specialized, no longer working in the operation, but with the inspection, short cable, etc.

In addition, workers acquire a number of bonuses for attendance, punctuality, *by years worked*, recruitment bonus promises, and seniority among others. The first three are part of workers' permanent records, while others are lost or increased depending on the crisis or boom sector in the locality, the product of the industrial situation in the international context, and the lack of bodies attached to labor law and strong and democratic unions. The minimum legally required benefits are offered to production workers for all plants.[9] Besides legal

benefits, some plants offer other benefits, such as free adult education at the plant, scholarships for workers' children, funeral assistance,
support for lenses, payment of one day's salary for their birthdays,
savings fund, and life insurance, which disappear (as with bonuses)
in times of crisis in the sector. The benefits that remain are essential
to the production process, such as transportation service, medical
service, and cafeteria service.[10]

Work Instability and Insecurity

Poor industrial relations, flexibility, and lack of association are
common in the harness plants in Juárez. Temporary employment
contracts contribute to job insecurity.[11] The right to labor union participation, enshrined in the Constitution and federal labor laws (Con-
stitutión de los Estados Unidos Mexicanos and the Ley Federal del
Trabajo [Art. 356 to 403]), has been virtually obliterated since the
advent of the *maquiladora* industry in the region. So, currently only
10 percent of the workers in this sector are union members.[12] Only
the Real Corporation/Real *maquiladora* plant has signed a collective contract with the Confederación Revolucionaria de Trabajadores
y Campesinos (CROC). This is a "subordinate" union without a
steward's presence at the facility or employees, as there is no interfer-
ence in the processes of recruitment, selection, hiring, training, and
coaching of direct production workers.[13]

Questions about employment and working process are best
answered and appreciated through observing and participating in
interviews with plant workers.[14] Recently, Real signed agreements
with the union labor CROC to enforce temporary unemployment
on 13,000 of its workers. They were instructed to report to work
for only two days per week.[15] This came about due to the American
Axle supplier strike, which led to the closure of 32 General Motors
plants in the United States further leading to a drop in orders from
local plants.

This gives us an account of the prevalence of a "retrograded
union" (Carrillo, 2001: 220–221) for this type of trade union—
"*Transparencia*[16] *Subordinados*"[17] and the domain of recruitment of
individual workers in export-processing production defeats the labor
movement advocated by weakening, factionalism, and apathy within
and between union and company against the attack by the unions
(Quintero, 2002: 21–22; De la O, 2002: 57; 1994, 127–128). In this
situation, the unilateral flexibility and/or labor relations are defined
by the enterprise in the four *maquiladora* plants. The work flexibility

and mobility between shift changes and plants are not as common as mobility between different areas in the plant, which are caused by the closure of the product business, absenteeism, turnover of direct production workers, and interpersonal relationships with group leaders and supervisors.

In the selection and recruitment process, discrimination continues to be practiced against pregnant women and men with *chola*[18] dress or appearance (also documented by Valdés-Villalba, 1983; and Lugo 2008, on *bien presentación*, the preference for young, pretty women). One observes gender discrimination when women who apply for employment are subject to reviews and interviews to determine if they are pregnant during the recruitment process and during the first three months of contract time;[19] denial of contracts to pregnant women, and abuse and coercion to intimidate a worker who is pregnant into submitting her resignation are not uncommon.

> After the interview, he sent me to nursing and the nurse told me that I was going to answer some questions while the doctor finished with the other operators who were doing the review hearing. The nurse asked me what was the date of my last period? Do you get premenstrual cramps? What methods do you use? Then the doctor asked if I had been pregnant or operated on
>
> P1, *Obrera*, Real Plant

In addition, new employees of the *maquiladora* plants (direct production workers and indirect staff) at Nipona/Nipona, Real/Real, and Arreos American/Arreos American Corp, are required to sign an established agreement to give a weekly "voluntary contribution" to Fondo Unido (United Way), part of the United Way global network. However, *plants* appear as donors rather than the 64,000 employees in the *maquiladora* industry who "donate" from $1 to $100 pesos of weekly salaries from Real, Arreos American, Nipona, and others. This is different from the civil association, the Chihuahuan Entrepreneurs Foundation (FECHAC), which receives a share of the public trust from the state government's share of payroll taxes collected—1 percent from all domestic and foreign firms in the state of Chihuahua.[20]

In the four plants studied, labor relations are governed by the Rules of Work based on management logic from rules and global mechanisms such as ISO, which impacts employment rights in the retreat of the state. These Rules of Work specify all the obligations of workers and the obligations that, by law, must meet the enterprise. Many reasons exist for the justified dismissals, relating to discipline, absenteeism, and the needs of production, but the four plants have added the lack of quality in production processes and the possible loss of a customer, causing a critical problem. The table below shows these rules, based on workers' testimonials in the plants studied. See the quote and the table below.

> "... Then the new girl who took out the wrong material was saying they'll give me a red card and I'm going to get fired ..." [P2(woman worker), Sushicon Plant]; "... well yes because they called my attention and told me that I need to focus more on my job and to check the materials better and they gave us a red card ... [P3 (woman worker), Arreos American Plant]; "... then given that the quality manager is coming and catch you for violating the control quality system, goes with the technician and can fire you for this ..." [P4, (woman worker), Arreos American Plant].

The latter are directly associated with quality requirements that play in global markets, which are controlled by global regulatory institutions.

Streamlined Recruitment

The four plants studied have recently streamlined recruitment policies. Since 2000, the Nipona Corporation/Nipona Plant decreased the initial trial period of three months to one month. The number of temporary contracts has increased, also the time at which the operator may have a contract for an indefinite period. At Arreos America Plant / Arreos American Corporation, operators are hired as "operators in training" for the first three months, after which the plant decides whether to offer a timed contract or casual employment awarded for an indefinite period as a general operator. In terms of numerical flexibility,[21] the plants still have the ability to modify the size of the workforce quickly in response to changes in demand, but this involves greater costs as specified in the Rules of Work. As for the flexible use of labor within the productive processes, there remains a high regulatory discretion afforded to the plants in the use and disposal of the labor force as shown above. The main aspects that have been adjusted to the demands of flexible production include working hours, mobility between jobs and job categories, mobility shift and plants of the same corporation. The chief criteria for promotion are work overtime and required work on rest days. Flexibility modifies employee functions according to the position and job category, enabling business decisions to move workers between jobs, shifts, work schedules, and plants in a city. Wage flexibility is low, since most workers' incomes in harness *maquiladora* plants consists of the tabulated weekly wage (around 65%), and economic benefits, bonuses and incentives, representing approximately (35%). In times of crisis, the industry may decrease benefits in type and quantity.

Working conditions: Resistance from workers
The intensification in high performance work productive is analyzed through the number of hours worked per week, the obligation of double shifts worked temporarily for vacation days and holidays, also for signing weekly overtime agreements. At Sushicon, Real, and Arreos American, working time is 43.33 hours weekly, while at Nipona Plant/Nipona Corp, it is 40.50 hours per week. The production workers are forced to work an extra shift in the plant for nonworking days, vacation and holidays as in the cases of Sushicon/ Sushicon Corp and Nipona Plant/Nipona Corp. Nipona. However, widespread "overtime" is common and routine in order to achieve improvements in income, show their "commitment to work," and gain approval of the head of group or supervisor for promotion considerations or for references if permits are required.

> "To move up a position: I must comply with what the company says: do not be absent, be punctual, do not be undisciplined, work extra time when the company requires it . . . To move up a position, the manager asks the group chief (woman): Tell me, is this one undisciplined, plays, and chats, dances and laughs? Because even laughter bothers them and sometimes they tell us: "You know, you laugh too much, please calm down" [P2, (man worker), Nipona Plant]; ". . . You say that if you know everything, you will have a better position and do things; well, because there are people that scream and the managers and chief dislike that, so we have to be disciplined. We need to have a good behavior. We almost sleep there. Ay, no!" [P2, (woman worker), Nipona Plant.]

In this process, women and single mothers who care for family and/ or for sick parents are caught between their commitment to work and their commitment to the tasks of social reproduction such as childcare and relatives. Thus, they generally do not work overtime, incurring the costs that this implies in their plant careers.

". . . for example, when I need a permit to be absent because my kid is sick, I prefer just to be absent because anyway they'll won't give me permission and they would count me as absent. They never give us permission; there is nothing we can do." [P7, Obrera Planta AAMSA]

While women are somewhat empowered in work, they are rarely promoted to managerial levels due to "the double elaboration of paradigmatic femininity—responsible and independent within the factory, 'naturally' retiring externally" (Salzinger, 2003: 98). In other words, the household does not promote the advancement of women in the ranks of the company. Sometimes, when they may ascend, they decline for fear of negatively affecting their relationships with their husbands at home, where the control of men over women is still assumed (Salzinger, 2003; see also Staudt and Robles Ortega in this volume).

Production workers pursue strategies to mitigate the process of streamling and flexibility. For example, they work slowly (*tortugüismo*). These attitudes reduce the number of tasks that do not relate to their work. When they are asked to increase the standard of production, operators of the line reached a tacit agreement not to do so, and those who decide do not say anything to the head of production line and supervisors of production. Also, they tell the supervisor and manager that they cannot produce more than they are currently producing.

Slow-down strategies have already been documented (Peña, 1997: 8). Peña showed how the unilateral flexibility of the vast majority of *maquiladoras* in Ciudad Juárez had answers for several cases of the workers, particularly in electronics plants. The first type of fight in this sector that Peña describes involves restrictions on the production, *tortugüismo* (slowdowns), and resistance to keep the production line.

Unlike decades ago, we found that Peña called the second form of resistance by workers through work stoppages and wildcat strikes. But in the eighties and particularly in the nineties, Peña showed that the rotation of the volunteer job was undoubtedly the main form of rejection of the working conditions in *maquiladoras*, as the turnover rates reached more than 10 percent a month since the nineties, except in periods of crisis that these drop, as in the 3.10 percent turnovers in December 2008 (AMAC, 2008b). *Maquiladora* employment reached its heights in 2000, with an average of 249,380 jobs, but in May 2009, only 163,020 jobs remained (CIES, 2005; IMSS, 2009) of which 60,000 are in work lay off.

During the early years of this century, absenteeism and turnover had not been as high as in previous decades because of the profound crisis of 2001. That has occurred since late 2007 to date, when Juárez still could not recover the total jobs lost due to the crisis; the levels that have occurred in 2002 (5.21%), 2003 (3.96%), 2004 (5.25%), 2005 (6.59%), 2006 (7.74%), 2007 (7.83%)[22] and 2008 (4.25%) have not exceeded 10 percent that were previously submitted (ibíd.). The workers claimed their voluntary turnover find bonuses more attractive benefits, and in those cases, worked with less time than employees worked at the plant, in the case of workers with more time in the plant to the lack of vertical mobility and fair mechanisms in the plant where they worked.

CONCLUSIONS AND REFLECTIONS

The harness *maquiladora* industry, located in Juárez, involves world-class production, but not world-class wages to match the efforts of innovation, organization, technology, and improving job quality. International subcontracting has enabled greater labor flexibility and a decrease in labor costs. Therefore, decentralization has become the principal strategy for adapting to competitive pressures in the autoparts sector. The factors that influence employment quality in the city involve subordinate union, the kind of collective and individual contracts supplemented by the irresponsibility of the Mexican state, out of compliance with workers' rights. Instead, global private institutes regulate rights.

About the analysis of working conditions in harness manufacturing in Ciudad Juárez, we find contradictory spaces of producing world-class with precarious employment and the shrinkage of the state (Sassen, 2007).

Working relations have a high component of labor flexibility unilateral, low wage flexibility, high functional flexibility, and high numerical flexibility, which translates into high volatility and job insecurity and inadequacy.

In the first case of instability and job insecurity, labor flexibility, numerical and functional flexibility are high, because the plants maintained individual contracts and collective labor and industrial relations centrally governed by the internal regulations of the workplace.

Second is the higher percentage of base salary from the salary, so that wage flexibility is low and characterized by low wages and poverty for about 85 percent of employees in this industry; as Ross said, globalization works very well with low wages (Ross, 1997).

The massive application of production practices of the so-called Lean Production Model have hit workers heavily in precarious working conditions in direct production. Yet this has been accompanied by the active participation of workers in the production process, labor intensification processes, resistance, and more control over their work.

NOTES

1. This part is part of more comprehensive research for my dissertation. See Miker, 2009.
2. According to Gereffi, this perspective: (1) incorporates an explicit international dimension to the analysis; (2) focuses on the power exercised by leading firms in various segments of the product chain and illustrates how the power is transformed over time; (3) considers the coordination of the chain in its entirety as a crucial source of competitive advantage that requires using networks as a strategic value; and (4) considers organizational learning as a critical mechanism by which firms seek to improve or consolidate their positions within the chain (1999:3).
3. Each is presented under a pseudonym, as are the corporations to which they belong, with the aim of safeguarding the identity of the same and cooperating with this investigation.
4. Currently, the number of electronic automotive parts is about 25 percent and will represent an estimated 40 percent in 2010.
5. Each type of car needs a different number of harness sets. On average, a passenger car needs 12 sets of harnesses. But some prefer integration of the entire assembly in one system or module. Therefore, some assembled harnesses are extremely large.
6. Electric Group in Juárez has the engineering and design center where they develop prototypes of new products with new technologies—everything from new applications for existing products and products manufactured, and its internal customers to plants and customers outside the major assemblers cars.
7. *Revista Expansión, junio* 2009.
8. On European manufacturing plants, plants in England recently moved to Central and Eastern Europe, with design in Germany, France, and Italy. Recently, factories have been established in North Africa (Morocco). In Asia, the company moved about 40 percent of their production from Japan to China and other countries.
9. The Federal Labor Law stipulates that in Mexico in its Title III, Working conditions, Chapter I to VIII regarding: hours of work (maximum 8 hours), salary (equal to or greater than the legal minimum), days of rest (1 worked six days per min), pleasure (6 working days per year minimum), and annual Distribution Utilities according to the law.

10. The average cost of personnel transportation in January 2008 cost 251.89 pesos per trip; the cost of cafeteria services according to shift, between 12.82 and 17.23 pesos (AMAC 2008a). Remember that the exchange rate then was 14 pesos to US$1.

11. To analyze the flexibility of harness *maquiladoras*, my research focused on "numeric flexibility" (ability of the company to increase or decrease the workforce), wage flexibility (Guadarrama 2004), and "functional flexibility" (ability of the company to change the roles of workers within the production process) (de la Garza 1993).

12. Sandra Montijo, President of the Maquila Association (AMAC) in Ciudad Juárez, said "Fortunately, Ciudad Juárez is a zone with very few unions and only about 10 per cent of the *maquiladoras* have one." *Maquiladora Industry Weekly*, February 22, 2007.

13. However, there is an association fee of one peso per working week, deducted via payroll and delivered to the union.

14. See p. 122.

15. *El Diario, suplemento manufactura, 12 de marzo de 2008*.

16. According to Carrillo, 2001, the *maquiladora* unions are "transparent" because they are subordinated to business.

17. Subordinate union is that it becomes an appendage of corporate power in the plant, which gives the union lost the essence of trade unionism. In this regard, see Quintero Cirila, 2003. Carrillo has called this kind of regressive union-functional as they seek to prevent any conflict in plants by controlling (on paper) of these unions, in this regard see Carrillo 2001.

18. Currently, *chola* clothing for men and women consists of trousers or Dickies jeans and loose shirts *guang*. Most men sport tattoos, tennis shoes, and short hair, and women tattoo their faces (delineating eyebrows and mouth) and most often have fringes and style their hair in a ponytail. For more information about life and dress in Juárez, see "Cholos view: Puro Barrio That, history," Arrecillas A, et al., 1991, the National Council for Culture and Arts, Department of Popular Culture, Regional Unit Chihuahua.

19. Women who are employed in the four plants were subjected to pregnancy testing as a condition of contract. In the first contract of employment—for the duration of a month—workers engage in the plant's internal regulations (RIT) to undergo the medical examination (examination of urine and then of the womb), to continue with the second and third months of work, and if they do not do this by default with the RIT, it serves as cause for dismissal. During the selection, recruitment, and hiring tests, doctors and nurses from the plants conduct tests (urine test, blood pressure, anemia, and diabetes), auscultation of the stomach, check the monthly menstrual period, ask intrusive questions about sexual activity, menstrual cycle, and the type of contraception the women use.

20. Diario Oficial del Estado de Chihuahua 29 de septiembre de 1979. Decreto No. 42907903016-P.E., Expedido por el H. Congreso Local, Impuesto sobre Nómina que sustiuye al impuesto sobre sueldos y emolumentos en el capituo indicado, Articulo 166–172.
21. This is defined as the ability of harness plants to determine the number of workers in accordance with the production process requirements.
22. This percentage was calculated from plants affiliated to Asociación Maquiladora, AC, Ciudad Juárez, and was consulted at AMAC, 2008b.

REFERENCE LIST

Arrecillas Casas, Alejandro, Telesforo Guillermo Contreras, Oscar Reyes Ruvalcaba, Ma. Eugenia Rentería Rodríguez, Gonzalo Gónzalez Acevedo, y Jorge Carrera Robles. (1991). *Puro Barrio Ese, Historias de vida.* Consejo Nacional para la Cultura y las Artes, Dirección General de Culturas Populares, Unidad Regional Chihuahua.

Barrientos, Stephanie. (2007). "Decent work in global production networks: Opportunities and challenges for social upgrading," in International Workshop *Global Production Networks and Decent Work: Recent Experience in India and Global Trends,* Bangalore, November 18–20, 2007.

Boyer, R., E. Charron, U. Jurgens, y S. Tolliday, eds. (1998). *Between imitation and innovation. The transfer and hybridization of productive models in the International automobile industry.* Oxford: Oxford University Press.

Carrillo, Jorge. (2001). Maquiladoras en México: Evolución industrial y retraso sindical. *En Cuadernos del Cendes,* Año 28, No. 47, Caracas, mayo-agosto, pp. 207–231.

Carrillo, Jorge, y José Carlos Ramírez. (1993). "Nuevas tecnologías en la industria maquiladora" en J. Micheli (compilador) *Tecnología y Modernización económica,* pp. 347–368. Conacyt-UAM Xochimilco, México 1993.

Carrillo, Jorge, and Raúl Hinojosa. (2001). Cableando el norte de México: la evolución de la industria maquiladora de arneses. *En Revista Región y Sociedad,* Vol. XIII, Núm. 21, Hermosillo, El Colegio de Sonora, enero-julio, pp. 79–114.

Carrillo-Viveros, Jorge Hector, y Martha Miker Palafox. (2009). "Importancia y evolución de los arneses automotrices en el norte de México" en Reporte Final de Investigación: Integración norteamericana y desarrollo: Impacto del TLC en la restructuración industrial y el empleo. Responsable Oscar Contreras, PIERAN-COLMEX, febrero, 2009.

Carrillo-Viveros, Jorge, Martha Cecilia Miker Palafox, y Julio César Morales Cruz. (2001). *Empresarios y Redes Locales: Autopartes y Confección en el Norte de México.* Editada por Universidad Autónoma de Ciudad Juárez y Plaza y Valdés Editores. México.

Castells, Manuel. (1999). Information technology, globalization and social development, UNRISD Discussion Paper No. 114, September 1999, United Nations Research Institute for Social Development. P23.

De la Garza, Enrique. (1998). *Modelos de Industrialización en México*. México, UAM- Iztapalapa.

De la Garza Toledo, Enrique. (1993). Restructuración productiva y respuesta sindical en México. Instituto de Investigaciones Económicas. Universidad Nacional Autónoma de México.

De la O Martínez, María Eugenia. (1994). Innovación tecnológica y clase obrera. Estudio de caso de la industria maquiladora electrónica RCA Ciudad Juárez Chihuahua, Universidad Autónoma Metropolitana-Iztapalapa, Miguel Ángel Porrua Grupo Editorial, México.

———. (2002). Ciudad Juárez: un polo de crecimiento maquilador. En María Eugenia De la O Martínez and Cirila Quintero Ramírez (coords.): Globalización, Trabajo y Maquilas: Las viejas y nuevas fronteras en México, Editado por Fiedrich Ebert Stiftung, Ciesas, Centro Americano para la Solidaridad Sindical Internacional, AFL-CIO y Plaza y Valdés Editores, México, pp. 25–71.

Diario Oficial del Estado de Chihuahua, 29, de septiembre de 1979. Decreto No. 429-79-3-16-P.E.

Freyssenet, M., A. Mair, K., Shimizu, y G. Volpato, eds. (1998). *One best Way? Trajectories and industrial models of the world's automobile producers*. Oxford: Oxford University Press.

Fröbel, Folker, J. Hinrichs, y Otto Kreye. (1980). *La Nueva División Internacional del Trabajo. Paro estructural en los países industrializados e industrialización en los países en desarrollo*, Madrid, Siglo XXI.

Gereffi, Gary. (1996). "Commodity chains and regional divisions of labor in East Asia,". *Journal of Asian Business*, 12(1).

Gereffi, G., Humphrey, J., Kaplinsky, R., and Sturgeon, T, eds. (2001). The value of value chains: Spreading the gains from globalization. *IDS Bulletin*, 32(3).

Gereffi, Gary, and Korzeniewicz Miguel, eds. (1994). *Commodity chains and global capitalism*. Westport, CT: Praeger.

González-Aréchiga, Bernardo, y José Carlos Ramírez. (1990). Subcontratación y empresas trasnacionales; apertura y reestructuración en la maquila, México: El Colegio de la Frontera Norte y Fundación Friedrich Ebert.

Guadarrama, Elena. (2004). Desarrollo de una industria manufacturera y relaciones laborales en la década de los noventa. Un caso regional de Veracruz en III Congreso Latinoamericano de Sociología del trabajo. http://www.alast. org/PDF/Galin1/RRLL-Guadarrama.PDF. Facultad de Economía. Universidad Veracruzana. Xalapa, Ver. México.

Guerra, Pablo. (1994). "La precarización del empleo: algunas conclusiones y un intento de operacionalización" En: El empleo precario y el empleo atípico; revisión bibliográfica y propuesta para el debate. Documento de Trabajo No. 105, PET, Santiago de Chile.

Harvey, David. (1996). "The city in a globalizing world," in *Social Theory: The multicultural and classic reading*, Charles Lemert, ed., second edition. Boulder, Colorado: Westview Press, pp. 622–626.

IMSS. (2009). Estadísticas Delegación Estatal del Instituto Mexicano del Seguro Social-Ciudad Juárez, junio de 2009.

Koido, Akijiro. (1992). "Between two forces of restructuring: U.S.-Japaneses competition and the transformation of Mexico's Maquiladora industry," PhD. Dissertation. Baltimore, Maryland: The John Hopkins University.

Kopinak, Kathryn. (1996). *Desert Capitalism: Maquiladoras in North America's Western Industrial Corridor.* Tucson: The University of Arizona Press, 232.

Lara Rivero, Arturo. "Arneses de tercera generación. La migración de firmas de Estados Unidos al norte de México." En Hecho en Norteamérica. Cinco estudios sobre la integración industrial de México en América del norte. (coord.) Oscar Contreras y Jorge Carrillo, México, El Colegio de Sonora, Ediciones Cal y Arena, pp. 109–135, 2003.

Lugo, Alejandro. 2008. *Fragmented lives, assembled parts: culture, capitalism, and conquest at the U.S.-Mexico border.* Austin: University of Texas Press.

Miker Palafox, Martha Cecilia. (2009). Aprendizaje laboral situado en la industria maquiladora de arneses automotrices en Juárez Tesis Doctoral. Universidad Autónoma de Ciudad Juárez, Ciudad Juárez, Chihuahua.

OIT. (1998). Teasuro OIT: Terminología del trabajo, el empleo y la formación. 5ta. Edición, OIT Ginebra.

Ortiz Bencomo, Victoria Eugenia. (2005). Proyecto de Intervención: Aprendizaje Organizacional: Análisis de los procesos de aprendizaje y rediseño de material de instrucción. Estudio de caso de los trabajadores directos de producción de la planta Fuentes de Lear Corporation Ciudad Juárez, Chihuahua. Universidad Pedagógica Nacional-Ciudad Juárez, 21 de noviembre de 2005, Ciudad Juárez, Chihuahua México.

Pelayo Martínez, A. (1992). Nuevas tecnologías en la industria maquiladora de autopartes en Ciudad Juárez. Materiales y observaciones de campo. Ciudad Juárez. Unidad de Estudios Regionales, Universidad Autónoma de Ciudad Juárez (Cuadernos de trabajo, 6).

Peña, Devon. (1997). The Terror of the Machine: Technology, Work, Gender, and Ecology on the US-Mexico Border, Center for Mexican American Studies, Austin.

Quintero Ramírez, Cirila. (2003). El sindicalismo actual en la industria maquiladora. Ponencia preparada para el 4o. Congreso de la Asociación Mexicana de Estudios del Trabajo, a realizarse del 9 al 11 de abril de 2003 en Hermosillo, Sonora.

———. (2002). "Relaciones Laborales en la Maquiladora: Balance y perspectivas," *El Cotidiano*, Noviembre-Diciembre año/Vol. 19, núm. 116, Universidad Autónoma Metropolitana, Azcapotzalco, Distrito Federal, México, pp. 16–27.

Revista Expansión. (2009). "Las 500 empresas más importantes de México" junio 2009.

Rodgers, Gerry. (1989). "Precarious work in Western Europe: The state of debate," in Gerry Rodgers and Janine Rogers, eds., *Precarious jobs in*

142   Martha Miker Palafox

labour market regulations: The Growth of Atypical Employment in Western Europe, ILO, Genf.

Ross, Andrew, ed. (1997). *No sweat. Fashion, free trade and the rights of garment workers*, Londres: Verso.

Salzinger, Leslie. (2003). *Gender in production: Making workers in Mexico's global factories.* University of California Press, 217.

Sassen, Saskia. (2007). Una sociología de la globalización, 1ra. Edicion, Buenos Aires: Katz Editores, traducida por Maria Victoria Rodil.

———. (2006). *Cities in a world economy, Sociology for new century*, third ed. University of Chicago: Pine forge Press.

———. (1998). *Globalization and its discontents: Selected Essays.* New York: New press.

Shaiken, Harley. (2003). "México, los estándares laborales y la economía global," en Enrique de la Garza y Carlos Salas (Coords.), *La situación del trabajo en México, 2003*, México, Instituto de estudios del Trabajo, Universidad Autónoma Metropolitana, Centro Americano para la Solidaridad Sindical Internacional (AFL-CIO), Plaza y Valdés editores.

Shaiken, Harley, and H. Brown. (1991). "Japanese work organization in Mexico," in *Manufacturing across borders and oceans.* San Diego, La Jolla: Center for US-Mexican Studies, University of California (Monograph series, 36).

Sturgeon, Timothy J. (2000). "How do we define value Chains and productive Networks?" in *Gloablization study industrial performance center*, Special Working Paper Series, MIP IPC Globalization Working Paper 00-010, present in The Bellagio Values Chains Workshop, Sep 25–Oct 1, 2000.

Valdés-Villalba, Guillermina. (1983). "Aprendizaje en la producción y transferencia de tecnología en la industria maquiladora de exportación" en Jorge Carrillo (comp.), Restructuración industrial: las maquiladoras en la frontera México-Estados Unidos, SEP-CEFNOMEX, México.

Wilson, Patricia. (1992). *Export and local development, Mexico's new maquiladoras.* Austin: University of Texas Press.

———. (1989). *The new maquiladoras: Flexible production in low wage regions.* Austin: Community and Regional Planning, University of Texas at Austin (Working papers Series, 9).

Electronic Pages Viewed

AMAC. (2008a). http://www.amacweb.org/Graficas%20de%20Encuesta%20Salario%20Enero%202008.pdf., accedida el 2 de septiembre de 2008.

AMAC. (2008b). Comité Estadísticas. http://www.amacweb.org/4%20GRAFICA-ROTACION-DIC-08.pdf

FONDO UNIDO. (2008). Fondo Unido Chihuahua. http://fondounido chihuahua.org/index.php?option=com_content&task=view&id=12&Ite mid=1.

CIES. (2005). Centro de Información Económica y Social, Gobierno del Estado de Chihuahua, con base en datos de INEGI, Dirección General de Estadísticas Económicas.

NEWSPAPERS CONSULTED

El Diario, Industria Maquiladora, Publicación semanal, 22 de febrero de 2007.

El Diario, Suplemento Manufactura, 27 de mayo 2008.

SECTION III

LIVING WITH GLOBALIZED RISKS: POVERTY, IMMIGRATION, AND EDUCATION

CHAPTER 7

CENTERING THE MARGINS:
THE TRANSFORMATION OF
COMMUNITY IN COLONIAS ON
THE U.S.-MEXICO BORDER

Guillermina Gina Núñez and Georg M. Klamminger

Colonias are nonincorporated communities located on the rims of larger urban centers throughout the U.S.-Mexico border. They are significant for understanding the inequities associated with elements of globalization such as free trade, industrialization, urbanization, and migration, for it is in specific places where the global becomes local. The analysis of cities adds to the "analysis of economic globalization," which allows us to "reconceptualize processes of economic globalization as concrete economic complexes situated in specific places" (Sassen, 1998: xix). In *Globalization and Its Discontents* (1998), Saskia Sassen refers to places bound to each other by the dynamics of economic globalization as a "new geography of centrality." Specifically, analyzing colonias offers scholars an opportunity to make the periphery the center of analysis in examining global phenomena, such as transnational migration and population settlement processes of immigrant enclaves within regions of the world that are critical to the transformation of capital, labor, and human interactions.

Colonias provide temporary and permanent housing for residents and transnational sojourners crossing the U.S.-Mexico border. Their strategic location within an important migration corridor, the El Paso del Norte Metropolitan region, makes the geography of colonias central to the transnational flow of people, goods, and other nontangible but equally palpable factors such as practices and behaviors influenced by racialized, class-based, linguistic, and gendered ideologies. By focusing on colonias, we make urban peripheries central to the analysis of inequality and underdevelopment. We also propose an alternative model to the stigmatizing "social problem" analysis of colonias by focusing on the community-building processes often associated with accessing and enacting rights to these places. This model is based on Setha Low's (1999) approach toward defining social spaces, which are constructed and produced by the inhabitants and users of such communities. This approach points to how specific locations are built on the landscape, as well as how these places are experienced and imbued with value and sentiment based on the social interactions, struggles, and personal histories of community members. The building of community through civic engagement, organizing, and political participation in colonias form a new border-cultural citizenship that is critical in bringing agency to the forefront of the decision-making arenas that directly influence the lives of colonia residents.

There are about 1400 colonias with over 1 million residents, primarily concentrated in the state of Texas, and in lesser numbers in New Mexico, Arizona, and California. These population settlements have both rural and urban characteristics, depending on their history, size, population density, and development trajectories. Although the concept of colonias literally translates to neighborhood, in the United States, these neighborhoods are actually unincorporated settlements and communities located within a close proximity of larger urban centers (Ward, 1999). Some colonias in the U.S.-Mexico region, particularly in New Mexico and Texas, may be traced back to early population settlements in the 1800s, while others are as recent as the late 1950's. The more contemporary configurations of colonias are mainly a result of a combination of factors including rapid urbanization, migration, and the lack of affordable housing. Other issues also contributing to the sprawl of colonias are the lack of government regulation in land transactions, discrimination against low-income Mexican populations, and the lack of attention and underinvestment in the social and physical infrastructure of these settlements (ibid, 1999). Investments in the U.S.-Mexican infrastructure were focused primarily in large urban centers with massive infusions of capital toward industry development, and much less attention was given to the region's rural and periurban sectors.

In this study, we take an urban anthropological perspective to examine the colonias in the El Paso Del Norte Metropolitan region. This work is written based on previous ethnographic research conducted in New Mexico, in a county located within the El Paso del Norte Metropolitan region. Through Núñez's ethnographic and Klamminger's ethnogeographical analysis of colonias as communities, this work contributes to the study of colonias as places and as social processes. The ethnographic analysis of colonias provides an experiential access to residents' opinions, ideologies, and behaviors, while the geographic component of this work examines the spatial aspects of colonias as zones fusing rural and urban communities in the borderlands.

In seeking to understand the growth and development of colonias along the U.S.-Mexico border, we aim to examine how urban cores and peripheries are engaged in both mutually beneficial and exploitive relationships of power. While colonias do offer a place where workers can live inexpensively and create their own homes and communities, they do so at the cost of jeopardizing the human and civil rights of low-income Mexican residents. It is on the fringes of larger urban centers of power, such as colonias, where residents' rights and humanity are often violated by economic depression, social isolation, and political alienation and repression. It is specifically in such places situated outside of centers of economic and political power where scholars and policy-makers may observe the consequences of international trade policies, immigration regulation policies, and the surveillance and protection of the nation-state at the cost of civil and human rights.

The existence of colonias has been primarily described in the public policy literature within an affordable housing framework, as colonia residents often seek refuge in these communities as "alternatives to affordable housing" in rural and periurban population centers. However, in a capitalist system, colonias are population settlements that heavily subsidize economic growth and development in the U.S.-Mexico borderlands, primarily as these settlements and communities house thousands of laborers that may be accessed as a labor pool seasonally and all year round to support industries that thrive on the backs of a low-wage workforce; a workforce that has very little time to expend trying to organize themselves to improve their living conditions.

Community development processes in the colonias of New Mexico have relied on the civic engagement of their residents, the organizing efforts of nongovernmental organizations (NGO's), as well as local, state, and federal government interventions. The successful partnership and the collective agency of residents, nonprofit organizations, and government entities contributes to the development of a new *border citizenship* that scholars, like Raymond Rocco (2002) and Cynthia Bejarano (2005) have noted, is involved in addressing social and environmental justice issues on the U.S.-Mexico border. This border citizenship involves the collaboration between U.S. citizens, in particular long-rooted *Hispanos* in New Mexico, U.S. residents, and immigrants—authorized and unauthorized—who have come to this land in search of refuge, opportunity, and hopes of fulfilling their dreams of homeownership and seeking success for their future generations.

Spatializing Culture: Urban Anthropology and the Study of Colonias

Urban anthropology and urban sociology have taken two primary approaches to the study of culture in urban settings by focusing on the study of life in the city and the life of cities (Gulick, 1989: 15). While earlier anthropological studies focused on indigenous and rural communities, anthropologists began to focus on "city life" as rural residents began to leave their homes in search of better opportunities in the city. As such, urban anthropologists and sociologists have long documented the ties cities have had with rural sectors (Foster and Kemper, 1979; Kemper, 2002; Zenner, 2002). As rural migrants have travelled to the "city" in search of work, they have reenergized cities by providing them with a consistent flow of labor and all of the accompanying cultural infusions associated with recent migrants and immigrants. Consequently, great urban centers are often infused with ethnic enclaves or neighborhoods, such as Little Italy, China town, and Korean town, where ethnography in the city can be conducted while studying smaller ethnic populations.

As centers of production and consumption, cities have been able to designate resources to the creation of larger bureaucracies and institutions of power and domination (Smith, 2002). Those on the margins are at best, dependent on the decisions and policy-making processes from those creating and operating rules and regulations from the core. What we have as a result is a making of an underclass, as population settlements on the margins of cities continue to depend on the labor opportunities and financial investment of dominant economic and political entities in larger urban cores.

The study of colonias within an urban anthropological framework begins from a broader discussion of the growth and development of the U.S.-Mexico border region. The border region's economic growth has been accompanied by significant population growth in Mexico's northern border and in the United States Southwest. The various types of industries located along the U.S.-Mexico border have drawn from Mexico's central and southern states migrants who are enticed to move to the border in hopes of higher wages. In the El Paso-Ciudad Juárez border region, the service sector and manufacturing plants or *maquiladoras*, have drawn migrants to the border region for more than four decades. Ganster and Lorey (2007: 123) indicate that the flow of migration settled in larger urban concentrations due in part to jobs in manufacturing, construction, hotels, restaurants, and services. Other more rural parts of the border attract migrants to emigrate across the border in search of work in agricultural and dairy industries.

The supply and demand for manufacturing and agriculturally produced goods in the U.S.-Mexico border region are shaped by national and international markets and by local demands for seasonal and year-round labor. This is an important economic factor influencing the growth of colonias, primarily because the industries that employ people are encouraged to recruit labor, yet are not necessarily responsible for providing housing for their workforce. As such, finding affordable housing within a relatively close proximity to their place of employment becomes an individualized responsibility for a low-wage workforce.

While some colonia residents are still involved in regional and transnational migration—moving back and forth across national borders, urban cores, and rural peripheries—others have now become more permanently settled as *fronterizos* or "borderlanders" (Martínez, 1994) in the U.S.-Mexico borderlands. Colonia residents surveyed by Núñez between the years 2002 and 2005 in Doña Ana County, New Mexico, narrated the experiences of previously working as migrant farm workers in the El Paso del Norte border region and returning to the region to look for work and to find an affordable place to live. This settlement process was particularly evident after the passing of the 1986 Immigration Control and Reform Act (IRCA), which allowed 2.2 million immigrants to gain amnesty and become authorized U.S. residents.

Many colonia residents were encouraged by local organizers to buy land and to start their immigration paperwork processes in hopes of becoming legal residents. As a former community organizer and housing specialist noted:

> We encouraged people to go and buy some land, anything that would prove they lived in the United States to support their requests for legal residency in this country. Colonias did not come after the Immigration and Reform Control Act of 1986, they started developing in the midst of it.
>
> Daniel Domínguez, Community Organizer
> as cited in Núñez 2006: 231–232

Thus, the push for Mexican immigrants to become U.S. residents and homeowners as part of a commitment to belong to the United States influenced residents to move into colonias in the mid 1980s. One of the impacts of IRCA was that it seemed to have increased the occupational status and the degree of occupational mobility among previously undocumented immigrants. Five years after IRCA, in 1992, researchers found that the population of unauthorized migrants who were legalized had jobs that were better than their first jobs and better than the jobs held in their countries of origin (Powers, Kraly, and Seltzer, 2004). In an effort to prove their loyalty and commitment to the United States, thousands of legal residents began to seek land to purchase and to call their home.

Formerly undocumented workers who had spent years "living in the shadows," hiding from the public eye (Chávez, 1992) came out in search of legitimate spaces they could define and lay claim to. With shifts in the economy and changes in immigration policies in the Untied States after the mid-1980s, newly "legitimized workers" came out in search of their place and space in the border landscape. Colonia-type settlements emerged as transnational migrants became rooted in the communities in which they labored. In the case of colonias in this study, residents often began as migrants, and then decided to stay in a place where they could find work in places they could afford to live. The decision to stay was then followed by a process of family integration and reunification. For legal residents and citizens, this reunification involves requesting permission to bring family members to the United States through immigration procedures. Evidence shows that the growth in the number of colonias along the U.S.-Mexico border has a direct correlation to the passing of IRCA in 1986 (Vélez-Ibáñez, Núñez, and Rissolo, 2000). As unauthorized immigrants sought to become legally recognized, they also sought out a place to call home within places closely associated with their life and labor histories. For many of these new U.S. residents, the U.S.-Mexico border offered them a place to call home within relatively close proximity to their relatives living in Mexico.

Another key event in the creation and classification process of colonias was the passing of the Gonzalez National Affordable Housing Act (NAHA) in 1990, which federally defined a colonia as an "'identifiable community' in Arizona, California, New Mexico, or Texas within 150 miles of the U.S.-Mexico border, lacking decent water and sewage systems and decent housing and in existence as a colonia before November 28, 1989." This definition, and in particular the cut-off date of November 28, 1989, was important in creating a rushed effort among local communities to seek to reclassify and coin local communities in need of physical infrastructure as "colonias." Although this classification would bring federal and state funding to local border communities, the "colonia" label also contributed to the stigmatization and their racialized perception as low-income communities of color in need of federal and state "set aside" funding—much like an affirmative action approach to border community development efforts.

In examining the community-building processes of colonia residents, we have followed Setha Low's framework for *spatializing culture* by "locating, both physically and conceptually, social relations and social practices in social place" (2005: 111). The social production of community entails the analysis of all those factors (social, economic, ideological, and technological) that constitute the physical creation of the material setting. The social construction of community addresses the phenomenological and symbolic experience of space as mediated by social processes such as exchange, conflict, and control. Understanding how colonias are socially produced and socially constructed is significant for understanding how larger issues of urbanization, migration, displacement, and settlement processes are experienced at the local level. The social production of colonias entails the population settlement processes that influenced people to seek land and homeownership in rural or periurban regions of the U.S.-Mexico border. The social construction of community deals more directly with the processes that colonia residents engage in to add value to the social relationships they have with each other as neighbors and with institutions of power in seeking recognition as legitimate communities. For outside observers, scholars, and policymakers, colonias may be viewed and defined in a deficit-model framework, for it is through definitions of what these communities lack (paved roads, water, wastewater systems, etc.) that the term colonias has been coined in public policy frameworks. In this case, the concept of spatializing culture is helpful in understanding how residents add value to their homes and properties by linking their historical trajectories and personal narratives of their community development struggles toward the inscription of memory and value in communities previously viewed as marginal and peripheral.

Ethnographic research conducted by Núñez from 2002 to 2005 focused on the community-building processes of five colonia communities in Northern Doña Ana County, New Mexico. Particular attention was paid to household and community interactions that exemplify what Ward (1999) refers to as "horizontal integration," which is the amount of interaction at the local level among individuals within a community or settlement to access services. Community-building in colonias is also made possible by the interaction and negotiations of power and resources between colonia residents, local leaders, nonprofit organizations and government organizations and their representatives. This negotiation of powerful relationships is defined by Ward (1999) as the vertical integration of community, which often involves tapping into powerful actors outside of colonias, primarily in the city, region, state, and federal government entities.

By examining how colonias have been produced and constructed by their residents, we are able to appreciate the value residents have placed on their homes and on their communities. This is an alternative perspective to most of the metanarratives traditionally associated with colonias within policy circles—as places of poverty and social ills (see Sarah Hill's, 2003 work to learn more about the issues contributing to the stigmatization of colonias). Analysis of colonia residents' life and labor histories in Doña Ana County, New Mexico, provide evidence of colonia residents who still maintain ties with their places of origin while also providing evidence that a considerable number of residents are no longer moving back and forth and now consider the United States as their permanent home. Evidence of colonia residents expressing interest in staying rooted in colonias indicates that they seem to be better invested in participating in local efforts aimed toward improving their communities, which is an important factor for understanding and facilitating community-building processes. A sense of ownership and stewardship is evident in residents who aim to become permanent homeowners and residents in colonias and who care to see their communities improve over the long run. This is in stark contrast to people who own properties in colonias, but are considered to be "absent landholders," and do not dwell on a permanent basis in these communities (Ward, Stevenson, and Stuesse, 2000). The number of empty lots within colonias contributes to the accumulation of desert brush, and the making of illegal dumpsites, which accumulate waste and pose environmental and fire threats to the communities, all the while adding to their aesthetic degradation.

Due to considerable power inequalities and imbalances of power among internal as well as external factors involved in the creation of colonias, the production and construction of viable communities involves the constant contestations of space and identity. Colonia residents are often plagued by social stigmas, such as illegitimacy and illegality. The peripheral location of colonias both in a geographical sense (meaning the physical distance from the nearest cities) as well as in a sociopolitical context (mainly the political distance from centers of power) marginalizes these settlements on various levels. Local communities are thus forced to respond to internal and external forces of marginalization, including economic, ecological, and political pressures. Residents within these population settlements are involved in challenging these forces by being engaged via interplay of the individual residents' experiences with one another and with external stakeholders that shape and define colonias. Colonias as population settlements can range from being settlements of households and individuals to well-defined and integrated communities with their own historical, political, and spatialized identities.

COLONIAS AS MIGRATION CORRIDORS

Colonias on the U.S.-Mexico border are situated within historical migration corridors. Migration and population settlement processes along the U.S.-Mexico border are deeply rooted in historical, economic, and political processes. Specifically, the El Paso del Norte region has been referred to as the Ellis Island of the Americas for its significant role in the movement of people and goods throughout the continent. The massive migration of peoples throughout the world and in the U.S. Southwest specifically involves processes of displacement, movement, and incorporation (Alvarez, 1987; Chávez, 1992). As communities located on the border, the growth and development processes of colonias are inextricably linked to historical, political, and economic forces influencing human migration, which may be examined as a process and as a response to the migrant populations' unfolding needs and aspirations.

Migration systems theory suggests that migratory movements generally arise from the existence of prior links between sending and receiving countries based on a history of colonization (Castles & Miller, 1998: 24). The migration systems approach further describes how migratory movements can be seen as the interaction of macro and microstructures. Macrostructures refer to larger global and institutional forces that include the larger political economy of the world, interstate relationships, the laws and structures and practices established by sending and receiving states controlling migration settlement; while microstructures involve migrants' local networks, practices, beliefs, and ideologies. Both macro and microlevel structural forces encourage migrants to seek to establish informal social networks in order to cope with the stress and challenges of the migration, settlement, and incorporation processes.

Migration from Mexico to the United States, originated in the southwestward expansion of the United States in the 19th century and the deliberate recruitment of Mexican laborers by U.S. employers in the 20th century (Castles & Miller, 1998, citing Portes and Rumbaut, 1996). More recent accounts of Mexican migration to the United States indicate how binational labor programs, such as the Bracero Program of 1942 to 1964, resulted in the border's population explosion (Alvarez López, 1988; Vélez-Ibáñez, 1997; Ganster and Lorey, 2008). Changes in U.S. immigration law in 1965 opened the United States to immigration from around the world as entries from Western Europe declined in favor of those from Asia and Latin America (Castles & Miller, 1998). Given their location along the U.S.-Mexico border—a corridor for the export and import of people, goods, and services—colonias are linked to transnational and transregional migration processes. For some, these communities represent a space within the migration route, for others, colonias represent destination points.

Migrants who cross the U.S.-Mexico border must decide whether to stay in the border region or cross the border region as one of the first steps before moving into other states and/or a place to return to work, rest, and reunite with family members. Research literature has long emphasized the importance between the role receiving communities have in the lives of migrants relatives and friends (Massey et al., 2002). Those colonia residents who are settled and have a home to live in can also offer refuge (Vélez-Ibáñez, 2004) and support to family members and *paisanos* who are still involved in the seasonal migration process. (Núñez, 2006). Ties with relatives in Mexico are maintained by a subsection of the population who visits family or owns property in their states of origin.

Through strong crossborder ties, residents of colonias are influenced by and sometimes share the values, ideas, customs, and traditions of their counterparts across the boundary line. This is partly a function of their peripheral location in the United States, which, together with their unique local culture and shared economic relations with other border communities, gives them a sense of both political and social separateness and otherness, of being culturally different from core and majority populations in their "national securities." Transnational populations are also involved in traveling through what Kearney (1996) refers to as hyperspace, between national boundaries of power and class hierarchies. While situated within local communities, the local hierarchies are made evident, creating boundaries between people based on class, ethnicity, and citizenship status.

Data collected through household surveys in five colonias in New Mexico's Doña Ana County during 2002–2004 indicates that a subsection of colonia residents are linked to international migration streams between Mexico and the United States. Of the 142 respondents surveyed, 33.8 percent indicated that they traveled to Mexico during short sporadic periods of time, while 59.2 percent of those surveyed indicated they did not travel to Mexico at all. The states most frequented were mainly Chihuahua, Zacatecas, Durango, and Guanajuato. Colonia residents who visited their states of origin did so once and up to three times a year to visit relatives and to check up on homes or small properties they had acquired over the years. During these short-term visits, people carry with them food, clothing, small used appliances, furniture, and other household items to offer as gifts to their family members. The heightened level of violence experienced by residents on the Mexican side of the border within the last three years (2007–2009) is sure to affect the visitation and migration strategies of U.S. border residents with family members in Mexico. A future study seems prime for gauging the links of border violence to decreased numbers of U.S. residents' crossing the border to visit and interact with family members in Mexico.

The colonia residents' relationship to migrants in Mexico and their links to immigrants in other regions of the United States make these individuals and these communities critical in the share of information and resources involving more profitable and sustainable labor opportunities. For example, a colonia resident in the El Paso del Norte border region might host family members from Mexico who are interested in work available in the state of Colorado. Being able to stay for a short period of time with a relative who is permanently living in a colonia allows individuals the time and energy necessary to strategize their migration routes and their future labor opportunities in other regions throughout the United States.

As Mexican migrant laborers have left their communities of origin, some have opted to stay and settle in border communities in the United States, while others have sojourned into states outside of the Southwest. As permanent or temporary receiving communities, colonias and their residents provide migrants with an anchor for building social relationships, while creating a place in which migrants can arrive and decide on their journeys to other areas of the United States or within the border region. Culturally, recent migrants reinvigorate local customs and traditions by importing skills, knowledge, and experiences of having lived in Mexico's rural and urban communities. Their experiences organizing community events, political meetings, prayer groups, and formal and informal neighborhood organizations are added to their experiences of building community in the United States. Besides bringing with them strong cultural preferences for Mexican music, medicinal practices, the Spanish language, and other religious or ritualized practices, migrants bring with them the optimism and character to build a platform for their social and economic advancement.

Colonias are also linked to internal migration streams within the United States. For many residents, living in the borderlands presents opportunities to connect with kin and social networks in other regions of the United States, including California, Alabama, Colorado, Kansas, Texas, Nevada, and Florida. While living in colonias, residents are able to work in seasonal farm labor locally, while at the same time communicating with kin and social networks in other regions of the United States to assess better employment opportunities in these other U.S regions. It is not uncommon for migrants in Kansas, Alabama, and Illinois to have previously lived in colonias in Texas or New Mexico. And vice versa, many colonia residents report having lived in areas like California, Wisconsin, Florida, and other states prior to settling in colonias. Núñez and Heyman (2007) provide ethnographic testimony of colonia residents who have narrated stories of hostility and discrimination faced while living in other regions throughout the United States, prompting them to move to colonias as a place where they can raise their families and perhaps even retire in their old age without facing as much racism, prejudice, and hostility.

Colonias as Buffers and Safety Valves

Colonias serve as a "buffer" for a number of clashes taking place at the boundaries of two nations: the clash between rural and urban, immigrants and citizens, authorized population settlement and unauthorized development, as well as many other social, political, and ecological outcomes associated with rapid urbanization and inadequate infrastructure. These populations on the margins of urbanized settings function as spaces and places of social tension and transformation. As buffers, colonias are the safety nets for the border region's low-income and working poor residents, migrants and local residents, people who are employed at or below the national poverty level in the border region's metropolises and its surrounding rural communities. Without colonias, the border region would arguably experience much higher rates of visible homelessness and despair. Yet, because of colonias, many of the U.S.-Mexican border's working poor, and their accompanying socioeconomic and environmental conditions, are less visible and less noticeable.

As buffer zones, colonias merge the urban cores and rural peripheries. As such, occupants of these settlements move in and out of zones of development and underdevelopment, negotiating everyday life in search of employment in the city, and in search of refuge and repose in their colonia populations. Although change is slow and gradual, colonias are usually under a continuous process of development and transition. Although factors such as the communities' history and completed infrastructure will vary from colonia to colonia, most of these communities continue to be in need of social and infrastructural services (health clinics, water, paved roads, sewage systems, etc.). For example, as of 2009, there are approximately 10,000 residents[1] in El Paso County without water services. This estimate may be compared to 1998 figures that estimated 75,000 residents living in El Paso County's colonias, a great percentage of these lacking in potable water services (Staudt, 1998: 114). The spatial distance of colonias and other rural communities from potable water lines and the extensive plots of empty space between colonias makes the delivery of piped water a highly costly ordeal. As such, colonia residents suffer from the social, geographic, and political distance and invisibility that is involved in living on the margins—outside of the visual horizons and mental landscapes of those operating within centers of power. The transformation of colonias as buffer zones surrounding larger urban settings is forging new social structures that are adapting around cities and reflecting the complex cultures resulting in this complex merger of cores and peripheries.

Another analogy that helps to describe the roles and functions of colonias within U.S.-Mexico border urbanization and globalization processes is that of "safety valves." As communities outside of urban centers, colonias provide a medium into which low income and working poor residents may be channeled and moved out of the urban core and into the rural periphery. In the border region, colonias, in essence, function as suburbs for the poor. As opposed to other large urban cities, where the affluent have sought to escape urban poverty by moving out to the suburbs, on the border, it is poor people who are pushed out, because they are not able to find employment with wages high enough to afford paying for housing in the city. This phenomenon of colonias as low-income suburbs was particularly evident after the passing of the North American Trade Agreement (NAFTA) in 1994. In El Paso County alone, estimates range between 14,000 and 20,000 people displaced by the closing of manufacturing plants in the textile industry. These manufacturing jobs in El Paso, Texas, offered laborers wages of about US$400 a week, while *maquiladoras* across the border in Ciudad Juárez, pay an average of US$50 a week. As corporations have exported their production-related jobs across the border into Mexico and elsewhere, laborers have been left stranded without opportunities to apply their job skills in new industries.

To note that people living in colonias exist in the margins is a major understatement. Their marginality is multiplied by larger structural and political issues, such as immigration raids, poor access to education and health care, and unemployment. These challenges are further aggravated by personal and individual experiences, such as lack of transportation, physical mobility, limited social networks, and lack of credit. We can thus also view colonias as "traps." Coronado (2003) notes that one of the primary reasons colonia residents are pushed to live in underdeveloped regions of the border is because many immigrants and natives lack access to credit lines offered by formal financial institutions. The lack of employment opportunities, and the levels of underemployment, makes colonia residents less likely to be able to maintain their lines of credit. As such, colonia residents are often involved in the informal labor market, as day laborers, and as seasonal migrant laborers. Poverty and limited economic mobility in the border region then trap residents in colonias. Those with the financial means to move elsewhere will often opt to do so, while others live in these communities because they have limited options to live elsewhere.

COLONIAS: THE IMPOSITION OF STIGMA AND DISCRIMINATION

The history of colonia settlement and development is marked by many empty promises and blown-up expectations associated with community development in the United States. Developers sold plots of land in colonias with promises that water, roads, and wastewater systems would soon follow. Many colonia residents purchased land and trailer homes to settle the land in hopes of gaining the promised services in the future. Residents were often led to believe that "the government" would soon provide the expected infrastructure services, such as potable water, electricity, and paved roads. However, these expectations were often ill founded. Instead of selling residential land with the necessary amenities for living on such property, many developers sold properties without investing in the necessary infrastructure.

To a great extent, land transactions in colonias were conducted between sellers and buyers without much government oversight. Buyers were often not aware of the lengthy bureaucratic process and costs involved in gaining infrastructure in colonias. In seeking clarification from the developers, many colonia residents looked for the developers who had originally sold them their plots of land only to find out that many were no longer around to be held accountable for their verbal promises and commitments.

Although colonias are broadly the result of emerging class distinctions in the U.S.-Mexico border region, their more specific antecedents are weak rural planning laws in border states (Paterson 1988). In New Mexico for example, rural landowners have been permitted to subdivide and sell land without plans to provide basic services. As a result, most colonias are isolated from nearby municipalities, which hesitate to annex them due to the costs of extending utility services outside of city limits. According to New Mexico State Senator, Mary Jane Garcia, most of Doña Ana County's contemporary colonias in southern New Mexico originated when subdividers began creating unimproved subdivisions within the county by taking advantage of the numerous loopholes in New Mexico's antiquated Subdivision Act. The 1996 New Mexico Subdivision Law required that certain infrastructure be in place before a development could receive preliminary plat approval. The loophole in the law made it so that titles to properties could not be issued unless the property has been properly subdivided with the county. Based on this Subdivision Act, a parcel of land could be legally divided into four parts (personal interview on file with authors). Each of these four lots could then be divided another four times. Subdividers used this four-lot-split provision on numerous occasions, resulting in large tracts of land being divided into as many as 200 residential lots parceled out without adequate roads, drainage, or other infrastructure improvements. These lots were then sold many times over via unrecorded real estate contracts to low-income people at low monthly payments (US$100–300) and high interest rates (up to 24%).

Guzman (2002) has documented the colonia residents' frustration and disappointment with the outcomes of this 1996 Subdivision loophole. In the colonias of southern New Mexico, there are resident landowners who have lived in colonias for 15 years without having the property titles that legitimately identify these families' claim to their properties. Without property titles, residents have no proof of their ownership, and lack the ability of engaging in future property transactions, which prohibits passing these properties down to their children, or selling these to anyone else. This is an unfortunate predicament shared by colonia residents in northern Doña Ana County as well as in other colonias throughout the El Paso del Norte region, in both New Mexico and Texas. Making things worse, many residents who purchased land to build their homes did not know they were doing so in a desert region impacted by a 100–year-old drought. That is, few residents actually knew that their properties were in ancient flood zones. It was not until the occurrence of flash floods that residents would learn they had purchased property in dried waterbeds, in the middle of arroyos, and in land highly volatile to climatic changes (Núñez-Mchiri, 2009). Few would consider these ecological conditions suitable and hospitable for human settlements housing thousands of people throughout the borderland region. Colonia residents are often tasked with the responsibility of making a living while facing serious threats to their personal and environmental health. Flash flooding, a "natural" ecological event, adds to the burden of poor and working-class communities who are vulnerable and susceptible to the repercussions of environmental disasters at much greater cost than most middle-class urban communities.

The environmental justice issues faced by colonia residents are compounded by local stigma and discrimination faced by Mexican-origin colonia residents. During a Village Council meeting in the Village of Hatch, Núñez heard a codes enforcement officer discuss the housing situation of certain residents in the community. Although he did not mention names, he often made references to "those people." Núñez learned that the codes enforcement officer was referring to Mexican families living in the community. In a public council meeting, the officer referred to "those people moving in and then bringing in all of their family members;" he further noted "you all know how those people are and how they live, but you all know I can't say more, because you all know how those people respond." Núñez listened in bewilderment, and later approached a local colonias organizer, who was also present at the meeting and asked if she had heard the same thing. The community organizer indicated that there was a long history of housing discrimination against Mexican residents in the region of study (it should be noted that these attitudes toward immigrants and marginal colonia dwellers are held broadly by both Anglo Americans and Hispanos living in the main settlements). These local attitudes make more difficult the extension of legal protections and infrastructure to colonias (Núñez, 2006: 238–239). Yet colonia residents and the nonprofit organizations they partner with demonstrate repeatedly their capacity for self-organization, both informally and formally, as a form of resistance to these discriminatory housing attitudes.

COMMUNITY FORMATION AND SOCIAL INTERACTIONS IN COLONIAS

U.S.-born colonia residents, U.S. residents who immigrated to the region, and other individuals living in colonias interact with one another on various levels: through informal family and community functions at various peoples' homes; through community meetings that bring residents together; and through the shared public community spaces. Colonias are part of regional border urban-rural and national-international-transnational continuums; as such people come into constant contact with one another and engage in face-to-face interactions to share information, exchange mutual aid, and build community. It is not uncommon to have U.S. residents and their children marry Mexican immigrants or their children. The children of both citizens and immigrants attend the same schools, participate in sports and other social events, and eventually begin to interact with one another on familial and social levels.

As colonia residents, whether U.S. born or immigrants, they all share the need for medical, educational, recreational, and business services more easily available in larger urban centers. Besides being unified by need for services, residents are pulled together in socially significant spaces such as churches, community centers, post offices, and home front businesses. Given the rural nature of colonias in Northern Doña Ana County, the limited public venues and shared social spaces are concentrated within the Village of Hatch or in much larger urban centers such as Las Cruces, New Mexico. As colonias scholars have noted (Richardson, 1999; Ward, 1999; Núñez, 2006), having public community spaces assists residents in having contact with one another and building more meaningful relationships as friends, neighbors, members of religious congregations, consumers, and as laborers. These mature colonias in southern New Mexico have several generations of residents who have been born and raised in these settlements with strong ties to their land and familial networks. Other residents have moved into these mature communities to share in this sense of belonging. The difference between mature and younger colonias is that time and slow growth permitted residents to buy inexpensive land and improve their housing stock and the supporting infrastructure over time (Simmons, 1997: 69–70). More mature colonias have had the opportunity to organize and structure their social organization and interactions with the creation and designation of public spaces. Mature colonias often have had key residents or what Kretzmann and McKnight (1993) refer to as "community assets" that build networks and partnerships with key elected officials and organizations that can mobilize resources for communities.

The history and maturity in community organizing in colonias is facilitated by the availability of public spaces used for community meetings and forums. For example, some colonias in New Mexico and Texas use former church structures as informal gathering spaces in lieu of formally constructed community centers. A historical colonia in New Mexico for example, has a portable double-wide trailer supported and maintained by the County of Doña Ana as a community center. Prior to the community center, residents of this colonia used to meet in the local water association's office, which was the largest space in the community to hold a public meeting. Another important space for the daily exchange of information is the small U.S. post office. For many colonia residents who do not receive their mail at home, going to the post office to check for their mail in the Post Office (P.O.) box becomes a daily ritual, many of whom share one post office box among a number of families. It is at the post office that residents often run into other local residents and catch up on all the local news or gossip. Hence, public spaces such as community centers and post offices are critical spaces for establishing a sense of community. Although colonia residents often reside outside of city limits, on old agricultural lands and in communities far from basic public services, they seek ways to fight their rural isolation by actively participating in everyday life events that ensure sociability and human interactions.

In his comparison of Mexican and Texan colonias, Peter Ward argues that on the U.S. side of the border, colonias exist much more as settlements than as communities (1999). He further argues that the U.S. colonia settlement process involves the individualized contracting between developers and settlers, making redundant the need for collective negotiation, as is usually the case among Mexican colonia residents. Ward's distinction between individual and collective negotiations of space is challenged by Paterson (1998), who reports that in the early 1990s, attempts to construct a "tent-city" for single, male seasonal farm-workers failed in Doña Ana County due to local residents' opposition. Similarly, as noted by Núñez (2006), when the local City Council of the Village of Hatch passed an ordinance restricting the placement of mobile homes within the village limits, it sparked a federal lawsuit against the town on the basis of racial discrimination. In this case, nonprofit organizations worked with residents in a lawsuit to challenge local housing codes implemented to preclude people of Mexican descent from living in older mobile homes within the city limits of Hatch, New Mexico. This partnership between the local nonprofit organizations and residents was successful in gaining the attention of the two federal agencies: the Department of Justice and the U.S. Department of Housing and Urban Development. As the outcome of this collaboration, residents were able to secure a moratorium that would halt their eviction and displacement. However, the continuous police harassment and the long and time-consuming legal process involving the suit affected several of the families involved, causing their subsequent displacement and relocation into nearby colonias. Although some residents were able to purchase land in nearby colonias in the region, the age and the structural conditions of their trailer homes prohibited them from moving their homes—leaving these families without adequate shelter. In spite of national policies against housing discrimination, colonia residents have often taken the brunt of local tactics of intimidation and discrimination. Nonetheless, this organized resistance of residents and nonprofit organizations provides an example of active political mobilization and collaboration.

As optimistic as this seems, the history of colonia development has also involved individuals and organizations who have approached residents in colonias with promises of services and benefits that have yet to be rendered. For example, a nonprofit organization, led by an internationally recognized individual, sought a loan on behalf of two colonias to implement a waste-water system, and never delivered the project. Colonia residents were later stunned to hear they had to repay the loan to a foundation they had never heard about. This matter left colonia residents skeptical about outsiders coming in to colonias offering to seek funding to help develop the communities' infrastructure (see Staudt and Coronado 2002 for a discussion of "poverty pimping"). Furthermore, the long and tedious process of forming partnerships to accomplish development projects make residents doubtful of institutions of power and their agents, who are often unable to deliver on their proposed promises. In a more recent case, a prominent colonia in Doña Ana County was awarded $450,000 to build a community center, and this money was recently pulled from the community and redirected toward a public transportation project. The County has since provided the colonia with a temporary portable trailer to use as its community center until a more permanent site is built. After years of seeking funding for a community center, residents have now experienced politics in action, which often involves taking resources from the margins to benefit greater numbers from the core.

Life in Colonias Post-9/11: Challenges to Political and Cultural Citizenship

The attack to the World Trade Center's Twin Towers and the Pentagon on September 11, 2001, and the United States' "War on Terror" have greatly influenced border populations and colonias in particular. As economic resources have been invested abroad to fight wars in Afghanistan and Iraq, national needs have been underfunded. Furthermore, the fear of terrorism has impacted how the United States has taken actions to police the border region. Efforts to curb the crossborder movement of migrants have been mixed in with the efforts to guard the border against potential threats to "national security." The heavy policing of the border region is part of what Donnan and Wilson (2001) argue to be part of a long-standing component to the processes of nation and state building. Scholars of the U.S.-Mexico Border (Andreas, 2000; Dunn, 1996; and Nevins, 2002), provide critical analyses of the federal policies and practices that have contributed to the culture of fear and psychosis in the border region caused by the heavy vigilance around and militarization of the region. These processes of militarizing the border reify nationalist endeavors to secure rights for nationals, while making evident the lack of rights for nonnationals.

Populations with large concentrations of immigrants are often faced by the stigmas associated with rights to benefits usually associated with citizenship status. Although the majority of the households in colonias are of Mexican ancestry, colonia residents represent a combination of U.S. born and naturalized citizens, legal residents, and visiting relatives, friends, or compatriots known as *paisanos*. Unauthorized immigrants, legal residents, and U.S. citizens are viewed and treated differently by state institutions and their representatives. These various categories mediate the lives of individuals and their families. For example, U.S. citizens are eligible to vote and be recognized by elected officials, while U.S. residents do not have this right. Colonia residents who are unauthorized to live and work in the U.S. are less likely to get involved in community-building practices for fear of being deported. U.S. residents and U.S. citizens are eligible for state-subsidized medical programs, while undocumented immigrants are not. Hence, the various identities associated with having a documented or undocumented status play key role in the recognition and validation of individual and community rights and entitlements.

The unbalanced distribution of power and economic resources between national centers of power and their borders is quite evident in the El Paso del Norte border region. Policies impacting immigration, economic policies, and political policies usually involving immigrant populations take place in larger centers of power such as Washington, D.C., and in Mexico City. Robert Alvarez (1995) notes that their postnational influences are such that when one nation's political and economic policies change, they tend to have consequential repercussions on the neighboring nation. The heightened national security measures taken by the United States governmental and nongovernmental entities, especially after the attacks of September 11, 2001, have made undocumented border crossings more difficult, costly, and dangerous for migrants willing to take such risks, while vigilante groups such as the Minutemen lined up along the border have taken the task of "guarding the line" in their own hands.

As locations within historical migration corridor, colonias within the El Paso del Norte Metropolitan region serve as a place or anchor in which migrants can arrive and adjust prior to sojourning into other areas of the United States in search of employment. Given the high concentration of Mexican immigrants in these communities, colonias have been particularly vulnerable to contemporary immigration enforcement practices that aim to detain and deport unauthorized residents. Mobility in and around colonias is restricted in the case of unauthorized residents or mixed-status households. These practices have taken place in the El Paso del Norte border region through the collaboration of local law enforcement with federal immigration officials. Routine traffic stops and violations have been the cause for the detainment and deportation of immigrants, who lack the adequate documentations to move around freely within these communities. As such, raids, *redadas,* or "round-ups," have been the cause of stress and panic for residents who have unauthorized family members living in colonias or moving in and out of these communities (Núñez and Heyman, 2007; Staudt, 2008). Family and household members transporting or harboring undocumented family members run the risk of being treated as *coyotes,* as human smugglers or transporters, a crime considered a felony in the United States. Geographically marginal settlements, such as colonias, are particularly vulnerable to unsupervised and unchecked border law enforcement and militarization

(e.g., Border Network for Human Rights 2007). Although colonias contain a mixture of U.S. citizens (both U.S. born and foreign
born but naturalized), legal permanent residents, and unauthorized
residents, they are stigmatized as being all immigrants and mostly
"illegals" and are subject to the imposed agenda of "national security"
that makes their communities more frightened, more fragmented, and
less secure.

The constant monitoring of colonias by immigration enforcement
agencies forces residents to become fearful of outsiders and government officials. This distrust toward outsiders creates considerable
challenges to the processes involved in the horizontal integration of
community development processes discussed earlier. Furthermore,
the climate of fear and psychosis created by immigration raids and
rogue immigration checkpoints forces colonia residents who might
have relatives unauthorized to live and work in the United States to
keep to themselves and avoid socializing or seeking aid from their
neighbors. This form of self-regulation censors the human body,
inhibiting movement and the active participation of residents as social
agents and as members of a community.

CONCLUSION

Anthropologist Eric Wolf (1982) recognized that the global movement of goods and people is not a recent phenomenon of the 21st
century, but rather a process that has been taking place for well over
500 years. What has changed within the last twenty years, however,
is the rate at which the world has undergone several changes, which
have influenced the movement of people and goods across borders.
World events such as the 1989 fall of the Berlin Wall, the European
Union's integration, major economic advancements in the Asian
Pacific Rim pressuring United States, the North American Free Trade
Agreement between Canada, the United States, and Mexico in 1994,
are examples of significant historical events that have influenced
how we view borders, migration, trade, and population settlement
processes.

While some colonias originated over a century ago as town sites
established by homesteaders in the mid 1800s, other communities
began as small settlements of farm laborers employed by a single
rancher or farmer. As the United States has created a demand for
labor, the border has not been able to keep up with the need for
affordable housing for its low-income, working-class populations.
Furthermore, dominant industries in the rural and urban regions

of the border have greatly benefitted from a year-round supply of available labor housed and "on reserve" in colonias. It is no longer sufficient to view colonias along the U.S.-Mexico border as marginal and peripheral communities, for they are central to the accumulation of wealth and capital in the border region's metropolitan areas.

Understanding colonias along the U.S.-Mexico border within the context of migration, urbanization, and globalization is a critical step in rehumanizing our discourse of populations on the margins and critically challenging the processes that have made them invisible and peripheral in the first place. Appreciating that colonias are actively involved in the vertical and horizontal processes of integrating as civically engaged communities brings to light their agency, perseverance, and resiliency in the midst of social, economic, and environmental injustices. Middle-class communities often have the benefits of more formal organizations that are in charge of addressing community development efforts via home ownership associations, whereas colonias do not. In colonias, much of the organizing is left up to the residents and the nonprofit organizations willing and able to work on the most immediate and pressing issues in these communities. However, as working-class members of a community of color, many colonia residents are faced with the challenges of making a living, while also trying to build their communities' social and physical infrastructure in the midst of a heavily monitored climate generated by the fear caused by the porosity of "open borders". By seeking to understand the processes in which residents are involved in the social construction and production of their communities, we are yielding an alternative framework for centering the marginal and peripheral within a wider analysis of global phenomena such as globalization, transnational migration, and population settlement processes.

NOTE

1. This estimate was provided by an El Paso Water Utilities representative during a "Drink Up?" Water Quality and Resources in the Texas-New Mexico Region Panel discussion at the University of Texas, El Paso, during Earth Week—Tuesday, May 21, 2009.

REFERENCE LIST

Andreas, Peter. 2000. *Border Games: Policing the U.S.-Mexico Divide*. Ithaca, NY: Cornell University Press.

Alvarez López, Juan. 1988. El medio ambiental en el desarrollo económico de la frontera norte de México. In *Cuadernos de Economía*. 3(5). Tijuana, MX: Universidad Autónoma de Baja California.

Alvarez, Robert R. 1987. *Familia: Migration and Adaptation in Baja and Alta California, 1800–1975*. Berkeley: University of California Press.

———. 1995. The Mexico-U.S. Border: The Making of an Anthropology of Borderlands. In *Annual Review of Anthropology*, 24, pp. 447–470.

Border Network for Human Rights. 2007. The Chaparral Report: A Testimonial Documentation of Wrongful Immigration Enforcement by the Otero County Sheriff http://www.nilc.org/DC_Conf/dc-conf2007/wrkshp_materials/4-5_ChaparralReport.pdf (accessed July 30, 2009).

Castles, Stephen & Mark J. Miller. 1998. *The Age of Migration: International Population Movements in the Modern World*. 2nd ed. London: Macmillan Press.

Chávez, Leo R. 1992. *Shadowed Lives: Undocumented Immigrants in American Society*. Case Studies in Cultural Anthropology. George and Louise Spindler, ed. Orlando: Harcourt Brace Jovanovich College Publishers.

Coronado, Irasema. 2003. La Vida en Las Colonias de La Frontera/Life in Colonias on the Border. *Latino Studies*, 1(1).

Donnan, Hastings and Thomas M. Wilson. 2001 (1999). *Borders: Frontiers of Identity, Nation and State*. Oxford/New York: Berg.

Dunn, Timothy J. 1996. *The Militarization of the U.S.-Mexico Border, 1978–1992: Low Intensity Conflict Doctrine Comes Home*. Austin: University of Texas, Center for Mexican American Studies.

Foster, George M. and Robert V. Kemper. 1979. Anthropological Fieldwork in Cities. In *Urban Life: Readings in the Anthropology of the City*. 4th ed. George Gmelch and Walter P. Zenner, 131–145. Long Grove, IL: Waveland Press, Inc.

Ganster, Paul and David E. Lorey. 2007. *The U.S.-Mexican Border into the Twenty-First Century*. 2nd ed. Lanham: Rowman and Littlefield.

Guzman, Gabriela C. 2002. "Landowners don't have titles or infrastructure." *Las Cruces Sun News*. Las Cruces, NM. November 27, 2002.

Hill, Sarah. 2003. Metaphoric Enrichment and Material Poverty: The Making of "Colonias." In *Ethnography at the Border*. Pablo Vila, ed. Minneapolis/London: University of Minnesota Press.

Kearney, Michael. 1996. *Reconceptualizing the Peasantry: Anthropology in Global Perspective*. Boulder: Westview Press.

Kemper, Robert. 2002. Migration and Adaptation: Tzintzuntzeños in Mexico City and beyond. In *Urban Life: Readings in the Anthropology of the City*. 4th ed. George Gmelch and Walter P. Zenner (eds.), pp. 193–204. Long Grove, IL: Waveland Press, Inc.

Kretzmann, John P. and John L. McKnight. 1993. *Building Communities from the Inside Out. A Path toward Finding and Mobilizing A Community's Assets*. Chicago: ACTA Publications.

Low, Setha M. 1999. Spatializing Culture: The Social Production and Social Construction of Public Space. In *On the Plaza: The Politics of Public Space and Culture*. Austin: University of Texas Press.

Martínez, Oscar. 1993. *Border People: Life and Society in the U.S.-Mexico Borderlands*. Tucson & London: The University of Arizona Press.

Massey, Douglas S., Jorge Durand, and Nolan J. Malone. 2002. *Beyond Smoke and Mirrors. Mexican Immigration in an Age of Economic Integration*. New York: Russell Sage Foundation.

Nevins, Joseph. 2002. *Operation Gatekeeper: The Rise of the "Illegal Alien" and the Making of the U.S.-Mexico Borderlands*. New York: Routledge.

Núñez, Guillermina Gina. 2006. The Political Ecology of Colonias in the Hatch Valley: Towards an Applied Social Science of the U.S.-Mexico Border. PhD. Dissertation. Department of Anthropology. University of California, Riverside.

Núñez-Mchiri, Guillermina Gina. 2009. The Political Ecology of the Colonias on the U.S.-Mexico Border: Human-Environmental Challenges and Community Responses in Southern New Mexico. In *Southern Rural Sociology*, 24(1), pp. 67–91.

Núñez, Guillermina Gina and Josiah McC. Heyman. 2007. Entrapment Processes and Immigrant Communities in a Time of Heightened Border Vigilance. In *Human Organization: Journal of the Society for Applied Anthropology*, 66(4), pp. 354–365.

Paterson, Kent I. 1998. "Colonias: Problems and Promise." *BorderLines*. 6(1). http://www.zianet.com/irc1/bordline/1998/bl42/bl42col.html. Accessed on 2/22/99.

Portes, Alejandro and Rubén G. Rumbaut. 1996. *Immigrant America: A Portrait*, 2nd ed. Berkeley and Los Angeles: University of California Press.

Powers, Mary G., Ellen Percy Kraly, and William Seltzer. 2004. "IRCA: Lessons of the Last US Legalization Program." Migration Policy Institute. http://www.migraitoninformation.org/feature/print.cfm?ID=223. Accessed 6/29/2005.

Richardson, Chad. 1999. *Batos, Bolillos, Pochos, and Pelados: Class and Culture on the South Texas Border*. Austin: University of Texas Press.

Rocco, Raymond A. 2002. Reframing Postmodernist Constructions of Difference. In *Transnational Latina/o Communities: Politics, Processes, and Cultures*. Carlos G. Vélez-Ibáñez and Anna Sampaio, eds. Maryland: Rowman & Littlefield Publishers, Inc.

Sassen, Saskia. 1998. *Globalization and its Discontents. Essays on the Mobility of People and Money*. New York: The New Press.

Simmons, Nancy. 1997. Memories and Miracles; Housing the Rural Poor along the United States-Mexico Border: A Comparative Discussion of Colonia Formation in El Paso County, Texas and Doña Ana County, New Mexico. *New Mexico Law Review*, 27, pp. 33–75.

Staudt, Kathleen. 1998. *Free Trade? Informal Economies at the U.S.-Mexico Border*. Philadelphia: Temple University Press.

Staudt, Kathleen. 2008. Bordering the Other in the U.S. Southwest: El Pasoans Confront the Local Sheriff on Immigration Enforcement. In *Keeping Out the Other: Immigration Enforcement Today*. Philip Kretsedemas and David Brotherton, eds., 291–313 Columbia University Press.

Staudt, Kathleen and Irasema Coronado. 2002. *Fronteras No Más: Toward Social Justice At the U.S.-Mexico Border*. New York: Palgrave Macmillan.

Vélez-Ibáñez, Carlos G. 1997. *Border Visions: Mexican Cultures of the Southwest United States*. Tucson: The University of Arizona Press.

———. 2004. Regions of Refuge in the United States: Issues, Problems, and Concerns for the Future of Mexican-Origin Populations in the United States. Malinowski Award Lecture. *Human Organization*, 63(1), pp. 1–20.

Ward, Peter M. 1999. *Colonias and Public Policy in Texas and Mexico: Urbanization by Stealth*. Austin, TX: The University of Texas Press.

Ward, Peter M., Robert Stevenson, and Angela Stuesse. 2000. Residential Land Market Dynamics, Absentee Lot Owners and Densification Policies for Texas Colonias. Austin: LBJ School of Public Affairs.

Wolf, Eric. 1982. *Europe and the People without History*. Berkeley: University of California Press.

Zenner, Walter P. 2002. Beyond Urban and Rural: Communities in the 21st Century. In *Urban Life: Readings in the Anthropology of the City*. 4th ed. George Gmelch and Walter P. Zenner, 53–60. Long Grove, IL: Waveland Press, Inc.

CHAPTER 8

SCHOOLING FOR GLOBAL COMPETITIVENESS IN THE BORDER METROPOLITAN REGION

Kathleen Staudt and Zulma Y. Méndez

> *With the objective of positioning Ciudad Juarez as one of the most competitive business areas in the world, a group known as Juarez— International Competitive City . . . recently conducted a study that measures the area's competitiveness and positioning versus some of the most competitive cities in the world*
>
> JuarezElPasoNow, 2008

"International competitiveness" is the discourse for business leaders in aspiring global cities posturing themselves for visibility and investment. In the trade magazine cited above, the language of business has an eerie resemblance to the language of educational reformers in both Mexico and the United States who advocate for competitive models focused on standardized testing to improve schools. But up to a half of the students in both countries live impoverished, economically marginal lives. In globalizing cities, a central question involves what students learn and are prepared for: informal, low-wage work or skilled, creative high-wage professional and managerial occupations? Our research, focused on the U.S. side of the metropolitan border region that is currently deeply enmeshed in standardized testing, is a way to anticipate trends on the Mexico side of the border.

The El Paso and Ciudad Juárez metropolitan region of more than two million people represents a complex system of schools that educate approximately half a million students, three-fifths of them in Mexico. Elsewhere in this collection, chapter authors advance Saskia Sassen's fine analysis of global spaces and globalizing cities, their links to international finance and manufacturing, and the ensuing inequalities in the labor force, yet she says nothing about the children in those spaces and the schools in which they are educated amid her attention to growing inequalities, informal and immigrant economies (2000; 2007). This chapter compares secondary education trends in neighboring El Paso and Ciudad Juárez, both of which contain large numbers of economically marginalized populations; this includes children, since schools have adopted standardized education and testing in varying degrees for an alleged "internationally competitive" model.

Mexico and the United States operate very different school systems in their self-proclaimed democracies. One educational system is highly centralized, with trends toward decentralization (Mexico), while the other, which long prided itself as decentralized, has become increasingly centralized at the state and national levels as a result of shifting rationales: equal opportunity, greater funding equity, and seemingly higher expectations as measured in standardized tests (United States). Theoretically, democracies that are accountable to the people provide space for individuals and organizations to press for and change public policies, including educational policies. Teachers' unions and parental and public interest groups typically represent the kinds of democratic organizations that have expertise and stakes in educational reform. Yet, in a global economy, such democracies may not only ignore this expertise, but also adopt the approaches of international financial institutions, such as the World Bank, and the ideologies of competitiveness that characterize the world economic system.

We contend that standardized testing regimes, contrary to the arguments of their national proponents, reinforce economic marginality through stigmatizing failures and driving students to drop out of school. Our analysis employs mixed methods, using secondary analyses, empirical data from the state accountability system, and participant observation in schools and community organizations (see appendix for more detail on methods). For the empirical data, we examine the El Paso region from the Texas Education Agency (TEA) (www.tea.state.tx.us). Our chapter also examines the extent to which activists in a seemingly democratic space can influence policy through a case study of a community social justice organization in El Paso, Texas, that sponsored "Listening Sessions" with 200 people, including parents, students, and teachers, in mid-2008. Our analysis examines a relatively shallow democracy at the border's edge in a state that prides itself on "limited" government.

I. Bordering the Language of Education Concepts

Contentious, politicized language often creates different meanings within and across two countries, e.g., standards, accountability, and standardized testing. For the last three decades, although the United States and Mexico have pursued different educational pathways, both nations share commitments to a standardized, measure-driven approach to teaching and learning, as we outline below in the historical section. The United States practices, especially in Texas with its high-stakes accountability testing including teacher and administrator bonuses for high pass rates, can marginalize students of low socioeconomic status, many of whom are (in U.S. discourse) "students of color," primarily Hispanic and African American.

Globalization promotes unifying concepts in market models that standardize procedures and practices in production and operations with a single assessment indicator: profit (or loss). One example is the International Organization for Standardization (ISO), which promotes modern, standardized methods (www.iso.org). ISO standards are adopted in the Paso del Norte region among the approximately 300 *maquiladoras* (export-processing factories) in what is proclaimed as the "*metroplex fronterizo más grande del planeta*" [the largest border metroplex of the planet] (www.desarrolloeconomico.org) in the *maquiladora* capital of the Americas. These global-linked manufacturing firms employ approximately 200,000 people (depending largely on U.S. economic demand) and pay weekly wages equivalent to a day's rate in the United States. Mexico's daily minimum wage in the border zone is 53 *pesos* or approximately US$3.75 a day at the current exchange rate of 14 *pesos* to US$1. ISO postings at plants and on vehicles proclaim modern, globalized business practices in the internationally competitive Paso del Norte border region, as noted in the epigraph. We believe that school standardized testing is linked to the modern standards deployed in the internationally competitive business marketplace.

U.S. Education: Historical Perspectives

The United States has long pursued a locally controlled, decentralized system for educational policy-making and funding. That began to change in the 1950s civil rights era through lawsuits that successfully challenged racial segregation, monolingual English education, and funding inequities. Despite changes, not all students encountered high expectations from teachers certified to teach in particular content areas. State governments gradually assumed more policy and budgeting responsibilities, but in 2001, the United States adopted a law with the curious title "No Child Left Behind" with consequences for leaving economically marginal children behind. We begin with the civil-rights-era critiques of the 1950s, connecting national themes to the border in El Paso.

In the United States, the critique of many public policies has been based on a paradigm of race and ethnicity rather than of class or poverty. Courts have responded to racial segregation charges—for example, Brown v Board of Education (1954) and at the border, Alvarado et al. v. El Paso Independent School District (1976)—but not to charges of income-based segregation, such as Milliken v. Bradley (1974). As these court cases show, decentralized and supposed democratic governance in itself does not guarantee responsive or equitable educational practices in regions with Hispanic and African American students and extensive poverty. Until the 1980s, in El Paso's limited democracy, for example, mostly white men served as school board trustees, despite the majority Mexican-heritage population (Rippberger and Staudt 2003: Ch. 2).

In Texas, school funding has historically been based on local property taxes. School board trustees set tax rates based on the value of residential and business property. In regions with low-value property, the funding system had produced low school expenditures for property-poor regions, such as El Paso, and generous funding for regions with valuable property. Due to lengthy lawsuits filed in the 1970s and 1980s, (*Rodríguez v San Antonio ISD* and *Edgewood v Kirby*), courts ordered the state to come up with solutions that would require more funding from the state budgets for underfunded schools. In most of the 50 states, a state income tax facilitates more equitable funding that is not based on property values. However, Texas is one of seven states without a state income tax, underlining once again the principle of limited government for which the state prides itself.

In schools that served low-income students of color, low expectations became a pressing concern in postcivil rights era schools. Some reformers promoted higher standards as a matter of school quality for all students. In Texas, progressive social justice reformers associated with the Texas Industrial Areas Foundation (IAF) organized to press for educational reforms that would set higher expectations for students, prepare them for higher education, and engage parents in school reforms (Shirley 1997: Ch. 2).

At the same time, national-level Reagan-era appointees, critical of big government, published a report entitled "A Nation at Risk" (1983) critical of low standards and unprepared teachers in a "rising tide of mediocrity. . . . If an unfriendly foreign power had attempted to impose on America the mediocre educational performance that exists today, we might well have viewed it as an act of war" (in Ravitch 1995: 52). While we agree that low educational standards are problematic for poor and rich students alike, we highlight, even then, the nationalist expressions in international competitiveness themes. Corresponding management solutions emerged in the late 1980s and 1990s.

State-based reformers brought a management-oriented corporate model to schools that would highlight students' and school performance with standardized data in the same way as profit in business performance measurement. With such data, low-performing schools could be more easily identified, fixed, and closed. Some reformers pressed to eliminate public school "monopolies," through school choice and private school tax voucher programs, in order to enhance internal U.S. competition. If public schools closed, due to low performance or an image of poor performance, opportunities would open for the private sector to establish schools and thereby offer "choices" to parents while simultaneously reducing the size of government. These changes took place within the context of a political culture that values limited government and maximized private market opportunities, especially prevalent in Texas.

In a federal system of government, where local and state policies govern education, the convergence of progressive reformers with those who advocated business models, privatization, and choice produced the political compromise of state-based standards and standardized tests that measured students' correct answers to mostly machine-graded, multiple-choice questions. Texas was a pioneering leader in this "accountability system" based on standardized tests in the 1980s and 1990s. As noted above, the public (including social justice organizations) supported such reforms in the hopes that their children might pursue pathways to higher education and better jobs.

With the passage of the national No Child Left Behind law in 2001, the federal government required Texas and all other states to develop "high-stakes" accountability systems in schools. All the standards and the tests are developed at the state level, but annual goals and penalties for nonachievement are set in Washington D.C. with consequences for low-performing schools that include threats of closure. Students and teachers are evaluated based on test scores, and the consequences for poor performance are substantial. Teachers and schools acquire monetary "bonuses" for raising test scores. High-stakes accountability systems reflect the essence of a business model, complete with competitive comparisons of schools, closure, and profits in the form of bonuses and penalty avoidance.

The public school accountability movement produced benefits and costs. On the benefit side, it gave educators no excuses for student failure: *All* students were expected to learn and pass tests, with serious consequences. Also, the accountability movement encouraged schools to hire qualified educators, certified to teach in their content specialization. All too often, uncertified educators had taught in schools located in impoverished regions. On the cost side, we identify several dysfunctions (as have other educational researchers, such as Valenzuela 2005; McNeil et al. 2008; Meier 2004), including a narrowed curriculum, an expensive bureaucracy that fuels the private testing industry, and the construction of large numbers of "failures," many of whom are impoverished students of color. First, teachers "teach to the test," resulting in narrower rather than broader focus on educational content. Schools prioritize content areas that are tested frequently (language and math); second, the bureaucratic and technological requirements for testing and reporting accountability data incur enormous expenses in time and taxpayers' money; and third, many students fail tests, especially those categorized as "economically disadvantaged" and "Limited English Proficient." Overall, the accountability system has not produced gains in national level tests, such as the National Assessment of Educational Progress (NAEP) and in standardized tests that students take for admission into higher education.

Mexico: Historical Perspectives

It may be argued that in Mexico, during the last half of the twentieth and the early part of the twenty-first century, the impetus for the reform of most social institutions—including the public educational system—has been related to globalization. In general, the rhetoric of the political class in the nation concurred with the notion that globalization required the modernization of the Mexican State.

Modernization, it reasoned, would be achieved via decentralization. Beginning with Presidents Echeverría and López Portillo, but most pronounced with Presidents De la Madrid in the late 1980s and Salinas in the early 1990s, decentralization was assumed to broaden the presence and scope of public schools and to guarantee access to educational opportunities (see also Rodríguez 1997).

The pervasiveness of a discourse of "quality" and "equity"— present too in debates over educational policy in Latin America and the United States—can be traced to three of the most important educational initiatives in the last 15 years. The first is the 1992 Acuerdo Nacional para la Modernización de la Educación Básica (ANMEB) or National Agreement for the Modernization of Basic Education; the second is the Programa Nacional de Educación (PRONAE) or National Education Program from 2001–2006 with President Fox; and, most recently, the Alianza por la Calidad de la Educación (ACE) or Alliance for the Quality of Education was instituted in 2006 and remains in place with President Calderón.

ANMEB involved three main foci: (1) reorganization of the educational systems vis-a-vis decentralization; (2) the reformulation of educational content and materials through the articulation of a curriculum that underscored the development of students' "attitude, methods, and skills" (Zorrilla 2004: 5); and (3) the revaluation of educators' social function via the expansion of opportunities for professional development, continuing education, and improved salary and compensation packages.

Though ample in scope, in its enactment, this initiative privileged the process of decentralization of the educational system and the broadening of its range and scope to make *secundaria*—middle school—an obligation of the State. The emphasis on decentralization was related to a concern with making the public educational apparatus modern and efficient by having each federal entity take responsibility for the education of its citizens. Signed by the governors of each of the states, the executive branch, and the national teacher union Sindicato Nacional de los Trabajadores de la Educación (SNTE), the ANMEB specified the role and obligations of the state and federal government in the provision of an equitable basic educational system for all (Zorrilla 2004). Moreover, by expanding the constitutional definition of basic education to include three years of middle school, the initiative sought to expand citizens' levels of educational attainment. This was particularly critical in a nation that sought to be modern and develop in accord with the demands for competitiveness that global processes of economic restructuring imposed.

Even though the efforts at decentralization and the expansion of public education were important victories for ANMEB, the quality of and equitable access to educational opportunity needed improvement (Zorrilla and Barba 2006). That the latter is the case is often explained by the differentiated socioeconomic conditions in each federal entity, municipality, and community. Yet, while basic schooling took place in varying socioeconomic contexts that shaped the kinds of educational opportunity available to students, teachers all across the nation continued to face adverse working conditions as a result of large classroom sizes and excessive course loads (Zorrilla and Fernández 2003; Zorrilla 2004).

Various observers note that the precariousness of Mexico's educational system was reflected in the results obtained in international measures of academic achievement (Zorrilla 2004; Giugale, Lafourcade and Nguyen [World Bank] with Vélez Bustillo and Vaqueo 2001). For instance, in her analysis of PISA[1] results for the year 2000, Zorrilla (2004) describes the preoccupying levels of student performance: "The few national evaluation studies show similar results as those in PISA 2000. That is, in the recent report by the Instituto Nacional para la Evaluación de la Educación (INEE 2003), 24 percent of students in *tercer grado de secundaria* show poor development in their reading competencies and half of the students exhibit an unfavorable performance in their ability to solve mathematical problems" (Zorrilla 2004: p. 14. Author's translation).

Challenged by the results on international assessments such as PISA, in 2001, under President Fox, the federal government launched a new initiative to address the achievement gaps in public education, and in particular, at the *secundaria* level. The initiative came to be known as the Programa Nacional de Educación 2001–2006, or National Program of Education 2001–2006. However, while PRONAE was described as an integral reform for middle school education, it mostly focused on three areas: (1) the clarification and deepening of the role and responsibilities of the state and federal government in public education; (2) the resolution of pending labor issues that arose with decentralization; and (3) the revision of teacher preparation programs.

Though both ANMEB and PRONAE might seem to place great emphasis on the administrative imperatives of public education, Zorrilla and Barba (2006) contend that from the 1990s to the present, a curricular and pedagogic reform has been underway. With ANMEB, for instance, there was a revision in the content and curricular organization of basic education. Thus, pedagogic approaches from a constructivist perspective were promoted, and the expansion in number and variety of material resources for teachers and students was supported.

With PRONAE, the curriculum—especially at the *secundaria* level—would undergo an "integral reform." The push for an integral reform was manifest in an initiative—in the context of PRONAE— that came to be known as the "Reforma Integral de la Educación Secundaria" (RIES), or Integral Reform for Secondary Education. Still present with RIES is the concern about expanding the reach of educational services and access to educational opportunity. In addition, issues of equity continued to be of concern. For instance, RIES called for the recognition of diverse educational needs and the achievement of comparable academic performance for all students. Attrition and time to completion were also areas of concern in the RIES policy documents. To achieve such goals, at the school level, RIES called for the transformation of the conditions under which schools functioned. Such transformation should propitiate the work of students and teachers (Zorrilla 2004).

An equally important element of PRONAE was the establishment of the Instituto Nacional para la Evaluación de la Eduación (INEE see www.inee.edu.mx) or National Institute for the Evaluation of Education in 2002. And though Mexico has a long history of participation in international assessments of student academic achievement (Giugale et al. 2001: 454, with Mexico "close to Latin American averages on language and math"), at the national level evaluation and assessment had not been emphasized (Zorrilla 2004). Notwithstanding, with the creation of INEE, an unequivocal sign that assessment would become more prominent in the development of educational policy was sent as well as the signal that data driven decision-making would carry an important weightage (PRONAE documents).

The use of assessments to measure student achievement was accompanied by a rhetoric of accountability and transparency that has gradually gained currency in official discourse in Mexico. In 2006, with the inception of Alianza por la Calidad de la Educación—the latest reform effort with President Calderón—teachers' salaries and economic incentives were subtly tied—at least on paper—to student achievement (refer to ACE). The move to employ student achievement measures as mechanisms to determine teacher salary increase and promotion has been received with great resistance on the part of teachers, who have mobilized against it in different states of the country (Léon Zaragoza 2008).

Student assessment as a mechanism to determine accurate academic achievement has been contested not only as means to determine teacher merit. The reliability of the recently adopted Evaluación Nacional del Logro Académico en Centros Escolares (ENLACE), a high-stakes exam administered to all Mexican students in grades 1, 3, 6, and 9, is also being questioned on other counts. On the one hand, reported ENLACE results present an intriguing pattern: students in overwhelmingly impoverished geographical areas performed poorly in the exam (see Cervera Gómez, Lizárraga Bustamante, and Sánchez Guillén, 2008, on Ciudad Juárez, on *insuficiente* and *elemental* categories; also noted in Giulagle et al. 2001: 454, 464 in rural areas of the country). Thus, questions have been raised about the validity of the assessment. Second, questions about curriculum alignment have surfaced. Alianza para la Educación, observers contend, advances a diametrically different curriculum than that which ENLACE tests. In sum, critics argue that ENLACE is an unreliable measure of student performance and that its implementation as a mechanism of accountability will have negative consequences on schooling.

In the World Bank report, the discourse of educational "efficiency returns," "benchmarking" and systematic standardized assessments is used to evaluate Mexico's development plans. The Bank raises issues about the quality and supervision of teachers as well as the "teacher-centered" model. Giugale et al. call the "nature of the mechanisms for teacher and school accountability" the "most critical issue" (2001: 13, also see them on "standard education assessment . . . quality assurance systems, which establish benchmarking" 457). This jibes well with the business model promoted by this banking institution.

Comparing the United States and Mexico, we see a convergence in emphases on standardized assessment models, albeit with impetus from different sources and through different pathways. The reform eras differ, beginning earlier in the United States and leading to a deeper institutionalization.

In the next section of the chapter, we focus on the relationships between poverty, students' test performance, and students leaving school before graduation (known as "drop out" or noncompletion in the United States) in the border region. In Mexico, the average number of years in school has been increasing, but the enrollment rate in secondary school and the percentage of 14-year-old children enrolled does not reflect full coverage: 72 percent (girls) and 78 percent (boys) in 1997 (Giugale et al. 2001: 449). The rate of *deserción* (desertion, a starker term) is another indicator.

According to statistics from the Servicios Educativos del Estado de Chihuahua (www.seech.com.mx), *deserción* rates for the state of Chihuahua were 7 percent in 2007–2008. Ciudad Juárez displays a 7 percent *deserción* for 2007–2008 (www.seech.com.mx). At the national level, *deserción* rates as reported by the Secretaría de Educación Pública (SEP) are 7 percent. Completion rate of *eficiencia terminal* for the state of Chihuahua is 78 percent, and for Ciudad Juárez, 78 percent. The SEP reports a completion rate or *eficiencia terminal* of 79 percent at the national level (all rates are for 2007). We believe that these seemingly excellent reported rates are somewhat deceptive, given that many 14-year-old students are not enrolled in schools (what the bureaucracy calls "coverage") and, therefore, unmeasured. Like bureaucracies in the United States, Mexican bureaucracies present the best image possible about performance.

In El Paso, where ethnicity overlaps with poverty (known as "economic disadvantage" in educational bureaucracies) and "Limited English Proficiency," the school accountability system constructs the image of Hispanic student failure and attrition at the highest rates in Texas. In a city with a Mexican-heritage population of 80 percent and a slightly higher student population, the systemic underdevelopment of student success is, we believe, a recipe for disaster even in a region that depends on—in global city terms—a sizeable economically marginal population.

II. Students' "Failures": Economically Driven?

In this section, we compare students, focusing on the ninth year in El Paso and on high school completion rates, differentiating schools based on the percentage of economically disadvantaged students. While efforts to establish standards and highly trained teachers are good for education, the narrow high-stakes accountability system adopted from business models appears to penalize low-income students with high failure and dropout rates, policy-induced failures to some extent.

In most parts of the United States, ninth grade is considered to be a year in which students study "at risk" for the failure to earn course credits and, subsequently, for decisions to leave school without completing their high school diplomas (grade 12). Students who do not graduate from high school live the rest of their lives with considerable disadvantages in earning power and work opportunities. After "dropping out," or what some term "pushing out," students can apply to be examined for a "GED," (General Education Development test, treated as comparable to high school completion), but data on EPISD from the TEA Web site for El Paso show that less than 3 percent acquire degrees in this way.

El Paso is home to nine spatially based public school districts, each with their own district superintendent and publicly elected school board of trustees who make major policy decisions, including those about educational leadership and budgets, within the constraints of national and state laws. Of approximately 200,000 students in the entire county of El Paso (larger than the city of El Paso in the fragmented federalism of the United States), 90 percent enroll in public schools as opposed to private-religious or secular schools with steep tuition fees. Of these nine districts, the El Paso Independent School District (EPISD) is the largest, enrolling approximately 62,000 students annually. In EPISD, 62 percent of the students are classified as economically disadvantaged, and 29 percent as "Limited English Proficient" (www.tea.state.tx.us/ aeis). Because of its size and its coverage in the heart of El Paso, we focus on the ten high schools in the EPISD.

We categorized the ten high schools into three groups based on the percentage of economically disadvantaged students enrolled. Students are required to enroll in schools in their own neighborhoods, a spatial construction that meshes with the different income characteristics in city regions. In Texas, school-related economic disadvantage is determined by household income forms that parents complete annually. "Economic disadvantage" is a low-income category that indicates the percentage of students who qualify for free or subsidized school lunches and is a measure of poverty in the spatially based neighborhood school-feeder pattern.

In Figure 8.1 below, we divide the ten EPISD high schools into "low poverty" (less than 50 percent economically disadvantaged), mostly on the more prosperous west side; "medium poverty" (50–74 percent economically disadvantaged), in all city regions; and "high poverty" (more than 75 percent economically disadvantaged), in the south, central, and northeast parts of El Paso. The percentage range is 28–35 percent for the two low-poverty campuses on El Paso's west side; 53–71 percent for the four medium-poverty campuses; and 75–93 percent for the four high-poverty campuses in south, central, and northeast regions of El Paso. Recognizing that poverty may require additional school resources, the federal government also makes money available, known under a provision in the Elementary and Secondary Education Act (ESEA) law as Title I. Only one high school is *not* a Title I campus—a low-poverty school located on El Paso's west side with a 28 percent economically disadvantaged student population.

EPISD categorizes five of these ten high schools as "priority schools"— four high-poverty campuses and one medium-poverty campus—because of failures to achieve annual progress rates in standardized test scores among all categories of students, as set by the U.S. Department of Education. Accountability data reports list students' standardized test pass rates in one or more of the following categories: African American, Hispanic, White, economically disadvantaged, and LEP (Limited English Proficient), the last of which overlaps with Hispanic students in El Paso. Approximately one fourth of EPISD students fall into the LEP classification, but not all of these Spanish-speaking students enjoy assignment to bilingual, dual-language, or ESL (English as a Second Language) classes. Spanish-language students face special challenges passing English-language standardized tests. The failure rate within the LEP group is the highest for any category of students.

Figure 8.1 shows the 2007–2008 pass rates for ninth grade standardized tests in two knowledge content areas: reading and math. We have averaged scores for the schools in each category of high schools. The data show gaps between schools with different poverty characteristics in both reading and math. Pass rates are low for math and reading at poverty schools and for math at all schools. For both areas, the gap between high- and low-poverty schools is 18 percent in reading and 27 percent in math.

The way that the state requires data to be reported conceals as much as it reveals. For example, "tracking systems" operate in most U.S. schools, which offer special courses and classes with college-preparatory material for select students, usually 10–20 percent of

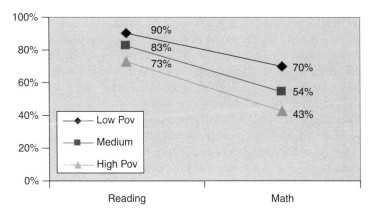

Figure 8.1   El Paso Independent School District 9th grade pass rates in low-, medium-, and high-poverty schools
Source: Texas Education Agency Academic Excellence Indicator System (www.tea.state.tx.us).

the student population. Thus, the circumstances under which economically disadvantaged students at low-poverty schools learn are questionable. In a thorough study of Los Angeles public schools, UCLA researchers Jeannie Oakes and John Rogers found that "students of color" rarely enroll in the college-preparatory courses, such as Advanced Placement courses (2006) wherein credits can be transferred to higher education classes *if* high scores are achieved on national-level examinations.

Ninth-grade students with a history of test failures often disengage with school, as researchers have noted. Yet definitions for and measurements of "drop out" are highly contentious. When the TEA first reported public accountability data, annual dropout figures seemed very low, at rates of 1–3 percent. Yet other researchers showed the gradual disappearance of sizeable numbers of students between ninth and twelfth grade (El Paso Collaborative for Academic Excellence chart, 2000).

Statewide, the Intercultural Development Research Association (IDRA) reports extremely high attrition rates of 35 percent for Hispanic students (www.idra.org). In other words, approximately 1 in 3 Hispanic students leaves high school before graduation. In response to growing criticism of the annual dropout figure, the TEA now also reports "completion rates" after four years, found in Figure 8.2. Some students may take five years to graduate, and others acquire a GED (as reported above). In the completion rate section of the accountability Web site, each campus reports an actual dropout rate, also depicted in Table 8.2. Given IDRA figures by campus and the lower figures from the TEA, the actual pushout or dropout rate may be as much as two to three times higher than on government reports. The discrepancy may be traced to the bureaucratic process associated with the categorization of data. If and when a student leaves high school, one of thirteen categories is checked, including transferring, moving, or dropping out. The real dropout rates may be concealed in the other twelve categories.

Drawing again on TEA publicly reported accountability data for low-, medium- and high-poverty high schools, we have averaged scores for each category of high schools. Figure 8.2 shows lower completion rates and higher dropout rates for high-poverty schools. Annual dropout figures in high-poverty schools are double those of low-poverty schools. Again, internal tracking systems conceal whether those students in the dropout categories are economically disadvantaged students living in pockets of wealthier neighborhoods.

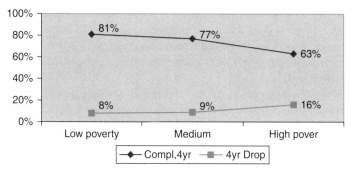

Figure 8.2 El Paso Independent School District completion and drop-out rates in low-, medium-, and high-poverty schools

After analyzing findings in this section, we conclude that standardized testing—prompting teachers to "teach to the test" of mostly multiple-choice exams—penalizes children for poverty and pushes them out of schools before graduation. Public policies produce both intended and unintended consequences. We believe that an unintended consequence of standardized testing policies, allegedly designed to raise standards using competitive business models, is that they enlarge the economically marginal population in global cities. Mexico's school reforms, albeit not yet as embedded in the business model as those in the United States, may be moving in that direction.

III. A CASE STUDY: BORDER DEMOCRATIC SPACE FOR CHANGE?

In this section, we examine a case study of popular efforts at educational reform, drawing on ethnography from an El Paso social justice organization. The case shows the space and opportunities available for voice, but the extraordinary challenges of influencing a deeply institutionalized mindset, bureaucracy, and organized material interests with stakes in maintaining standardized testing.

Community Organizations: Efforts to Reform

Texas Republican Governor Rick Perry created the Select Committee on Public School Accountability. He recruited Republican legislators and educational and business leaders, including former Dallas school board trustee, lawyer and lobbyist for the testing industry,

Sandy Kress, who coauthored No Child Left Behind. The Committee traveled to several locations around the state in 2008 in order to hear testimony from experts of their own choosing and from the public in cities they visited. Their findings would lead to new bills in the 2009 legislative session.

U.S.-style democracy prizes a process whereby nongovernment organizations (NGOs) represent their interests in competition with one another and in engagement with government. This is known as the "pluralist model"—a model that contrasts with an "elite model" whereby elite interests use government to advance their own interests. Money matters in U.S. democracy, whether that money involves campaign contributions or funding to organize groups with professional staff to lobby government. The power of numbers, what we call "people power," can counteract the power of money, but people power requires extraordinary time commitments, unpaid volunteers, and activists who organize to engage with government and to vote for representatives that advance their interests. Can they effectively "compete," as in the pluralist model, with politicians, experts in the bureaucracy, and paid lobbyists with material stakes in perpetuating the testing industry? The answer we develop below: maybe.

In the 1930s, new forms of popular organizations grew in the United States to "organize the unorganized" for responsive government. Saul Alinsky founded the Industrial Areas Foundation (IAF) in working-class neighborhoods of Chicago, Illinois, where residents had few voices or limited engagement with local and state government (see selections in Orr 2007). Over time, the IAF grew into a nationwide organization with groups in many cities as well as statewide organizations. IAF develops and empowers leaders, many of whom were once voiceless and unorganized in public affairs. IAF builds its organized people power on the foundation of community institutional coalitions, mostly faith-based congregations with social justice commitments.

The Texas IAF network links strong community organizations in major cities around the state, recruited through their congregations. When the Governor's Select Committee on Public Accountability took testimony around the state in 2008, leaders and clergy from different IAF affiliates testified about their members' experiences with high-stakes accountability educational systems.

In El Paso, two community organizations are affiliated with the Texas IAF: El Paso Interreligious Sponsoring Organization (EPISO) of 22 Catholic parishes and a thirty-year track record of public policy accomplishments in water, sewer, and workforce training; and Border Interfaith (BI), a newer organization of 12 diverse congregations, including a synagogue and Protestant and Catholic congregations. In El Paso, BI leaders (including one of the authors) decided to hold three "Listening Sessions" in summer 2008, to gather data about the perceptions of parents, teachers, and students on the public accountability system. Approximately 200 people attended one of three sessions at Temple Mount Sinai, Western Hills United Methodist Church, and San Patricio Catholic Church. They provided mainly negative testimony about the ways that high-stakes testing standardizes teaching and encourages students to drop out, especially low-income, Spanish-speaking English-language learners. Listening forums produced a great deal of testimony about young children who became sick and vomited on high-stress testing days. BI leaders heard much detail about a narrow testing system, using multiple-choice questions, that drove teachers to encourage memorization and "teaching to the test" in ways that did not prepare students for higher education and, moreover, pushed students—especially English-language learners—to leave school before graduation.

The Select Committee's meeting in El Paso on August 4, 2008, illustrates the possibilities and shortcomings of U.S.-style democracy that aim at a pluralist model but often privileges the elite. The day itself involved both tedium and drama, as we outline below with some ethnographic detail.

The University of Texas at El Paso hosted the Select Committee in the Student Union building, and the morning began with typical introductions and welcomes from local dignitaries such as the university President Diana Natalicio, the EPISD Superintendent Lorenzo García, and the State Senator Eliot Shapleigh. The Select Committee, with its male and female cochairs from east and north Texas, opened the formal, taped proceedings. After some banter, they took testimony from three nonlocal "experts" they had invited, one of them via a videoconference from Washington, D.C. Hours passed.

After a long wait of three hours, Select Committee members listened to testimonies from the live audience of approximately forty people, including a journalist from the *El Paso Times*. Each formal testifier was allotted three minutes, timed carefully. The first testimony came from four Hispanic educators who flew in from South Texas, who were troubled with patronizing, seemingly racist interactions they had when the Select Committee met in Brownsville. Select Committee members listened and then exchanged words with the educators in a patronizing manner. After the Brownsville group, six BI leaders testified: one university professor (Staudt), two clergy, one retired expert (school administrator), and two teachers.

By this time, nearly four hours after the meeting started, several Select Committee members became somewhat restless. A few moved in and out to retrieve a boxed lunch in the room next door. The cochairs chatted with one another in whispered tones. BI leader Rosa, a teacher and mother of a child with special needs, gave her testimony about how her young son worried about test failure and how she encouraged him anyway. As a special-needs child, he was entitled to a special standardized test. Teachers, also under great stress on testing days, gave her son the wrong test and he failed. Rosa came to tears as she gave her moving testimony. Meanwhile, the chatting cochairs had been laughing, probably not at Rosa and her son, but at their own conversation. The impression they left, however, was one of unmistakable disrespect. With her strong leadership assets, Rosa stopped her testimony, focused her anger, and stated forcefully, "this may be funny to you, but it was not funny to me or my son." Her stunning comment brought an eerie, respectful quiet to the room, as the chatty cochairs apologized profusely. Committee members listened carefully after that.

In the selectively open and transparent government of Texas, clerks duly taped testimonies and posted summaries online. The summary appears to grant credence to some of the issues raised in public meetings around the state. See: http://www.senate.state.tx.us/75r/ Senate/Archives/Arch08/p102108a.htm.

In another example showing possible responsiveness, as a Texas teacher association report indicated, committee members acknowledged the "over-emphasis on testing, the excessive number of tests, and the use of test scores in ways that were never intended when the accountability system was originally developed, putting unreasonable pressure on schools and students" (Texas AFT 2008). They also criticized Mr. Kress for his lobby ties with the testing industry and for arguing that stronger tests are necessary to prepare students better for college.

Yet, in an unpublished paper by Sandy Kress (lead author) and four of his colleagues entitled "Common Ground: A Declaration of Principles and Strategies for Texas Education Policy," he emphasizes the necessity of continued accountability for college/workplace readiness without higher educational remedial systems through a new tracking system with a "career/technology" industry certificate. The only accommodations with public testimony involved the need for more budgetary resources, a reduction of the testing system's bureaucratic complexity, and the attention to English-language learners, or as Kress et al. said, "largely illiterate older immigrant children" (2008: 13) who should not be grouped with other students for accountability evaluations.

The 2009 Texas legislative session did not produce significant educational reform. Less than a fourth of bills introduced are passed into laws, and the low-paid Texas legislators meet every other year for just five months. In the meantime, high-stakes standardized testing continues, pushing out as many as a third of low-income Hispanic, Spanish-speaking students. If a three-track system is installed, the career/technology track will prepare non–higher education bound graduates into jobs; and perhaps the sizeable number of "drop outs" will provide the underclass that Sassen discusses as so common, perhaps essential, to international capital in global cities.

This case study reveals the strengths and weaknesses of US-style democracy. The legislature and its Select Committee provided limited space in which social-justice organizations could engage in a reform process. It provided an open atmosphere and visibility on the government Web site. The press covered the meeting in one short article, without follow up. BI leaders strengthened their own skills, learning, and power in the process. Yet in the end, the seemingly democratic process privileged the voices of those appointed and the interests they serve, including the bureaucracy and the private testing industry. Thus, the ostensible "pluralist" system seems more like a disguise for elite rule, albeit elites with plural minds about educational reform who occasionally "listen" to the public.

CONCLUSIONS AND FINAL REFLECTIONS

In this chapter, we examined public school reforms and practices in the Paso del Norte global region. We compared the history of recent educational reforms in two sovereign countries, each of them moving toward a standardized approach, such as that used in business models. However, schools are not businesses, and students' test scores are not equivalent to profit and loss statements. On the El Paso side of the border, where standardized testing is deeply embedded in the assessment of schools and teacher practices, standardization policies construct a large class of failing students who drop out of school. Most of them are economically disadvantaged Hispanic, English-language-learning students.

Mexico's diagnostic ENLACE has not become a similar push-out/ high-stakes operation like that in the United States. Links between the curriculum and the testing system pose potential assessment problems (see Méndez on an "empty" curriculum in this volume). However, poverty and economic desperation also take their toll on the ability of students to remain in school and acquire skills to compete in the global economy rather than serve as its underclass. In the much proclaimed internationally competitive border metropolitan region, with its laboratory of mirrors, we worry that the future of Mexican educational reforms will reflect those of the United States and its business model: teaching to the test and an approach to learning based on the "bubbles" students mark on multiple-choice exams.

The ethnographic case study of attempts at reform, with all its drama and tedium, demonstrates the limited space for people's voices in a highly controlled semipluralistic democratic system. In such a system, the voices of those with stakes in the business model prevailed far more pervasively than those in civil society. Despite people's hopes for education as the key to overcome poverty, our analysis of reformism in the globalized metropolitan region shows instead an educational system that constructs failed students who will likely sustain the polarization of globalizing cities: a future of many informal, low-wage workers coupled with a decreased number in professional and managerial positions.

APPENDIX: METHODOLOGY

We both teach at the University of Texas at El Paso, a border university of 20,000 students with approximately 10–15 percent commuter students from Ciudad Juárez, with research and teaching missions that stress engagement with community organizations and public schools. Together, we each have studied and taught at the institution for at least a decade and participated in many conversations with teachers and in teacher-training activities. Méndez has conducted ethnographic research in a *secundaria* in Ciudad Juárez (see other chapter, this volume). Staudt served as former cochair of BI, a social-justice organization affiliated with the Texas Industrial Areas Foundation. For four months in mid-2008, she planned and collaborated with BI leaders to organize three "Listening Sessions," each of which were two hours long, with two in English and another in Spanish. She presented testimony at the legislative hearings.

Acknowledgment: Thanks to Susan Rippberger for her comments on this article.

NOTE

1. PISA stands for Program of International Student Assessment (PISA). The assessment, supported by the Organization for Economic

Co-operation and Development (OECD) measures students' "knowledge" and "skills" in three areas: reading, mathematics, and science. Students who take the assessment must be 15 years of age regardless of their grade level (Base de Datos www.inee.edu.mx).

REFERENCE LIST

Cervera Gómez, Luis Ernesto, Gilberto Martín Lizárraga Bustamante, Claudia Paloa Sánchez Guillén. 2008. "Estudio georreferencial de la Evaluación Nacional de Logro Académico en Centros Escolares (ENLACE) en el Municipio de Juárez, Chihuahua: análisis especial." REDIE 10(1). http://redie.uabc.mx.

El Paso Independent School District (EPISD). www.episd.org.

Giugale, Marcelo M., Olivier Lafourcade, and Vinh H. Nguyen. 2001. Mexico: A Comprehensive Development Agenda for the New Era. Washington, D. C.: World Bank.

Gobierno Federal (México). Alianza por la calidad de la educación.

Hunt, Woody, et al. 2009. Report of the Select Commission on Higher Education and Global Competitiveness. January. Austin: State of Texas.

Instituto Nacional de Estadística Educativa. (INEE) www.inee.edu.mx, (Accessed numerous times, 2008).

Intercultural Development Research Association (IDRA). www.idra.org (Accessed numerous times, 2008).

Kress, Sandy, Don McAdams, Mike Moses, David Thompson, and Jim Windham. 2008. "Common Ground: A Declaration of Principles and Strategies for Texas Education Policy," Unpublished Paper, November 6.

León Zaragoza, G. 2008 (November 24). Insisten profesores: la alianza educativa, a consulta nacional. La Jornada. Retrieved January 9, 2009, from http://www.jornada.unam.mx

McNeil, Linda, Eileen Coppola, Judy Radigan, and Julian Vásquez Heilig. 2008. "Avoidable Losses: High-Stakes Accountability and the Drop-Out Crisis." Educational Policy Analysis Archives, 16, 3 (January). http://epaa.asu.edu/epaa/v16n3/

Meier, Deborah et al. 2004. Many Children Left Behind: How the No Child Left Behind Act is Damaging Our Children and Our Schools. Boston: Beacon Press.

Oakes, Jeannie and John Rogers. 2006. Learning Power: Organizing for Education and Justice. NY: Teachers College Press.

Orr, Marion, ed. 2007. Transforming the City: Community Organizing and the Challenge of Political Change. University Press of Kansas.

Ravitch, Diane. 1995. National Standards in American Education: A Citizen's Guide. Washington, D.C.

Rippberger, Susan and Kathleen Staudt. 2003. Pledging Allegiance: Learning Nationalism in El Paso/Juarez. NY: Routledge/Falmer.

Rodríguez, Victoria. 1997. Decentralization in Mexico: From Reforma Municipal to Solidaridad to Nuevo Federalismo. Boulder: Westview Press.

Sassen, Saskia. 2000. *Global Cities*. Princeton University Press.
———, ed. 2007. *The Sociology of Global Cities*. Routledge.
Secretaría de Educación Pública. www.sep.com.mx. (Accessed numerous times, 2008).
Servicios Educativos del Estado de Chihuahua. www.seech.com.mx. (Accessed numerous times, 2008).
Shirley, Dennis. 1997. *Community Organizing and Urban School Reform*. Austin: University of Texas Press.
Texas AFT. 2008. Texas AFT Legislative Hotline. October 2.
Texas Education Agency, Academic Excellence Indicator System. www.tea.state.tx.us. (Accessed regularly, 2008).
Valenzuela, Angela, ed. 2005. *Leaving Children Behind: How "Texas-style" Accountability Fails Latino Youth*. Albany, NY: SUNY Albany Press.
Zorilla, M. & Barba, B. 2006. Reforma educativa en México. Descentralización y nuevos actores. Fronteras Educativas. Comunidad Virtual de la Educación. ITESO.
Zorilla, M. & Fernández Lomelin, M. T. 2003. Niveles de logro educativo de español y matemática en alumnos de escuelas secundarias públicas. Revista Electrónica Iberoamericana sobre Calidad, Eficiencia y Cambio en Educación, 1, 1.
Zorilla, Margarita. 2004. La educación secundaria en México: Al filo de su reforma. Revista Electróncia Iberoamericana sobre la Calidad, Eficacia y Cambio en Educación, 2(1).

CHAPTER 9

ALIANZA PARA LA CALIDAD DE LA EDUCACIÓN AND THE PRODUCTION OF AN EMPTY CURRICULUM

Zulma Y. Méndez

In the midst of a pervasive rhetoric about the purported declining quality of public education (Noriega Chávez, 2000), México recently adopted a series of measures to reform its public school system. These changes, embodied in Alianza para la Calidad Educativa (ACE),[1] restructured public schooling through a process of decentralization and the revision of the national school curriculum. In the mind of the reform's two main stakeholders—the federal government and the Sindicato Nacional de Trabajadores de la Educación (SNTE)—transferring the responsibility for school centers was necessary to make the educational system more "equitable." Similarly, reformers reasoned, by establishing an intricate accountability system that tied teachers' salaries and school funding to students' performance, public schools would be more "transparent" and "efficient."

In this chapter, I present a case study of a reformed language arts classroom in a middle school in the border city of Ciudad Juárez, México. The classroom, like other ninth-grade language arts and mathematics classrooms, was targeted by Alianza. Concerned with the study of curriculum, I was initially intrigued by the resemblance between many features of Alianza and other standard-driven policies such as No Child Left Behind (NCLB) in the United States. Familiar with the debates and criticisms leveled at the current U.S. educational policy, I wondered about the import of Alianza for public schooling and education in México; but most particularly, I wondered how—in the geographical and socially complex context of Ciudad Juárez—a reform like Alianza would be translated and enacted, and with what consequences to teachers, students, and the educational enterprise. In México, the inception of Alianza, like the adoption of NCLB in the United States, was a point of contention. On the one hand, critics of the reform asserted that behind claims of a public funding crisis were the pressures from the business and the conservative government sector to reduce the state's obligation to provide its citizens with free quality education. Reformers, on other hand, argued that public education, like other public goods, required a level of investment that demanded tighter systems of accountability.

Notwithstanding Alianza's mixed public reception, empirical research on similar initiatives implemented in other nations raises intriguing questions about the outcomes of such reforms. In the United States, for instance, an extensive body of research has documented the perverse effects that NCLB and its push for curriculum standardization and high-stakes testing has had on public schools (McNeil, 2000). In México, research documenting the impact of Alianza is incipient given the recent adoption of the reform. However, such research is critical. Empirical studies documenting how reform initiatives are enacted and experienced in classrooms are necessary to guide scholars' and practitioners' assessment of the import of Alianza since it is to prepare citizens that can contribute to the future and viability of the nation and its communities.

EDUCATIONAL RESEARCH AND THE STUDY OF CURRICULUM REFORM IN MEXICO

México and its public school system have experienced a long and complex history of educational reform. A close analysis of the process of educational policy and change exhibits the recurrence of concerns with centralism, teacher preparation, curriculum, and (an absence of) standards and assessment (Calvo, 1994; Levinson, 2001; Velez Bustillo and Paqueo, 2001; Zorrilla, 2004; Zorrilla and Barba, 2006).[2] That reform efforts incessantly aim at these recurring concerns suggests the obdurate nature of the problems of public basic education, or the failure of policy makers to adequately address them.

A reflection of the chronic problems of Mexico's educational system, some contend, is student underperformance in international measures of academic achievement such as PISA;[3] and most recently, in ENLACE (*Encuesta Nacional del Logro Académico en Centros Escolares*),[4] the mandated national academic assessment in México. Both international and national measures reveal the achievement gap of students in the areas of language arts and mathematics across the nation in general and most particularly in public school centers (Cervera et al., 2008; Velez Bustillo and Paqueo, 2001).

While some see the critical socioeconomic conditions in the nation as an explanation for the low scores in assessments, other factors that are inextricably related to the curriculum might also explain students' levels of achievement (Velez Bustillo and Paqueo, 2001: p. 455). Problems in the realm of curriculum are multiple, and the literature amply enunciates them. For instance, often cited is the outdated curriculum that conceives learning as memorization of facts and formulas; a "disconnect" between the curriculum as mandated and the enacted curriculum; teacher quality and a purported resistance to embrace change; desultory teacher supervision resulting in insufficient feedback or coaching; lack of administrative supervision resulting in high rates of teacher absenteeism; deteriorating school facilities; and unreliable student achievement assessments that result in opposition from school personnel to participate in them (Velez Bustillo and Paqueo, 2001; Zorrila, 2004).

However, while the long history of curricular reform has been widely documented and empirically examined in nations such as the United States, in México, the processes of curriculum change have been chronicled, but most empirical questions about implementation remain largely unanswered. The bulk of the literature concerned with curricular reform describes the various reform movements, but few works specify and document *how* educational policies fare on practice, and *how* school administrators, teachers, and students experience them. Such gap is not inconsequential considering the mixed results that efforts attempting to improve the quality of public education have yielded, and given that increasingly limited resources are devoted to particular educational interventions, the public demands and should be able to access more information about their efficacy.

An Interpretive Perspective of Curriculum Reform in Secundarias

My study takes on a more nuanced approach to the study of curriculum reform and its enactment. With an interpretive perspective that focuses on meaning, process, and context (Erickson, 1986), I offer a detailed account of ACE with a close focus on classroom practice. In particular, I examine a ninth-grade or *tercero de secundaria* classroom to understand how a reformed language arts curriculum is enacted in everyday classroom interaction. Through my analysis of curriculum enactment, I consider the import of the curricular reform to the students and teachers who experience it directly.

Given my interpretive perspective, I am attentive to the nexus between meaning and context. Thus, I treat classroom participants as actors engaged in meaning-making, the language arts curriculum as shaped by the wider sociopolitical context and the local school conditions; and school knowledge as an entity that classroom participants define and enact (Apple, 1990/1979; Erickson, 1986; Martin, 1994; Page, 1991). Moving away from rational conceptions, which conceive the curriculum as a set of mandates that are straightforwardly implemented in the classroom, I analyze educational reform and policy as a contextualized social construction that teachers and students negotiate sometimes achieving unintended outcomes.

Design and Research Procedures

I spent the 2008–2009 school year conducting an ethnographic study of curriculum reform. In it, I focused on school knowledge as an unstable social production (Apple 1990/1979; Martin, 1994) and curriculum as a "translation" by classroom participants of academic, social, cultural, and political meaning (Page, 1991: p. 21). Thus, as I describe and analyze how curricular translation occurred in a classroom, I am attentive to both the written and the enacted curriculum. I distinguish between the two given that classroom life is fraught with more complexity than educational policy makers anticipate, and than their policies suggest (Cohen, 1990; Page, 1991).

To gather data, I engaged in long-term participant observation in two *secundaria* or middle-school classrooms during the 2008–2009 school year. I recorded extensive field notes of lessons and everyday life in the classroom and in the school. I conducted and audiotaped formal interviews with teachers, students, and school administrators. In addition to this, I collected samples of students' work, lesson plans, the ninth-grade language arts textbook, newsletters, and other handouts available at the school. I also consulted documents from the Secretaria de Educación Pública (SEP)[5] that described Alianza, and accessed public government databases containing demographic and assessment results for the border city of Ciudad Juárez.

Participant observation occurred in two of the five ninth-grade or *tercero de secundaria* language arts classes offered at a middle school I will call Secundaria Vespertina.[6] All of the five language arts groups for that grade level were taught by Maestra Laura. During the fall, I observed in the classroom labeled 3ero C. During the spring, I observed in 3ero E. Both classes, like all of Maestra Laura's language arts courses, followed the same curriculum. In this account, I only focus on 3ero C, a classroom of 31 students.

Given that an interpretive perspective posits the curriculum as socially constructed, my project also involved extended participant observation to seek an understanding of the wider contextual forces that shaped the production and enactment of the reformed curriculum. Thus, as a participant observer, I visited *Vespertina* twice a week. During my school visits, I observed and documented various aspects of school life, became acquainted with students, and had the opportunity to converse formally and informally with various administrators, teachers, and students. I also attended various school functions such as the Mexican Independence ceremony, the Día de la Candelaria teacher dinner, and witnessed student council elections among other activities in the busy school calendar.

Though I became a familiar face in Vespertina, most of my time in the school was spent in the classroom. In there, my focus was on classroom participants' words. The documentation of those utterances in fieldnotes and transcribed audiotaped interviews comprised most of the data set captured during my fieldwork. Hence, because classroom participants' words and utterances make visible, according to Page (1991), the systems of power that structure schooling and culture, I was especially attentive to what and how topics were presented and studied in the classroom. Systematic documentation of curriculum enactment allowed me to understand how the teacher and her students constructed their unique version of the curriculum.

Participant observation activities also helped me to become acquainted with students who quickly baptized me as Maestra UTEP. Some befriended me and I received invitations to *quinceañeras*, heard stories about girlfriends and boyfriends, and learned about their quarrels with others in the classroom. Taken together, participant observation, informal and formal interviews, and the collection of documents afforded me the opportunity to learn more about the world of *secundarias*, the adolescents and teachers in them, and their attempts at defining the self and the other as they collectively enacted and experienced their unique version of the Alianza curriculum.

Setting and Background

Secundaria Vespertina[7] is among one of the oldest middle schools in the border city of Ciudad Juárez. It is a two-story building with approximately 15 austere and, for the most part, overcrowded classrooms. The classrooms are adjacent to a patio, and the school ground is surrounded by a tall brick wall painted white. Two decades ago, the school ground was delimited by an iron-gate that was replaced as incidents of outsiders mingling and drug dealers offering their merchandise through it surfaced. Today, even though the school is located in an area where the incidence of petty crime is high, Mr. Arenas, the principal, attributes its high enrollment numbers to the parents' perception of Secundaria Vespertina as a safe school facility.[8]

School safety is an important consideration for the working-class parents who send their children to Vespertina. The latter is particularly true in the context of a city that is positioned as one with the nation's leading heroin consumption market, has alarmingly witnessed and suffered from femicide,[9] most recently has witnessed a massive number of executions,[10] and is subject to the surveillance and patrolling of its streets and neighborhoods by the 7,500 and more soldiers deployed by the federal government in the so-called war against drug cartels. In addition, given the recent emergence of extortion threats against teachers and school personnel who are being coerced to give their salaries and bonuses in exchange for "protection," (Felix, 2008; Felix, 2009) school safety is not a small matter to weigh in when deciding what school one's children should attend.

Students often complain about the lack of extracurricular activities and the strict rules enforced by school personnel. Grooming and attire are closely monitored at the door. Girls, for instance, are not allowed to wear makeup and boys' shirts must be tucked-in and their hair must be short. Those infringing school regulations are detained until they tuck-in the shirts in the case of boys, or wash their make-up off in the case of girls. If a boy's hair is long and he is a repeat offender, he might be sent back home. However, the fact that enrollment is high despite the strict rules and the long-distances students' must travel on foot, riding the school bus, by *rutera*,[11] or in their parents' modest cars, signals to Vespertina's reputation.

Yet, as one enters the school through the iron door jealously guarded by the only female of three *prefectos*,[12] no apparent signs of the innovations advanced by the recent reforms effort are visible. Far from Alianza's rhetoric regarding the "modernization of school infrastructure" and measures to "dignify" school centers, as one walks the school corridor, it is easy to hear teachers' recitations as they stand in front of their students who listen from their old, beaten desks tightly arranged in rows. Alianza's promise of innovative instructional technology and teachers' training on how to use it are not observable. In fact, technology in the form of overhead projectors, computers, or media sets are not found in Vespertina's classrooms, or in the small school library. Teachers rely on white boards to instruct and some present lessons using construction paper or other materials that they purchase with a limited allowance that is included in teachers' biweekly salary check. Classrooms walls are almost bare with only a few pieces of students' work taped on the wall for display and hand-written signs admonishing students to keep their classroom clean, or to not damage other students' work.

The socioeconomic precariousness of the urban context of Juárez—paradoxically Mexico's leading manufacturing export zone—is reflected in the school grounds. But the precariousness of the school's context is only comparable to the weak academic standing of students of the city of Juárez in general, and at Vespertina in particular. For instance, in their analysis of students' performance in the *ENLACE* administered in 2006, Cervera et al. (2008) found that the majority (53%) of students taking the language arts portion of the assessment in Juárez scored at the "elemental" level of achievement, 26 percent fell in the "insufficient" level of achievement, 19 percent performed at a "good" level, and only 2 percent achieved at the "excellent" level. Data regarding level of achievement by school was not found on the databases available for public consultation. However, in 2008, Vespertina ranked in the last quarter among a total of 127 middle schools that tested in the city. In Juárez, the highest achieving school scored 707 out of a total of 800 points, and the lowest achieving school scored 434 points. Vespertina scored a few points above the lowest score in the city.

At the city and national level, the continuation of Alianza rests on the federal government's claim that students' achievement on the assessment instrument warrants the changes promoted in the reform. First piloted in 2006 under President Felipe Calderón, at the core of the educational policy are five major foci: (1) the "modernization" of school centers; (2) the professionalization of teachers and school authorities; (3) students' "well-being" and "integral development"; (4) a curricular reform "oriented toward students' achievement of "competencies and skills"; and (5) evaluation for the improvement of educational services (Alianza por la Calidad de la Educación. Funcionamiento General, Secretaría de Educación Pública [Alliance for Quality Education. General Functioning. Ministry of Public Education.], 2006; p. 1).

Like previous educational policy to reform public schools, Alianza was broad in scope. However, in contrast to previous efforts that aimed mostly at schools' administrative structures, Alianza targeted the school curriculum. It mandated a new mathematics and language arts curriculum that advanced a student-centered pedagogic approach and privileged an activity-driven curriculum. It also called for tighter measures of accountability via the administration of high-stakes assessment of students' academic performance in mathematics and language arts.

Two years after it was piloted, *Secundaria* Vespertina implemented Alianza. To do this, teachers were required to attend a weeklong workshop where they were introduced to the reform. Subsequently, as the school year progressed, teachers were required to attend day-long workshops on pedagogical training. Teachers also attended work sessions to share and get feedback on practical problems regarding instruction.

At Vespertina, Maestra Laura was responsible for implementing the reformed ninth-grade language arts curriculum. Although she communicated a favorable opinion of Alianza, she acknowledged the difficulties in its adoption. In her opinion, the most challenging aspect of the reform was its call for the implementation of curricular and pedagogic approaches that were new to her and to most other teachers. Shifting from a teacher-centered approach was difficult. In the past, as Maestra Laura said, "the teacher explained and then [students] obeyed and completed the activity that was assigned." With the reform, teachers were no longer solely responsible for "providing all the information" or content. Instead, she said she was expected to "coordinate" and support students by "clarify[ing] their doubts, or concerns."

Notwithstanding the challenges in implementing Alianza, Maestra Laura saw the reform as a learning process that had its rewards: Mostly, it had lessened the demands placed on her. She was no longer the sole source of knowledge or "information" as she called it. And because students were supposed to work in groups, they submitted group as opposed to individual assignments, lessening the burden of grading endless piles of papers. In short, the work of teaching, as described, was more efficient.

For the students, however, understanding their new role as stipulated by Alianza was a challenge. This was mostly because, as Maestra Laura explained, they were used to individual work in classrooms, recitation being the prevalent mode of instruction. With the reform, students were now expected to be self-directed learners, who "collaborated." Even though groups distributed roles and responsibilities among its members, problems sometimes aroused. This was true, for instance, when a student was asked to be in charge of finding sources or supplies to develop a group's project and he or she failed to bring them on the specified day. Or, when a group was scheduled to present their work to the class and their spokesperson was absent. Or worst, when a group's project was left at the home of a forgetful member on the day that it was due.

From the beginning of the year, Maestra Laura allowed the formation of groups on the basis of *"afinidad"* or affinity and the students chose with whom they wanted to group. In addition, roles for each group member were specified and visible on a sign taped to the wall, describing the task a given student would carry out: "Group leader, coordinates; secretary, writes down agreements; [person responsible for] materials; timekeeper; spokesperson" (author's translation). As the year progressed, however, there were smaller-size groups with students refusing to continue to work with certain group members. There were also larger groups with students insisting on working with their friends. Regardless of the groups' sizes, they remained organized in the same way throughout the reminder of the school year.

To guide her work in the classroom, Maestra Laura used the adopted textbook, Proyectos de Español or Language Arts Projects. The text advanced a curriculum that posited language as "a social practice" and conceived its acquisition and study as a means for students to achieve an "integral" preparation (Murillo, 2008; p. XI). It organized language arts into three domains or *ámbitos* titled "Citizen's participation," "Research," and "Literature." Work in each of the domains involved the completion of a project or *proyecto*.

During the fall, students completed a number of projects from the three domains. For instance, the first two months of the academic year, under the Research domain, the teacher adapted the suggested textbook projects, "How will we read and compare different treatments of a single topic?" and "Let's debate!" A third project under that same domain titled "How do we write a research report?" was assigned later in the academic year. As part of the "Citizen participation" domain, the class completed the projects "How does publicity influence our purchase decisions?", and "How to fill out various application forms?" Under the "Literature" domain, students completed three projects including "How do we trace a genre, thematic, or poetic movement?", "How do we elaborate a literary anthology with a prologue?", and "How to read a piece in medieval or renaissance Spanish?"

The activities within each project, as specified in the textbook, were divided into three stages. Each project included a set of activities that were part of an "introductory," "development," and "closing" stage. Moreover, it was assumed that as the teacher "modeled" and "demonstrated" certain skills embedded in the activities and, as students worked through the various stages, they would acquire the "competencies" or formal knowledge embedded in each set of activities.

As her classes worked on each of the projects' activities, Maestra Laura was always patient, and unrelenting in her desire to help students complete their work. She demonstrated a willingness to support all of her students including those in 3ero C whom she considered a challenging group in terms of academics and discipline. Notwithstanding the difficulty that working with such a group of students posed, the teacher's commitment to her students earned her the respect of the school principal and other administrators who regarded her as one of Vespertina's best. But also, in the context of a school experiencing underfunding, understaffing, and overall neglect as the impetus in the state grew to eliminate the *escuela vespertina or* afternoon school modality, her dedication stood out.

Students in all of her classes seemed to like her. As she made her way to the various classrooms in which she taught,[13] students–mostly girls—greeted her with a kiss on cheek. Others would walk her to her next classroom and chat about their day, classes, and personal matters. Because she usually carried an assortment of papers and books, students often volunteered to help her carry her teaching materials.

Once in the classroom, students, cued by her presence, arranged their desks in preparation for the group work that Maestra Laura and Alianza expected of them. As they noisily gathered in their groups, students usually took out their notebooks, laid out their materials, and chitchatted, as they began the work in their projects. Some students consulted with each other, monitored the work that was being produced, loudly argued over differing opinions, confronted whoever was not fulfilling their expectations, talked or played, and a few expressed their disinterest by simply not participating with group tasks. When a student was tardy, he or she was allowed to come in only after asking and gaining the teacher's permission to enter the classroom. When the student came in the classroom, it was expected that he or she join in group work or activities that could have been interrupted or delayed as a result of the student's lateness.

The environment in Maestra Laura's 3ro C was lively. For most of the 45-minute period, the teacher walked around monitoring groups and answering questions. Rambunctious students moved freely from one place to the other borrowing markers, pens, papers, books, and other materials that they supplied for the completion of their group's activities. Often, the teacher was forced to reprimand students who were off-task playing with their cell phones, working on another class's assignment, not working in their designated group, or were unwilling to do any work. But even in those cases, Maestra Laura was soft-spoken and never overbearing.

Alianza and the Production of an Empty Curriculum

At the outset of my study, I had anticipated that the enactment of Alianza would be fraught with complications, given its broad scope, lofty objectives, unclear directives, limited funding, and the tight system of accountability that drove the curriculum. However, what I found was baffling. Contrary to the "drill and kill" routines of teaching to the test, or the highly scripted, teacher-centered approaches that critics of NCLB have documented in the research literature, Maestra Laura and her students followed a student-centered approach and favored an activity-driven curriculum. Yet, as classroom participants worked to execute the assigned activities, engagement with language arts was forestalled.

This puzzling enactment of the language arts curriculum could be traced throughout the various projects assigned in Maestra Laura's class. In this chapter, I focus on three learning activities embedded in one of the assigned projects. The detailed description and analysis of the two learning activities illustrate the conflicting curricular approaches and practices that surfaced as teacher and students worked throughout the year. Unlike the "mélange" of the new and traditional approaches that others have documented (Cohen, 1990: p. 312), or the "hybrid" curriculum described by Page (1999), in Maestra Laura's classroom, language arts was emptied from the curriculum.

Enacting the Empty Language Arts Curriculum

Aiming to deepen students' literacy skills, the textbook's version of the project titled "How to compare various treatments of a topic?" prescribed a set of activities to get students to "compare and evaluate" the treatment of a given topic in diverse texts (Murillo Paniagua, 2008: p. 47).

In general, the activities were meant to teach students how to recognize an author's point of view through the identification of certain literary devices employed in a text to convey an argument or point of view. Moreover, various "products" were expected at the completion of each of the six interrelated group activities (ibid: p. 48).

The textbook project's activities and products were varied and they involved student engagement with both formal and substantive content in language arts. As listed in the textbook, the activities for the project included the following:

1. Read various texts on a topic of the students' choice and produce a number of bibliographic index cards referencing consulted sources.
2. Identify and analyze each of the texts' arguments, develop a comparative analysis by preparing an outline identifying the different arguments in the texts.
3. Synthesize the information obtained from the consulted sources in a short essay.
4. Organize a group presentation to "share what was learned" with the entire class.
5. Evaluate all activities in the project by using the student self-assessment rubric that the textbook provided.

Moreover, like most competent language arts teachers (see Kaufman, 1994; Rockwell, 1996), Maestra Laura made the pedagogical choice of modifying the projects stipulated in the textbook. Adaptations, often intended to meet the unique learning needs of students, are often seen as a display of teacher confidence, command over the subject matter, and thorough knowledge of students' abilities (Cohen, 1990; Page, 1991). Common in Maestra Laura's class, adaptations often involved the redesign of a number of activities in a given project. Sometimes, however, they included the modification of a project focus or learning objectives.

Maestra Laura's modified version was titled "How to investigate a project?" The activities involved only subtle changes and the inclusion of a few extra activities that were carried out in a period of three weeks. By way of introducing the project, as she specified them, she also wrote them on the board (author's translation):

1. Select a topic related to something studied in other classes.
2. Search for information.
3. Analyze and organize the information.

4. Compare the various points of view.
5. Prepare a synopsis of the information.
6. Prepare bibliographic index cards documenting: author, title, editor, place, year, and page number.
7. Write an essay on the topic.
8. Prepare visual material for a presentation.
9. Organize a presentation to share the information.

Maestra Laura's adaptations, like the textbook's suggested activities, seemed thoughtfully and tightly organized. In practice, however, the procedures and the systematic manner in which the activities unfolded vacated language arts from the curriculum. This was possible, as the teacher, attempting to implement the modified curriculum, found herself caught between both a rational and subjective view of teaching. Acting from a rational view of her obligation as a teacher, Maestra Laura emphasized hard work and the completion of the project's activities. Yet, frustrated with the students' behavior, and her view of students as both unwilling and unable, she resorted to an emphasis on the formal aspects of the curriculum. Such a practice, she often described as an attempt to "ease" students' "restlessness" and ensure the completion of the activities. In the end, as the enactment of the two activities described next show, her adaptations pervasively avoided engagement with language arts.

Completing Activity Three: Analyzing and Organizing Information

A week into "How to investigate a topic?" student groups began to struggle. Maestra Laura had asked them to search for multiple sources containing information on their chosen topics. Many, the teacher anticipated, would not have access to books at home. Consequently, anyone who requested it was given permission to go to the school library during the class period. Some groups would come back from the library with a book or two; others, empty handed, joined the choir of students openly voicing their impatience with locating materials on their topics.

Unrelenting, despite the fact that a few groups did not have any sources with which to work, Maestra Laura moved on to activity three. The activity, as she had specified on the board, required that students identify and analyze information on the group's topics. To guide students' work, the textbook suggested that the teacher model the identification of an author's point of view by focusing on the use of various literary devices that authors employ to make an argument.

Yet, amidst a roomful of adolescents, some of whom were off-task chatting, texting, or attempting funny remarks, Maestra Laura reverted to dictation. Providing a definition of concessive expressions, she said—in her usual low-pitch—that concessive sentences contained an "action-consequence" linked by a conjunction such as "que" or "tan que." As she patiently proceeded, Maestra Laura asked students to provide possible examples using the conjunctions that she had identified. Some provided a few examples but none of those related to the materials they had consulted or their group projects.

Not explicitly linking her dictation of concessive expressions and the students' examples to the activity at hand cast language arts as disconnected and even unrelated to the task of reading. By teaching about concessive expressions not as a literary device but as a grammatical figure disconnected from the particular endeavor of reading for understanding and analysis, language arts was deemphasized.

The shift to an emphasis on the formal aspects of the curriculum was also exacerbated by a sense of urgency to complete, in a timely fashion, the various activities. This was especially true as constant interruptions, such as students' requests to go to the restroom, chatting, and students' remarks unrelated to coursework that the teacher ignored began to impinge on the focused completion of activities. In the end, practice for the reading skills they needed to be able to analyze and synthesize the information in their sources was omitted.

Consequently, during the subsequent class period, unable to analyze and synthesize the texts they had gathered, students—seemingly puzzled—stared at each other. A few leafed through the various books and materials, but most complained about the task of looking for information, about their books' lengths, and about what some considered as the authors' lack of clarity. A couple of students, visibly frustrated with the activity, disengaged from the task.

Pressed with time, confused about the task at hand, and with the teacher's insistence that the activity needed to be completed, most groups simply copied entire passages from the sources they had collected. Then, checking on whether they were doing what the activity called for, groups repeatedly called on the teacher to have her read what they had written. Monitoring the work that groups were doing could have been a signal to the teacher that students' were confused or simply did not know how to read for understanding. Yet, Maestra Laura, did not explain the concept of concessive expressions as a literary device again, nor did she model how to recognize them when attempting to locate an author's perspective on a topic. Instead, once she read through the few paragraphs that groups had copied on their notebooks, she would instruct each group to simply "use their own words" when writing the synthesis.

Completing Activity 4: Preparing Bibliographic Index Cards

Writing a synthesis that draws from multiple sources required skills that students had not mastered yet. However, her eyes set on the next activity, Maestra Laura asked the students to prepare bibliographic index cards referencing the sources that each group had consulted. Instructing them on the mechanical aspects of the preparation of the cards, she mentioned that she required each card to contain specific information, such as the book author's name, title of text, publisher, place of publication, year, and the page number from which the information had been cited.

However, while some had used a book or two to complete the project's activities, and had located the information to reference the pieces on the index cards, most had consulted store-bought *planillas* to get information on their particular topic. *Planillas*, as it turned-out, were not authored pieces, did not show a year of publication, and were not paginated. Thus, because the teacher did not seem to require or show students how to reference nonbook material, the logic by which they began to understand the task of documenting their consulted sources was related to whether or not the pieces contained the information the teacher had required them to provide. If a consulted source did not show an author's name, page, or publication date, groups would not reference it.

Teaching students to acknowledge and recognize an author's contribution to the written discourse on a particular topic by referencing the work is a critical component of the ninth-grade curriculum. However, as this skill was taught and practiced in the classroom, referencing turned into a mechanical task that was practiced only if the information they had been instructed to provide was readily available. In the end, mirroring the teacher's emphasis on the formal aspects of the curriculum, the preparation of bibliographic index cards became one more activity that groups were pressed to complete.

Completing Activity Nine: Organizing a Presentation to Share with the Class

During the third and last week of the project's activities, students arduously worked on the "closing" phase of the project that, according to Maestra Laura, culminated with a presentation to the class.

As she had planned it, groups' presentations would be based on the information contained in a final essay that would build from activity three and which would summarize what each group had learned about their respective topic. In addition, groups would prepare various visual materials for their display during the presentations. In practice, activities unfolded in an unexpected way. The syntheses each group had prepared as part of activity three suddenly replaced the summary that Maestra Laura had originally planned as part of the closing activities. In addition, instructed to focus on the preparation of the visual materials that would go with the group presentations, students spent two class periods cutting, gluing, pasting, and coloring the visual work and labeling it with intricate handwriting. Omitting the final activity—an essay where students would practice and display the language arts they had acquired—was puzzling. However, her decision to devote two class periods to the creation of visual materials illustrated her changing imperatives. No longer focused on language arts, Maestra Laura aimed to move this challenging class through the projects, by emptying language arts from the curriculum.

Hence, when presentations were finally delivered, students' talk mirrored the curriculum that Maestra Laura had emphasized throughout. For instance, a group of girls presenting on the topic of "plants as living organisms" displayed a series of leaves they had collected from trees found in their neighborhoods. Glued to a colorful construction paper, they had titled their poster "Las hojas/Plantas," or "Leaves/Plants." As the *vocero* or speaker for the group delivered the presentation, however, none of what she mentioned alluded directly to the leaf samples that the girls had collected. Instead, the presentation focused on the anatomy of plants and the functions of each of its parts.

Because it was obvious from the vocabulary employed during the presentation that the student was reading from a textual passage in a science or botany source, Maestra Laura, seemingly exasperated, interrupted the presentation and reiterated what she had told them but not taught them: to communicate their information "using their own words." Thus, as the presentation ended with the student hurriedly reading through her notes, Maestra Laura asked her a basic question, which her presentation had covered: "What is a leaf?" The student, not really understanding what she had just read to the class, simply responded pointing to her group's poster: "This is a leaf."

That the students had not sought information on the leaves they had collected was revealing of the disconnected ways in which the project's activities were carried out. Rather than acquiring and practicing the language arts involved in reading for understanding and analysis, documenting the evidence that supported the various arguments about a topic, and effectively communicating, through writing and verbally, the knowledge they gained, groups engaged in activities that to them were unreasonable and disconnected.

Conclusion

Focusing on the details of a classroom practice reframes the central issues of curricular reform. Thus, rather than focusing on whether Alianza "works" or not, this account raises a series of critical questions about the meaning of Alianza to specific individuals who experience it in particular classrooms. In the case of the city of Juárez, the community that Vespertina serves, questions about the merit and the worth of curricular reform are not trivial. In fact, the viability of the city as a sustainable community, particularly in this complex social, political, and economic juncture, depends in large measure on the quality of education its citizens are afforded.

However, if the story of Maestra Laura's classroom is carefully considered, then a series of critical questions must be raised: How does curricular reform work and with what intended and unintended consequences? And, what is the import of reform in shaping the knowledge that schools are to teach and distribute? In Maestra Laura's classroom, these difficult questions uncover complex answers. Set out to implement Alianza's high-minded but contradictory postulates, Maestra Laura's modified curriculum appeared demanding with a tight schedule of projects and activities to be completed. Upon analysis, however, the arduousness translated into a series of tasks emphasizing the formal aspects of the language arts curriculum but not deepening students' language arts. The arduous tasks of copying text, filling-out index cards following a template, and creating visual material pertaining to the topic not only kept students busy, it also kept language arts at bay.

This pattern of classroom interaction was possible as Maestra Laura navigated between the contradictory views that informed her practice. As a committed teacher, she was unwilling to abdicate what she conceived to be her role and responsibilities in the classroom; yet, as other classroom research has documented, she—like many teachers—acted on her subjective views of students' limited academic and behavioral skills. What ensued was an overemphasis on mechanistic and laborious activities that worked to produce an empty curriculum.

Notes

1. Alianza para la Calidad Educativa translates as Alliance for Quality Education.
2. Refer to the 1992 Acuerdo Nacional para la Modernización de la Educación Básica (ANMEB); the 2001 Programa Nacional Para la Educación (PRONAE), and Reforma Integral para la Educación Secundaria (RIES); and the 2006 Alianza para la Calidad de la Educación (ACE). More on the reforms may be found in Staudt and Mendez's chapter in this book.
3. PISA is the acronym for Programme on International Student Assessment, a measure used by the Organization for Economic Cooperation and Development (OECD) to determine academic competencies of students from around the world.
4. ENLACE is the National Survey on Academic Achievement of School Centers that was introduced as an assessment instrument under ACE.
5. Secretaria de Educación Pública is the equivalent of the Ministry or Department of Education.
6. To protect participants' anonymity, their names and the school's name have been given pseudonyms.
7. *Escuelas Vespertinas or* evening schools where first established to ensure sufficient coverage without the need to build more school facilities.
8. México, unlike the United States, does not have a neighborhood feeder system in place to determine which school a student must attend. Parents and students are able to choose which school to enroll in. In particular, *secundarias* where high demand exists and problems of coverage are very real, students are admitted through what is known as an *exámen de admision*, or an admissions exam that is administered by school personnel in any given school.
9. For more on the topic, see Monárrez Fragaso & Bejarano and Staudt & Robles Ortega in this volume.
10. Just in December of 2008, statistics reported by *Diario de Juarez*, one of the local newspapers, indicated that more than 1,500 persons had been killed in "drug-related" executions in the city.
11. Ciudad Juarez' public transportation buses are known as *ruteras*.
12. In *secundarias* in Mexico, *prefectos* are in charge of disciplinary matters. During my fieldwork, the work responsibilities of Lupita, the *prefecta* at the door, increased. She, like other school personnel across schools in Juárez, was instructed to only allow inside the school grounds employees students, and other previously authorized visitors as the number of kidnappings, and extortion threats increased and became more public. Hence, those coming to the school—including parents—would first knock on the iron door and wait for Lupita to check who it was through a gap between the door and the wall so that

she could approve entrance. To leave school grounds, she would open the gate and shut it closed, just as soon as visitors stepped out.

13. In Mexican middle schools or *secundarias,* teachers change classrooms as opposed to students moving between classrooms.

Reference List

Apple, M. W. (1990/1979). *Ideology and curriculum.* New York and London: Routledge.

Calvo, B. (1994). Modernización educativa: una perspectiva desde la frontera norte de México. Unidad de Estudios Regionales, Universidad Autónoma de Ciudad Juárez.

Cervera, Luis, G. Lizárraga, and C. Sánchez. (2008). "Estudio georreferencial de la Evaluación Nacional de Logro Académico en Centros Escolares (ENLACE) en el Municipio de Juárez, Chihuahua: análisis especial." REDIE 10(1). http://redie.uabc.mx.

Cohen, D. (1990). *A revolution in one classroom: The case of Mrs. Oublier. Educational evaluation and policy analysis,* 12, pp. 479–502.

Erickson, F. (1986). Qualitative methods in research on teaching. In M. C. Wittrock (ed.), *Handbook of research on teaching.* New York: Macmillan.

Felix, G. (2008, November 11). Exhorta Educación a no autodefenderse. *El Diario de Juárez.*

Felix, G. (2009, January 11). Piden tener escuelas cerradas y llevar registro de visitantes. *El Diario de Juárez.*

Kaufman, A. M. (1994). Escribir en la escuela: Qué, cómo y para quién. Revista Latinoamericana de Lectura. Año 15. No.3.

Levinson, B. (2001). *We are all equal: Student culture and identity at a Mexican secondary school,* 1988–1998. Durham, NC: Duke University Press.

Martin, J. R. (1994). *Changing the educational landscape. Philosophy, women, and curriculum.* New York: Routledge.

McNeil, L. (2000). Contradictions of school reform: Educational costs of standardized testing. New York: Routledge.

Murillo Paniagua, G. (2008). Proyectos de Español 3. Ediciones Pedagógicas. McGraw-Hill.

Noriega Chávez, M. (2000). Las reformas educativas y su financiamiento en el contexto de la globalización: El caso de México, 1982–1994. México, D.F.: Plaza y Valdés Editores.

Page, R. N. (1991). *Lower track classrooms: A curricular and cultural perspective.* New York: Teachers College Press.

———. (1999). "The uncertain value of school knowledge: Biology at Westridge High." *Teachers College Record,* 100(3), pp. 554–601.

Rockwell, E. (1996). Los usos escolares de la lengua escrita. In Ferreiro, E. & Gómez Palacios, M. (eds). Nuevas perspectivas sobre los procesos de lectura y escritura. México DF: Siglo XXI.

Velez Bustillo, E., and V. Paqueo. (2001). Education Sector Strategy. In Lafourcade, O. & V. H. Nguyen (eds.), *México: A comprehensive development agenda for the era*. Washington, D.C.: Guigale, M. M.

Zorrilla, M. (2004). La educación secundaria en México: Al filo de su reforma. Revista Electrónica Iberoamericana sobre la Calidad, Eficacia y Cambio en Educación. Vol. 2, no. 1.

Zorilla, M., and B. Barba. (2006). Reforma educativa en México. Descentralización y nuevos actores. FronterasEducativas. Comunidad Virtual de la Educación. ITESO.

SECTION IV

TOWARD NEW GOVERNANCE?

CHAPTER 10

CROSSBORDER GOVERNANCE IN A TRISTATE, BINATIONAL REGION

Tony Payan

During the administration of Mayor John F. Cook, the city of El Paso revived an old effort to establish a close cooperative relationship with its sister across the U.S.-Mexico border, City of Juárez, Chihuahua. Mayor Cook put Mr. Robert Andrade, his Executive Assistant, in charge of putting together a group of El Paso residents, one appointed by each City Council member and one by the mayor, to do just that. This group of residents of El Paso, known by city ordinance as the Committee on Border Relations (CBR), was primarily charged with putting together a program "to enhance relations with Ciudad Juárez and with the border area in proximity to El Paso."[1] The ultimate and more political goal of the CBR was to ensure that the local governments in the region coordinate their actions so that they: at a minimum, not operate against the interests of the other and the region as a whole; and, at a maximum, aid each other to profit from the natural advantages of the region.

I was appointed to the CBR by El Paso Council Member Steve Ortega in February 2007[2] and served in it until February 2009—a two-year term. The most important activity I was engaged in while still a member of the CBR was to put together a meeting of the City Councils and mayors of all three cities of the Paso del Norte region (El Paso, Texas; Ciudad Juárez, Chihuahua; and Sunland Park, New Mexico). If we were to accomplish the goals of the CBR, the reasoning went that, at minimum, we had to get the local politicians to talk to each other. The task soon proved to be a colossal endeavor, akin to moving an elephant with a feather. We ran into a series of obstacles that had to be resolved before the meeting could take place. First, were the legal obstacles: the Texas Open Meetings Act, for example, forbids City Councils to meet outside their jurisdictional territory.[3] To resolve this obstacle, we came up with the idea of meeting at the exact point where the three states (Texas, Chihuahua, and New Mexico) and cities (Ciudad Juárez, El Paso, and Sunland Park) meet, each within their own territory but facing each other. We scouted the area physically after we conducted a satellite search of the exact border point where the three states met. On the stark, empty space—which can be located on satellite photos on the Internet—one can see a semipaved road, a clump of trees that grows near the river, and a line of stones painted white (not a fence or wall) that marks the boundary line. Having determined the exact point where the meeting would take place, we had to search for the consent of all the parties that may object to such a meeting: Customs and Border Protection, the Border Patrol, El Paso County Water Improvement District No. 1, the El Paso Police Department, the Ciudad Juárez Police Department, the Juárez Distrito de Riego No. 9, the legal teams of the cities involved, the American Consulate in Ciudad Juárez, and the Mexican Consulate in El Paso, Texas, the fire departments of all three cities, etc. Then, we had to remove the physical obstacles, including clearing the land, removing stray boulders, drawing the border lines on the ground, beautifying the place, make the location accessible to the handicapped to comply with the law, etc. Then we had to find the funding required for renting the equipment, the furnishings, a large tent that would straddle the borderlines, etc. Then we had to negotiate the agenda; draft the resolutions to be considered by the City Councils; harmonize the protocols; and advertise the meeting to the local, national, and international media.

The entire affair went relatively well and received moderately good media coverage, but it represented a gargantuan effort from many parties, over several months, and a carefully choreographed ceremony which, in the end, produced little, because it did not amount to building a permanent crossborder political or policy-making network to bridge policy coordination, cooperation, or collaboration. It represented at most, a one-time event that did not reformulate or restructure the relationship between the cities in the region and did not symbolize a reorganization of the crossborder governance capacity of any government.

For this reason, after the meeting, many wondered if the enormous amount of work put into this meeting was worth the effort just to get the City Councils to pass three resolutions which, in the end, had no teeth and were mere expressions of good will and good intentions. What does governance in the Paso del Norte region mean, then, in the face of the obstacles of territory and sovereignty? Is it possible to build and expand crossborder networks between two subnational units that can produce real governance and material results for the residents of both cities? Is it possible to speak of the Paso del Norte region as a single "transnational urban system" (Sassen, 2007)?

SO MUCH FOR SO LITTLE: THE PUZZLE

The enormous amount of time and energy invested by the members of the CBR and others in trying to craft a lasting and effective governance relationship among the most important local governments of the Paso del Norte region, across mutually exclusive spaces and divided sovereignties (two nations and three states), and the poor results it produced constitute a testimony that *governance* in a crossborder region must be affected by a number of variables, permanent and temporary, that need to be examined carefully.[4] That is the purpose of this chapter, to answer the question: What are the factors that operate against local efforts by the residents of El Paso, Ciudad Juárez, and Sunland Park to bridge their differences? How can these three communities achieve, at a minimum, coordination of their local policies; at a higher level, effective cooperation in solving common issues and problems; and at a maximum, collaboration in building a common regional vision, with common goals, and common policy instruments?

ARGUMENTS AND THEORETICAL PERSPECTIVES

To answer these questions, I appeal to some of the ideas articulated in three major works by Saskia Sassen. These are *Territory, Authority and Rights* (2008), *A Sociology of Globalization* (2006), and *The Global City: New York, London, Tokyo* (2001). Sassen argues in *Territory, Authority, and Rights* that to understand the dynamics of the modern nation-state (its creation, its evolution, its current condition, and its "coming end"), we have to examine three elements: *territory*, *authority*, and *rights*—TAR. In fact, to understand the processes of globalization today, we have to understand how TAR evolved over time, how its component parts coalesced, and how it operates in our institutions and our daily practices. For Sassen, TAR took centuries to meld but eventually came to constitute a powerful assemblage known as the *nation-state* that is still hard to transcend for most people. Indeed, TAR is a hardened structure. In the modern nation-state, the *centripetal* forces—those that push toward the preservation of the nation-state—are still stronger than the centrifugal forces—the forces of globalization, which Sassen describes in her work. In other words, the *nationalizing* balance is still tilted against the *denationalizing* forces and neither of these forces is felt the same everywhere by everyone. Still, Sassen posits that the forces of globalization—the denationalizing forces—are gaining momentum, and adds that many of them are in fact the same forces that gave the nationalizing processes of old their impetus. Sassen's work is of course focused on the denationalizing forces, but it is very likely that the interests and instruments that resist the pull of *nationalizing* processes are still weaker. Hence, one should expect the underlying sentimental correlative of nationalizing forces—phenomena such as nationalism, patriotism, etc.—to be stronger than concepts such as world citizen, the right to universal mobility, etc. Assemblages that swim against the nation-state, such as bilateral or, even better, binational institutions, are likely to remain weaker for quite some time, even if, as Sassen argues, they keep getting stronger. What does that mean for border contexts? How can these concepts be applied in such contexts and help us explain poor levels of crossborder governance in the Paso del Norte region?

With regard to most borderlands in the world, no matter how integrated the markets, the peoples, the language, the culture, etc., may be along a borderline—that is, how territory, citizenship and authority may be challenged on the ground by those who live in borderlands—TAR ultimately determines what is possible and what is not possible for locals to accomplish vis-à-vis each other.[5] The constrictions of TAR are phenomenal: they impose what each can and cannot do within and outside a given territory, under whose authority or authorities they can act, and what their rights are. Thus, although the concept of TAR is familiar to all the citizens of a nation-state, it is probably felt more strongly in border contexts because it is there where the possibility of acting or interacting under a different TAR is a daily experience. At borders, citizens cross into foreign territory, fall under a different authority, and enjoy different rights and privileges, depending on where they are at any given minute. I propose, therefore, that TAR is likely to be one of the greatest obstacles to creating crossborder structures, processes, and issue linkages[6] that can help transcend the pull of the nation-state. In the end, what actors can and cannot accomplish is constrained by this powerful assemblage. Thus, TAR is in and of itself a principle that, at minimum, divides loyalties and, at its worst, breaks down any potential good intentions in favor of the creation of crossborder governance mechanisms, particularly those with the potential to promote *good* crossborder governance.

In *The Global City: New York, London, Tokyo*, Sassen argues that it is economics—more specifically market forces, accompanied by technological developments—that is redefining space and reshaping the dynamics and processes on a global scale. This affects, in her view, markets for goods and services, financial investments, people migration, etc. The result of this market- and technology-driven transformation is the creation of clusters of power (large globalized cities) and vast expanses of weakness (peripheral, dependent areas). These clusters of power or large globalized cities, she writes, "concentrate control over vast resources, while finance and specialized service industries have restructured the urban social and economic order" worldwide. Sassen argues that it is the *economic* or *market* forces—some of the very forces that she sees as operating for centuries in favor of the nation-state assemblage—that are reorganizing our conception of territory and space, authority and jurisdiction, and human/legal rights and mobility. Many of our domestic and global institutions today are, in fact, attuned to the administrative and legal orchestration of *market* power. Unfortunately, these same forces are increasingly deaf to the personal plight of human beings. That is, the primary motivation is material self-interest rather than issues of social justice or humanitarian substance.[7] The new global arrangements—with a number of key cities at the core, a number of cities at the periphery, and vast expanses of *no man's lands*—destroy the unity of the dispossessed and create two classes of citizens. One is a class of citizens that is highly mobile, transnational, and wealthy. This group of individuals can travel around the globe, invest, live, work, and move at will. The second is a group of individuals that is territorially embedded, a "nationally-rooted" class that participates only as hired hands—what Sassen calls "low-value individuals" engaged in "low-value" service activities. The global village or rather the network of key global villages (New York, London, Tokyo, Paris, Berlin, and a few others, perhaps Mexico City, Rio de Janeiro, Buenos Aires, etc.) is propelled, by definition, by the doctrine of neoliberalism: laissez-faire, laissez passer at its best. What does *The Global City* have to contribute to understanding governance in crossborder contexts, such as our region Paso del Norte?

In borderland contexts such as ours, Sassen's observations in *The Global City* have enormous implications. This is in part because the "framers" of the concept of "border"—its evolving definition, its physical appearance, and its meaning for each person on the ground—are primarily those who have *market* power rather than those that are dependent on market forces, that is, those who own nothing but their labor, who can provide nothing but "low-value" service activities. The economic devastation that market forces can work on the most vulnerable along the border—precisely those who enjoy no crossborder mobility because they are denied passports or visas or resources to study, travel, or immerse themselves in high-value activities—is hardly ever considered in a highly interdependent economy, where the focus is on *macro*economic health and unshackled production. In this context, the microeconomic, often meaning the personal, becomes less and less important (Staudt, 2008). The many are mere "cannon fodder" for the guns of the market-driven environment. Many of the global dynamics along an *economically unequal* or *uneven border*, such as the region Paso del Norte, are expressed in the form of internal concerns and struggles with capital and production, with development and advantage-taking, and with nationalized struggles that look at their respective centers (capitals) and only secondarily on noneconomic transborder networks and dynamics. This a consequence of the nationalism that is often reinforced along borders by technology, patrols, fences and walls, and a permanent police presence, where the intent on dividing is as powerful as or more powerful than any integration process and where *economics* is at the driver's seat but local democracy takes a backseat.[8]

But Sassen's potential contributions to explaining what happens in a crossborder region, such as Paso del Norte, do not stop there. It is necessary to explain how the macro is translated into the micro. In that regard, we appeal to her work *A Sociology of Globalization*. In this piece, Sassen explores how the global and the local interact. Sassen argues that globalization processes are linked through global institutions but these are manifest in the form of interconnections at the local level. Monetary policy affects the purchasing power of the local residents; migration policies determine who can move and who cannot; legal frameworks determine who can network with him among activists etc. Thus, the effect of the global is manifest at the national and local levels in the form of monetary, immigration, fiscal, and development policies—and likely in the possibilities of local actors and activists. In other words, the global affects the subnational by imposing on it a complex system of small interactions that serve the larger scale of the global. In border contexts, this is further exacerbated because the global, the national, and the subnational take on a particular glow as local actors interact and clash.

A FEW *CROSSBORDER* HYPOTHESES

To bring Sassen's theoretical perspectives to bear on our case, I formulate a number of hypotheses. First, the CBR, a weak, advisory, all-volunteer body was clearly well over its capacity to create and maintain regularized processes and issue linkages, and more so to constitute a formal structure, for crossborder governance in a region characterized by divided loyalties (TAR and its emotional equivalent, nationalism) and shaped primarily by market forces, where the local economic activity is based on a maquiladora industry that is plugged into the global market but sits atop a nationally anchored working class. A corollary of this hypothesis is that in an uneven border, where the flows are also heavily influenced by inequality, new priorities emerge, such as the protection of the market from those who would infringe on it. Law enforcement, therefore, becomes the armor designed to protect the market forces from an avalanche of intruding forces, say, undocumented workers. Law enforcement, which begins as the material correlative of TAR, takes on the defense of the market logic. A logic of law enforcement, and its consequent escalation,[9] as local residents act and react, becomes a central component of the dynamic of a border context. Law enforcement actors have thus become central players in what can and cannot be done by local residents along the border.

Second, I propose that the center-peripheral arrangement of the modern global city, as Sassen describes it, not only creates spaces along borders where citizens are deeply constrained by TAR—where they can and cannot go; under whose authority they fall; and what rights and privileges they enjoy are all determined by TAR, but more and more they are viewed almost exclusively as economic factors of production, rather than as human beings. Their welfare and happiness depends somewhat on their performance (read, productiveness) as factors of production but also on the market priorities of individuals and forces located away from the border. Thus, the maquiladora industry of the U.S.-Mexico border is *dependent* on decisions made away from the border, rather than on decisions made at the border by local residents.

Third, the imposition of TAR and the global market logic on the local represents a diminished level of democracy, where local

participation in truly important decisions is diminished and consultation with the region's residents is low and decreasing. In the end,
local border residents have lesser levels of autonomy in decision
making around their own policy issues. Clearly, building crossborder
governance by local leaders and local activists in an increasingly centralized context, particularly one that privileges the economic over
the humanitarian, is quite complicated.

If all this is true, then Sassen's arguments can help explain the relative weakness of the CBR and any such efforts, including the Border
Governors Conference, etc., and shed light on their failure. The CBR
exercise on 20 May, 2007, was akin to giving a man a wooden sword
to go out and fight a valiant battle against an enormous, well-armed
battalion.

These concepts propounded by Sassen and the hypotheses derived
from them help sharpen our focus in an examination of governance in
the Paso del Norte region. They guide the kinds of questions that we
have to ask. Some such questions are: What is crossborder governance
like in the region? What are the formal or informal institutions, that
is, the structures and processes that facilitate crossborder governance?
What are the mechanisms by which these institutions create and
maintain crossborder governance in the region? How are the region's
interests aggregated and decisions made and for whom? Who are the
actors that provide governance in the region? What kind of crossborder governance do we practice? Is governance in the Paso del Norte
region *good* governance?

DEFINING GOVERNANCE FOR THE PASO DEL NORTE REGION

Starting from the experience of the CBR, we have to ask what
crossborder governance means in a region such as Paso del Norte.
Crossborder governance is here defined as the ability of the local
governments (and the political leadership) of the region, that is, of
the several mutually exclusive systems of administrative and political
control that exist in the area, to create joint structures, to implement
common processes, and to establish mutual issue linkages that produce optimal results in terms of human security, economic prosperity
for all, community political empowerment, and a robust social fabric
for their residents. This definition, of course, is not unique to the
Paso del Norte region. It could apply to nearly any geographic region
that straddles two or more administrative and political entities. This
definition implies that crossborder governance is more complicated

than governance of a region contained wholly within a nation-state because it applies to a context where policy problems straddle *international* borderlines and the structures, processes, and issue linkages that allow policy coordination, cooperation, or collaboration cannot easily but should be carefully articulated up against the complexities of mutually exclusive sovereignties, defined by separate territories, divided authority, and disparate rights (TAR). That is, such mechanisms should not only create effective and efficient interfaces among these mutually exclusive administrative and political jurisdictions but also ease out the concerns created by the concept of national sovereignty while simultaneously possessing enforcement mechanisms to fulfill all policy agreements. In this sense, this definition is common to all international border regions. Put this way, the CBR was bound to fail, as it has no capacity to create coercive mechanisms, all of which are, in border contexts, monopolized by central governments. The CBR was not only a toothless tiger; it was no tiger at all.

But even as we struggle with the idea of crossborder governance, we must push ahead and demand good crossborder governance. In other words, we can no longer stop at simply defining *crossborder governance*. In the end, governance can also be accomplished by tightly closing a border, repressing nearly all crossborder interaction, as in the North Korean-South Korean border, and focusing all energies toward the nation-state, away from all borders. In such a milieu, all issue linkages are repressed and crossborder structures and processes are largely irrelevant. This situation would correspond to what Martínez (1994) calls an alienated border. The Paso del Norte region is well past that. It is a more "interdependent" border. Thus, it becomes necessary to examine what good crossborder governance could possibly mean. For our purposes, the meaning of good crossborder governance must include all the characteristics of crossborder governance as defined above plus all the characteristics of good governance as generally understood. Thus, good crossborder governance must be defined as the ability of the local governments of the border region, that is, of the several mutually exclusive systems of administrative and political control that exist in the area, to create structures, to implement processes, and to establish issue linkages that produce optimal results in terms of human security, economic prosperity for all, community political empowerment, and a robust social fabric for all of the region's residents. In addition, these structures must be participatory, accountable, transparent, responsive, equitable, inclusive, effective, and efficient. Good crossborder governance must, therefore, seek to provide human security, economic prosperity, political empowerment, and a solid social fabric for the entire *binational* community and not just for one side or for a few groups whose power and mobility enables them to straddle the borderline. The methods of governance must involve the entire binational community.

Unfortunately, given our definition of crossborder governance and specifically our definition of good crossborder governance, this essay argues that the Paso del Norte region falls well short of both standards. Its crossborder governance structures, processes, and issue linkages are either non-existent or defective and deficient. Whatever crossborder governance mechanisms do exist do not add up to good governance, because they fall well short of the universal characteristics of good governance, that is, they are not participatory of the entire binational community, accountable to all, or transparent, because there are so many other forces at work that are not visible to the naked eye. Finally, they are not responsive to, equitable with, or inclusive of the entire binational community.[10]

This means that governance-producing structures, processes, and issue linkages in the region, when they exist, do not serve the binational community's interests or aspirations well, principally because they are not created or maintained by well-articulated *political* actors accountable to the people through a democratic process, namely elections. In other words, only a few, —i.e., two—actors provide the structures and processes for crossborder governance and the issues are viewed through very narrow logics. Thus, to add insult to injury, the bulk of the benefits produced by whatever crossborder governance exists are reaped by only a few individuals and groups (investors, maquiladora owners, land speculators, importers and exporters, etc.) through a very narrow vision of what the border should be. The vast majority of the population is left out, serving mostly as low-value labor and service providers. Moreover, in the last quarter of a century, crossborder political actors have emphasized issue delinkage rather than issue linkage.

Agency and Governance in the Region Paso Del Norte Region: Who Governs?

After a brief analysis of the concept of governance, we must turn to another question: Who governs?[11] That is, what are the actors that provide the axis on which crossborder governance in the Paso del Norte region revolves? Moreover, under what logic or vision is crossborder governance provided in the region? Who defines and links the interests of the region? How do they do it? Whose interests are served by the structures and processes of crossborder governance in the region? These are questions that require an examination of the region's principal actors. Fortunately, one does not have to dig very deeply for the answers to emerge. Using Sassen's concepts regarding the global city, mobile elites, and the markets, a picture emerges that reveals that crossborder governance in the region Paso del Norte is provided by two principal actors: economic actors and law enforcement actors. In that sense, it is hardly crossborder governance; it is *bad* governance.

The answers to these questions are at once simple and perverse. It is these two nonelected actors, and thereby, nondemocratically accountable, nontransparent, and noninclusive entities, that provide much of the governance in the region through processes that serve their own narrow interests: (1) the market-based actors and their interests in a binational community (Ciudad Juárez, El Paso) inserted in the context of an enormous manufacturing/export global network; *and* (2) the border law enforcement communities. Many of the constraints that are faced by local, elected political actors and community activists are the product of these two logics (market and law enforcement) that act as straitjackets on them, tying their hands and limiting their ability to create a shared vision of the region, to use the same instruments in public policy, and to cooperate in public policy implementation processes. The CBR, in fact, had to work very closely with both important actors, *particularly* law enforcement actors, just to be able to plan a meeting among city councils. Any one law enforcement agency could have derailed the entire project.

Market and law enforcement actors define and articulate the "interests" of the region under a very narrow logic: (1) economic gain (global markets) organized around the maquiladora industry, which is in turn plugged into the global chain of production; and (2) national security (a resultant of TAR), organized increasingly around U.S. interests regarding the war on drugs, border security, immigration, terrorism, etc. These actors generally leave the region's *elected* leaders, that is, its policy makers and the bureaucrats that work for them, and the local residents to merely react and adjust to the realities imposed by these two formidably well-organized, well-funded players. The logic through which these actors organize their vision of the border and their interests is one where the border is fully open to the powerful economic interests of the global manufacturing industry and allow for the flow of capital, goods, and services in an expeditious manner, but where all border activity remains organized under a *gateway scheme*, with all ports of entry under the tight control of the law enforcement community. Everyone and everything must flow through the hands of the law enforcement community. But economic forces are privileged. This turns the border into an "open" border for the global economic interests of the maquiladora industry but into an increasingly "closed" border for the local binational community, including the local, elected officials. In other words, the structures and processes of the border are subsumed by the powerful economic interests lodged in the region, particularly those of the manufacturing industry, but the human beings (the community) are increasingly split asunder by the physical construction of the border. The ultimate arbiter of what crosses and what does not cross rests in the hands of the border law enforcement agencies. The building of the wall is but one more expression of this.

This does not mean that there are no other actors that attempt to insert themselves in the processes of governance in the region or even in the much larger context. Different regions may have different local noneconomic and nonlaw enforcement actors, such as the Border Governors Conference, etc., but in general these are much less powerful than market and policing actors.

A quick analysis of the two main actors (market and law enforcement) that produce the region's structures and processes through which everything and everyone is judged and passes or is blocked clearly reveals that crossborder governance in the region Paso del Norte can be said to be *bad* crossborder governance. It is not designed to satisfy the wants, needs, aspirations, or desires of the people that live in the region. Instead, it is designed to operate under a logic of global economic or market integration without local social integration and without political empowerment of the residents of the region (Staudt and Coronado, 2002). Similarly, it is designed to operate with the law enforcement community at the core of the crossborder system, ensuring that capital, goods, and services cross, but not people, who have acquired the characteristic of being largely undesirable.[12] In this sense, crossborder governance in the region cannot be said to be participatory, accountable, transparent, responsive, equitable, or inclusive, inasmuch as it is built around the narrow, nonlocal logic of the market forces with the law enforcement community as its guarantor on the ground. The structures and processes serve the interests of the two sets of actors, whose "instructions" come from away from the border and who define the region's "interests" according to those instructions. It is not possible to even claim that the border structures and processes that exist are efficient and effective either because they do not provide overall economic and social welfare for the binational community.

An analysis of the history of the border tells us that this should not come as a surprise. Not only are border regions naturally different from regions within a sovereign nation-state because border regions is where jurisdictions, authorities, controls, and influences end and begin and where their mutual exclusiveness is most obvious, but also because the U.S.-Mexico border has been moving in that direction since its inception (Payan, 2006a). Border regions constitute the very places where the identification of the state and its borders is the strongest and sovereignty dictates reinforcement in the form of separation. It is where the "gatekeepers" of sovereignty operate and often where identities clash. Very often, it is where political, economic, and social institutions are split asunder by the gatekeepers, precisely because it is where they are questioned the most. In this sense, border regions suffer from weaknesses that interior regions do not, given that such regions are at the outer reaches of a nation-state and their economic and infrastructural development is weak and do not always participate fully and actively in the political decision making of the national core.[13] Sassen (1998) already intuited that the two basic elements of the modern nation-state, territoriality and sovereignty, whose limits are most observable at border regions, were operating against people rather than for people, because they signified, first, a forced fragmentation of space in the face of globalizing or integrating forces (e.g., export-manufacturing) and, second, an unnatural separation of peoples in the face of a desire for human mobility (e.g., exclusive and privileged citizenship held up against law enforcement).

INSTITUTIONS AND GOVERNANCE IN THE REGION PASO DEL NORTE

To further demonstrate that crossborder governance in the region Paso del Norte does not rise to the level of good governance, we must also examine some of the crossborder structures and processes themselves. In this regard, it is appropriate to ask: What are the structures and processes that provide governance for the entire Paso del Norte region? As with our examination of the main actors, it does not take very long for an answer to emerge from our empirical observations. The Paso del Norte region is noticeably lacking in crossborder institutionalization—a key component of good crossborder governance anywhere. In fact, few areas are linked sufficiently across the border so as to operate in tandem to improve the quality of life for the entire binational community. For the most part, each entity in the region pursues its own interests independently of the others.

It is not enough, however, to state that the region Paso del Norte has low levels of institutionalization. Greater precision is required. So, what exactly is meant by low levels of institutionalization? To answer this question, we must first create a typology of *crossborder governmental* interaction that might be useful to operationalize what is meant by low, medium, or high levels of crossborder institutionalization. Although the terms coordination, cooperation, and collaboration are often used interchangeably, they are not interchangeable at all. They signify a clear difference in the way structures, processes, and linkages occur in any given context. Let us see what we mean by drawing a table (see Table 10.1 below) that can help us define what each term implies.

Now let us see where the region Paso del Norte fits in this table. On the great majority of issues affecting the binational community, the governments of the region are not engaged in any of the three levels. Decision making and implementation is almost entirely localized within each community even when problems are shared: crime, delinquency, and fugitives; air and water pollution; land use ordinances; urban planning; economic development; signage standards;

Table 10.1 Border typology: Coordination, cooperation, and collaboration

	Coordination	Cooperation	Collaboration
Objectives	Generally different and not jointly articulated	May or may not be the same; when they are the same, it is purely coincidental	Same objectives, previously defined as common by all actors
Vision	Different understandings of self-interest, meaning and purpose	Partial coincidence in understandings of self-interest, meaning and, purpose and joint action is possible in those areas where these intersect	Shared understanding of interests, meaning, and purpose
Acknowledgment of interdependence	Nonexistent or low, except for the acknowledgment that they need to stay out of each other's way	Medium; actors need to acknowledge that they need each other to accomplish their goals	High; goals are the same

(*continued*)

Table 10.1 Continued

	Coordination	Cooperation	Collaboration
Mechanisms of interaction	Designed to stay out of each other's way so as to accomplish different goals—much like drivers on their way home are coordinated by road rules and lights; each actor needs to understand what he/she must do and when	Designed to maneuver in tandem on a temporary basis in order to achieve different goals; actors must understand the rules well as they work together; such synchronization is likely to die after the goals have been accomplished	Designed to be permanent and clear; actors are bound by the rules and procedures and there is a degree of certainty in the outcome because everyone works toward accomplishing the same goals; the work is synergistic
Purpose of the system	To ensure that different entities stay out of the way of each other so that they be free to accomplish their individual goals. Action is sporadic, based on need, and temporary agreement	To work together to accomplish goals that may or may not coincide but which cannot be accomplished without each other's involvement. Action is linear, along predetermined rules and procedures that are more or less permanent but still in flux	To work together to accomplish the same goals, which the actors defined prior to taking joint action.
Requirements	Minimal trust, some information sharing, and maybe some consultation	A good deal of trust; ample information sharing, particularly while the work is ongoing, and frequent consultation to clear obstacles to action	Absolute trust, continual information sharing, and ongoing consultation
Physical location of participants	Dispersed and isolated with little interaction	Regularized meetings but separate location	Same physical location or very well regularized processes of interaction

international traffic; bridge infrastructure; disaster and emergency management, etc. And although occasionally there may be some coordination and perhaps even some cooperation in one or another area, this is largely ad hoc and primarily reactive to a particular issue that arises and neither community can deal with it without the other. The default position, however, is always dealing with an issue independently of the other communities and involving them only after it becomes absolutely necessary. Thus, crossborder interaction is nearly absent in most areas. It is sometimes merely coordinative, as in the case of the Memorandum of Understanding of 25 June, 2007, between El Paso, Ciudad Juárez, and Sunland Park, where each city commits to "notify" its sister cities if any disaster were to occur within its territory.[14] It is cooperative at best in certain aspects at certain times, such as when the need arises for new infrastructure, namely, an international port of entry, where neither can accomplish its goals without the other.

The most advanced level of crossborder institutionalization can be found in the International Boundary and Water Commission (IBWC), which includes a sophisticated binational treaty and solid, long-standing offices on both sides of the border. The IBWC can correctly be considered a bilateral institution. It holds regular meetings and the two sections work together to ensure that the treaty is fully implemented. In this sense, the IBWC correctly fits a "cooperative" profile. The Border Environment Cooperation Commission (BECC), an organ of the North American Development Bank (NADBANK) in charge of vetting environmental repair projects along the border, more likely fits a "collaborative" profile, because it is a binational agency with a single office, staff, and budget (Peña, 2004).

The Border Governors Conference also has some bearing on the region by the various largely informal agreements that the ten border governors sign in their annual meetings. However, there is not much evidence that these agreements have an effect on state policies and, in the end, they amount to nothing more than joint declarations, with the same teeth as good intentions.[15]

The relationship between the mayors and city councils in the region is even less effective than the Governors Conference. It may not even rise to the simplest level, given that the two governments not only fail to coordinate most of their actions but often operate at odds with each other. One example of the latter relates to the tolls charged at the international bridges. During the 2008 budget crunch, the city of El Paso chose to raise the crossing fee without consulting the city of Juárez or the Mexican federal government (who ultimately collects the fees on the Mexican side), provoking some protests from the city of Juárez's government, but to little avail since El Paso needed the revenue for its own projects and did not *have* to consult with the Ciudad Juárez. Within two years, there is yet another attempt to increase the fees unilaterally.[16] Another example is the work on the new international bridge to be built somewhere between the Córdova de las Américas (free) bridge and the Zaragoza bridge. In this case, the local governments made an enormous effort first to establish the need for a bridge that had been in the planning for nearly twenty years. On this project, some representatives of community came together to support that project and the local governments determined to coordinate their actions so that each worked with their respective federal governments to obtain the right permits and conduct the right studies to eventually build the bridge. Some plausible coordinative work was conducted, but it was also because an external actor brought the local governments together. Another example was the Christmas season of 2007, when Steve Ortega, a member of the El Paso City Council, and others correctly perceived that the border law enforcement community was particularly inflexible and the wait times at the international bridges were too long. The downtown economic community in El Paso saw that as a threat to their Christmas season profits and City Council member Ortega took their cause to the plenary session of the city, which in turn attempted to negotiate with the border law enforcement agencies mechanisms to expedite the crossings at the international bridges. The law enforcement community, specifically Customs and Border Protection, was able to place some conditions on the City Council, such as conducting a campaign to warn border crossers that they had to be ready when they came up to the checkpoint, including not holding cell phones, having their documents ready for presentation, not talking, etc. Even some university students, recruited by me, participated in handing out flyers with instructions for drivers and pedestrians at the international bridges in order to comply with the "requests" of the CBP so that they could reduce the wait times. This particular example leaves it clear that any action in favor of the community is generally motivated by economic interest and circumscribed by the law enforcement community.

All of these examples show that local governments have little power to establish solid and lasting mechanisms for crossborder collaboration in defining their destiny. Or rather that they show that they have few incentives to do so and the processes of interaction are more in accordance to what Charles Lindblom called the process of "muddling through" (1996).[17] The organizational architecture for crossborder governance of the Paso del Norte region is therefore relatively primitive, compared to the European Union's. The national-to-national relationship overwhelms the architecture of the local-to-local and generally the priorities of the national cancel out the local. The local arena is characterized by spontaneous governance, largely under an economic and law enforcement logic and individual actors, and the result is often very narrow or temporal objectives. In this sense, not even Robert Putnam's (1998) logic of two-level games applies. The border governance game is a much more simple, one-logic game, where the federal does not respond to the views of the local. Governance on the border obeys a federal logic with an economic undertone, neither with inclusion of the local community and its desires, needs, or priorities, nor with any mechanisms for accountability to the population itself. This implies that most crossborder functions are heavily centralized in the law enforcement community, which in turn serves as a funnel and everyone and everything must go through its agents' hands. In this scenario, local governments are continuously left to appeal to the higher sovereign and to self-help within a very constrained environment, because the mechanisms for defining problems jointly, creating common visions, and collaborating in achieving shared goals are simply absent.

GOVERNMENTAL STRUCTURES AND GOVERNANCE

It has long been known that a major obstacle in policy coordination, cooperation, or collaboration in the Paso del Norte region—as anywhere along the U.S.-Mexico border—is the fact that there is a lack of structural harmony between governments on both sides of the boundary, in addition to the fact that, because the constitutions are different, local governments are not allowed to harmonize their governmental structures. This lack of structural harmony between governments in the region makes it considerably difficult to establish a permanent dialogue for coordination, cooperation, or collaboration on almost any policy issue, as disparate entities hold jurisdiction over different policy issues. Thus, although most residents of the border region do not realize it, the actors, jurisdictions, powers, authorities, and even the terms, are quite different, even as the policy issues continue to converge (Staudt, 1998). The lack of harmony between governmental structures and policy practices clashes powerfully with the fact that policy problems know no boundaries. Here is a table of differences:

These differences—and there are considerably more—are quite significant as they make interface quite complicated and largely

Table 10.2 Comparative governance structures: Mexico and the United States

Issue	El Paso, Texas	Ciudad Juárez, Chihuahua
Federalism	Less centralized form of government, with strong powers deposited in the states. Counties operate as the arms of the state government. Limited but effective ordinance powers deposited in city governments.	Considerably more centralized, although there has been an increase in the power in the hands of the states. In theory, the municipal governments should possess greater powers than in the United States, as they are constitutionally autonomous entities. In practice, they are weak and dependent on the states and the federal government.
Representation	District-based representation, resulting in greater accountability to the public.	Proportional representation at the local level, resulting in less accountability to the local public and greater responsiveness to the political parties' agendas.
Terms	Previously, two-year mayoral terms; now four-year mayoral terms. Reelection possible. Policy priorities in the hands of a more professionalized bureaucracy, making project continuity possible. Nonpartisan elections.	Three-year terms at the local level. No consecutive reelection possible. Policy priorities are highly dependent on the current mayor, not on a permanent professionalized bureaucracy, and project continuity is nearly absent. Partisan elections.
Revenue	Property tax and service fees revenues, with relatively effective tax-collecting mechanisms.	Property tax revenue and federal and state contributions, but ineffective tax-collecting mechanisms.
Governing entities	Creation of various boards to handle specific issues, such as water, sewage, transportation, infrastructure, etc., is possible. This allows for a decentralization and depolitization of issues.	There is no possibility of creating independent boards to handle any policy issues. All issues rest squarely on the hand of the elected officials, centralizing power, enabling a spoils system to operate, and heavily politicizing most policy issues.

dependent on very disparate entities, with dissimilar agendas, unequal powers, unalike interests, and unalike jurisdictions. The task of bringing together these differing policy coordinating mechanisms can prove to be gargantuan. A result of this is the fact that much of what can be done depends heavily on the personal relationship between mayors, their individual priorities, and the time and energy that each may want to invest in cultivating a relationship with the other. Add to this complicated brew the natural zealousness and turf-protection of the federal bureaucratic entities that hold the ultimate word on all policy issues touching the borderline (Payan, 2006a) and you have a nearly impossible task in bringing about effective and efficient local governance—forget the idea of *good* governance itself. In this regard, the CBR was well over its ability to call a meeting of actors of all three levels of government to sit at the table and talk policy. This means, clearly, that governance in the crossborder region Paso del Norte is not only difficult but it is also *bad governance*.

GOVERNANCE IN THE PASO DEL NORTE REGION: THE PRIVILEGE OF THE MARKET

In accordance with Sassen's arguments, crossborder governance on the Paso del Norte region is based on a hierarchy of actors, with the market-based actors atop this hierarchy. Each of these employs a number of narrow mechanisms that aggregate interests and produce decisions for the collective in the form of maquiladora plants openings and closings (Fatemi, 1990); in hiring, firing, and skilled labor mobility decisions (Hausman and Haytko, 2004); and in lobbying for expeditious border crossings for goods and services. The region's interest aggregation, from its organizational architecture to its actors and integrative mechanisms, favor economics over politics, culture, society, or human rights (Staudt and Coronado, 2002). Tourism, shopping, exports/imports, investment, etc., are favored over human security and even over public safety and social networks (Tuttle, forthcoming). The crossing requirements, the infrastructure, the operating procedures, the introduction of new technologies, and the overall dynamics are scaled to fit economic integration while excluding the social and political integration of the binational community. This helps explain in part the inability of the CBR to establish local political or policy issue linkages between the two communities' elected leaders and to move the local governments to act jointly. Such are low priority items in the region's structures.

The literature on the maquiladora industry, which dominates the region's economic development, shows how the global economic command and control functions are fully operable at the Paso del Norte region. Hundreds of thousands of people are plugged into the maquiladora matrix, including the production processes, the warehousing activities, and the transportation networks (Skalir, 1993). The entire manufacturing industry is fully plugged into the global network of production. The economic system is fully consolidated and much political rhetoric is designed to satisfy the requirements of the economic integration of the region. Governmental investment in infrastructure, particularly in Ciudad Juárez, is also designed to satisfy the requirements of the capital flows. As predicted by Sassen (2001), the dominant logic is that of capital. Similarly, border crossers are also seen as economic entities that shop, consume, and spend, rather than human relationships that reinforce trust, human security, and cross-border intimacy. Thus, whether at the macro level or at the micro level, economics prevails over political or social concerns.

LAW ENFORCEMENT: WHEN EVERYONE IS SUSPECT

Over the last century, the United States government has defined the meaning of the United States-Mexico border (Payan, 2006a). In this process, the logic has been one of escalation of law enforcement (Andreas, 2009). Over the last decade alone, the United States has multiplied the resources and the number of agents posted along the U.S.-Mexico border. The Border Patrol shows this trend quite starkly, a trend that predicts that by the end of 2009, the Border Patrol will have over 20,000 agents. Similar increases apply to Customs and Border Protection (CBP).

This token statistic shows that a law-enforcement logic prevails in the Paso del Norte region. Behind this logic is the presumption that anyone who wants to cross the border into the United States is suspect.

Moreover, the new passport requirements for U.S. citizens that entered into effect on 1 June, 2009, further emphasize that it is law enforcement agencies that impose all sense of order in the region and determine who can move where, when, and how. This in turn drives more and more border residents into illegality—if we accept the premise that what is "illegal" is also socially constructed, as much as what is legal. In the end, everything and everyone *must* necessarily pass through the hands of a law enforcement agent and must be vetted by him/her before the person, vehicle, merchandise, etc., is allowed to circulate. In effect, law enforcement agencies serve as a gateway and little can now cross without their consent.

This trend is not exclusively an American one. Clearly, when the mayor of Ciudad Juárez, José Reyes Ferriz, decided that he could no longer manage the police force in Ciudad Juárez due to its deep, structural corruption and the violence that gripped the city through 2008, the Mexican federal government sent 10,000 military and

2,500 federal police to take over all policing activities in the city.[18] This militarization of the local law enforcement implied that the logic of escalation also applies on the Mexican side of the region.

THE SYMBOLIC-COGNITIVE DIMENSION

Law enforcement contains within it the seeds of division, because it constitutes the arm of the state that ensures its integrity. It does provide *stable*, though not necessarily *good*, governance. It does so because, by nature, it includes and excludes. By nature, it rewards and punishes. By nature, it draws divisions among those who would be in and those who would be out. In this sense, the logic of law enforcement escalation in the region Paso del Norte has reinforced the divisions among the local population. There are those who cannot aspire to cross the borderline and there are those who enjoy complete mobility. This is how law enforcement provides governance: it invents communities (Anderson, 1991) by projecting its power onto spaces in highly organized ways (Liepitz, 1994), from which some are excluded and in which some are included. In this sense, law enforcement also forms identities, which in turn tell residents who can access what, when, and how. Whereas Europe is facing the decline of borders as identity-forming phenomena, in the Paso del Norte region, borders are emerging as the principal identity-forming phenomena, particularly in the face of the fact that the population is well over 90 percent Hispanic of Mexican descent. Law enforcement is the last stronghold to distinguish between those who are Mexican-Mexicans, those who are Mexican-Americans, and those who are Americans. Today, more than ever, borders are being redefined and shifted to create identities, which in turn facilitate crossborder governance. They do so, however, by dividing, rather than uniting, by weakening the community rather than empowering it. The reinforcement of the border is, therefore, becoming the strongest organizing principle in regional governance, mediated of course by law enforcement agents. Accordingly, law enforcement is the main barrier to any kind of political project that attempts to provide crossborder governability at a much higher level of crossborder institutionalization.

Moreover, there is a certain sense of self-deception that becomes internalized as territory becomes identity and borderlines become separation. Thus, the community's interests are divided and its destiny drifts further and further apart. This internationalization of identity ordered by the borderline and enforcement by agents becomes, therefore, a challenge to the institutionalization of governance.

THE DEMOCRATIC DEFICIT: WHEN FEDERALISM TURNS INTO ITS OPPOSITE

The most important institution that should intuitively come to the aid of locally focused governance is the principle of federalism. Federalism is a system designed to stimulate local solutions to local problems. It is a system that is meant to imply the devolution of powers to the local communities to shape their policies in response to their own unique problematiques. But at the borderlands, such is not the case. In fact, federalism seems to operate against people rather than for people, to obstruct good crossborder governance rather than work for it. It does so because when a policy problem, no matter how small, touches an international boundary, in both the United States and the Mexican political systems, it becomes a federal issue and local governments are shoved aside and seldom, if ever, consulted on the matter. Thus, the principle of federal supremacy drowns the principle of federalism privileging nationally determined solutions to local problems along borderlines. This endows the federal governments with powers even over the smallest of policy problems, and local governments are not able to achieve crossborder arrangements that will work for them and their local communities. Often, this implies a democratic deficit because solutions to policy problems are imposed from above, rather than emerge from below.

Thus, the concept of federalism in a border context is much more complicated than it is often thought. In other words, TAR is not something that local governments can influence. TAR is in a way a *federal* principle, meant to reinforce the nation-state not the devolution of powers to the local governments. It is a legal and political structure designed to foster local solutions to local governments but in a border context, it appears to get in the way of *good* crossborder governance rather than facilitate it. That is because the response to a local problem is usually an imposition from above, with no local participation, no accountability, no inclusiveness, no transparency, and no responsiveness to the local visions of the region.

RESCALING GOVERNANCE FOR A BORDER CONTEXT

In order to rescale crossborder governance and turn it into good governance in a region such as Paso del Norte, we have to start by recognizing that its structures, processes, and links are inadequate and require transformation, a sort of rescaling. As Young (2002) puts it, the Paso del Norte region is in dire need of revising its governance scales and perhaps considering a multiscalar governance framework. Its leaders must begin by restructuring the mechanisms through which they define policy problems and create and implement solutions. In other words, the Paso del Norte region must move to a functional strategy to achieve good governance and it must begin at the local level. A second step is to learn from other experiences how to rescale crossborder integration in order to structure cooperation issues, such as urban planning, public transportation, infrastructure, the environment, etc.[19] Now, because the formal processes for crossborder collaboration can only be authorized by national treaty, it is necessary that the subnational units lobby their central governments to negotiate treaties that devolve powers to local governments in border contexts to determine much of the public policies that deal with local problems.

Besides the political constraints faced by the local governments, that is, those caused by the impacts of disparate and mutually exclusive administrative systems, language and culture do seem to make it quite difficult as well. But there is a relatively good base of bicultural, bilingual, and even binational individuals that can make this work. Crossborder issues are becoming more and more important and the Paso del Norte region, since the North American Free Trade Agreement entered into effect, has lost its structural advantages in the globalization process, namely, that it enjoyed a privileged status within the United States-Mexico economic integration process. In fact, there is some evidence that the region is losing this comparative advantage to other cities within Mexico and even in places like China, Vietnam, and Central America, etc. The region needs to band together if it is to recover some of that comparative advantage taken away by NAFTA. Anderson and O'Dowd (2003) remind us that "the drawing of any given state border represents an arbitration, and a simplification, of complex geo-political, political and social struggles. It seldom, if ever, offers a coincidence of economy, policy and culture."

CONCLUSION

If locally driven crossborder governance is to happen, it must be done through a constructive process that is likely to be determined in a top-down approach. Moreover, it will require much more than good will and volunteer work by a group of well-intentioned citizens. The CRB could not accomplish such a feat. Crossborder governance requires the creation of concrete capacities for interface, backed by political will, but also institutionalized within the local governmental entities.

It also requires devolution of powers to the local governments: a true federalism. In addition, these capacities must take the form of clear structures for joint work, explicit processes for collaboration, all of which must be legitimized by a common understanding of the issues between the various administrative and political entities that participate. Only such structures, processes and issue linkages can allow for effective collaboration across the boundary line to produce crossborder governance. In other words, crossborder governance in a binational (and tristate) context requires a system of institutional incentives that create, formalize, and legitimize interactive mechanisms, which in turn reinforce the institutional incentives to continue with the process of creating and developing concrete capabilities for collaboration. Such structures, processes, and capacity for issue linkages are, for all practical purposes, absent.

NOTES

1. http://www.elpasotexas.gov/muni_clerk/_documents/ordinances/008262.pdf.
2. http://www.elpasotexas.gov/muni_clerk/city_council_021307.asp.
3. http://www.oag.state.tx.us/AG_Publications/pdfs/openmeeting_hb2008.pdf.
4. The City Councils passed three resolutions, all of some importance but without the force of law. One was a resolution against ASARCO's renewal permit application—which was denied in the end but on account of considerable activism by the community itself and probably economic considerations within ASARCO; a second was an agreement to request that the river be maintained—which the International Boundary and Water Commission eventually did; and a third was a commitment to create crossborder relations committees in all three cities. The last of the three was never implemented. In any event, it was left up to the participating governments to implement them.
5. The European Union is excluded here because there has been a conscious effort by the European Governments to erase the border and to create border regions that are specifically endowed with the capacity to collaborate in the creation of crossborder governance institutions. See *New Borders for a Changing Europe: Crossborder Cooperation and Governance*, edited by James Anderson, Liam O'Dowd, and Thomas M. Wilson (London: Frank Cass, 2003); and *Crossborder Governance in the European Union*, edited by Olivier Kramsch and Barbara Hooper (United Kingdom: Routledge, 2004).
6. The literature on the importance of these three elements (structures, processes, and issue linkages) and the centrality of agency (individual

and organization actors) in international relations is quite developed. See, for example, *Agency, Structure, and International Politics: From Ontology to Empirical Inquiry*, by Gil Friedman and Harvey Starr (United Kingdom: Routledge, 1997); and many other books, articles, and papers. Not all the debates, however, have been settled. A large question, for example, remains which is whether issue linkages facilitate institution-building or whether institution-building makes issue-linkages easier.

7. *The Economist*, a preeminent journal in the defense of markets and globalization, recently published an article asking this very question. See "Responsibility to Protect: An Idea Whose Time Has Come—And Gone?" in *The Economist*, 23 July, 2009. The entire article can be found at the following link: http://www.economist.com/world/international/displayStory.cfm?story_id=14087788, (Accessed 13 August, 2009).

8. Volk, Tyler. 1995. *Metapatterns: Across Space, Time and Mind*. New York: Columbia University Press. Chapter 3: *Borders*.

9. See Peter Andreas, *Border Games: Policing the U.S.-Mexico Divide* (Ithaca, NY: Cornell University Press, 2009).

10. For a short but good discussion of the concept of good governance see the United Nations ESCAP website at this site: http://www.unescap.org/pdd/prs/ProjectActivities/Ongoing/gg/governance.asp.

11. An important assumption behind this question is that it is important to ask "Who governs?" if one is to discern how governance is provided in any given place. Who governs and governance are intimately connected.

12. The disadvantage of the poor and the most vulnerable is increasingly evident as the centralization of law enforcement on the U.S.-Mexico border continues apace. Recently, Immigration and Customs Enforcement, within the Homeland Security Department, has made it clear that the delegation of immigration authority to local law enforcement agencies will be pushed forth under Section 287(g) of the Immigration and Nationality Act. See http://www.ice.gov/partners/287g/Section287_g.htm, (accessed 13 August, 2009).

13. Leibenath, 15.

14. See the Binational Hazardous Materials Emergency Plan MOU signed by the three parties at the following website: http://www.epa.gov/border2012/regional/chi-sister.html, (Accessed 13 August 2009).

15. See the Border Governors Conference Web site at http://www.bordergovernors.ca.gov/, particularly the link regarding the numerous joint declarations. It is hard to believe that governors as powerful as those of California, Texas, and Nuevo León, have so little power to affect crossborder governance.

16. See http://newspapertree.com/news/4144-wilson-defends-budget-and-rising-bridge-tolls-parking-meter-fees-to-central-business-association, (Accessed 13 August, 2009).

17. See Sergio Peña's "Crossborder Planning at the U.S.-Mexico Border: An Institutional Approach" in the *Journal of Borderlands Studies*, Vol. 22, No. 1 (Spring 2007). In that article, Peña propounds that the institutions for crossborder planning are few and weak and that they must be strengthened through an incremental approach. I adhere to a more extreme view: they hardly existent at all.

18. See http://www.cnn.com/2009/WORLD/americas/03/06/mexico.troops/index.html, (Accessed 13 August, 2009).

19. One example of the kind of studies that regional leaders can learn from is that of Gabriel Popescu, "The Conflicting Logics of Cross-Border Reterritorialization: Geopolitics of Euroregions in Eastern Europe," in *Political Geography*, Vol. 27, No. 4 (May 2008); 418–438.

REFERENCE LIST

Anderson, Benedict. 1991. *Imagined Communities: Reflections on the Origin and Spread of Nationalism*. London: Verso.

Anderson, James, Liam O'Dowd, and Thomas M. Wilson, eds. 2003. *New Borders for a Changing Europe: Crossborder Cooperation and Governance*. London: Frank Cass.

Andreas, Peter. 2009. *Border Games: Policing the U.S.-Mexico Divide*. New York: Cornell University Press.

Fatemi, Khosrow, ed. 1990. *The Maquiladora Industry: Economic Solution or Problem?* Santa Barbara: Greenwood.

Hausman, Angela and Diana L. Haytko. 2004. *Examining Key Factors of Supply Chain Optimization: The Maquiladora Example*. Working Paper #2004–20 (May 2004). Entire document found at http://ea.panam.edu/cbes/pdf/s20.pdf.

Kramsch, Olivier, and Barbara Hooper, eds. 2004. *Crossborder Governance in the European Union*. United Kingdom: Routledge.

Leibenath, Markus et al., eds. 2008. *Crossborder Governance and Sustainable Spatial Development: Mind the Gaps!* Berlin: Verlag-Berlin-Heidelberg.

Liepitz, A. "The National and the Regional: Their Autonomy vis-à-vis the Capitalist World Crisis," in Pallan, R. and Gills, B (eds.), *Transcending the State-Global Divide*. Colorado: Lynne Rienner.

Martínez, Oscar J. 1994. *Border People: Life and Society in the U.S.-Mexico Borderlands*. Tucson, AZ: The University of Arizona Press.

Payan, Tony. 2006a. *The Three U.S.-Mexico Border Wars: Drugs, Immigration, and Homeland Security*. California: Praeger Security International.

Peña, Sergio. (2004). "Planificación Transfronteriza: Instituciones Binacionales y Bilaterales en la Frontera México-Estados Unidos" in María Socorro Tabuenca and Tony Payan (Eds.) *Gobernabilidad Ingobernabilidad en la Región Paso del Norte: Reflexión Desde Distintas Perspectivas*. (pp. 59–84). México: El Colegio de la Frontera Norte, NMSU, UACJ & NEON.

Peña, Sergio. "Crossborder Planning at the U.S.-Mexico Border: An Institutional Approach" in the *Journal of Borderlands Studies*, Vol. 22, No. 1 (Spring 2007).

Popescu, Gabriel. "The Conflicting Logics of Cross-Border Reterritorialization: Geopolitics of Euroregions in Eastern Europe," in *Political Geography*, Vol. 27, No. 4 (May 2008).

Putnam, Robert D. "Diplomacy and Domestic Politics: The Logic of Two-Level Games," in *International Organization*, Vol. 42, No. 3 (1998), pp. 427–460.

Sassen, Saskia. 1998. *Globalization and Its Discontents*. The New Press. New York.

———. 2001. *Global Networks, Linked Cities*. New York, NY: Routledge.

———. 2007. *A Sociology of Globalization*. NY: W. W. Norton.

———. 2008. *Territory, Authority, Rights: From Medieval to Global Assemblages*. Princeton, NJ: Princeton University Press.

Staudt, Kathleen and Irasema Coronado. 2002. *Fronteras No Más: Toward Social Justice at the U.S.-Mexico Border*. New York, NY: Palgrave Macmillan.

Staudt, Kathleen. 2008. *Violence and Activism at the U.S.-Mexico Border*. Austin: The University of Texas Press.

Staudt, Kathleen. 1998. *Free Trade: Informal Economies at the U.S.-Mexico Border*. Philadelphia, PA: Temple University Press

Tuttle, Carolyn. *American Factories in Mexico: Liberation or Exploitation?* (Forthcoming).

Young, Oran R. 2002. *The Institutional Dimensions of Environmental Change: Fit, Interplay and Scale*. Cambridge, MA: MIT Press.

About the Contributors

Cynthia **Bejarano** (PhD, Arizona State University) is Associate Professor of Criminal Justice at New Mexico State University. She is the author of *Qué Onda? Urban Youth Culture and Borders,* numerous articles on feminicide, migrant students, and border surveillance, along with a forthcoming book that follows the feminicide trail in the Americas.

César **Fuentes** Flores (PhD, University of Southern California, Urban and Regional Planning) is a Research Professor at El Colegio de la Frontera Norte in Ciudad Juárez, Chihuahua, Mexico. He wrote the book, *Inversión Pública y Productividad Regional de la Industrial Manufactura en México* (2007), and authored more than twenty articles on urban themes at Mexico's northern border. He is a Level I research in Mexico's National System of Researchers. Fuentes teaches regional economics at the University of Texas at El Paso.

Georg M. **Klamminger,** M.A., PhD student at the University of Graz, Austria.

Zulma Y. **Méndez** (PhD, University of California at Riverside) is Assistant Professor of Educational Research and Foundations. She teaches graduate seminars in curriculum theory, qualitative research, and the production of knowledge.

Martha Cecilia **Miker** Palafox (M. A., El Colegio de la Frontera Norte, Tijuana, in Regional Development) is a Researcher at El Colegio de la Frontera Norte in Ciudad Juárez. She authored four articles on export-processing in the auto-industrial employment sector of northern Mexico. She will complete her PhD dissertation in social sciences at the Universidad Autónoma de Ciudad Juárez in 2010.

Julia E. **Monárrez** Fragoso (PhD, Universidad Autónoma Metropolitana—Xochimilco, Sociology) is a Research Professor at El Colegio de la Frontera Norte in Ciudad Juárez, Chihuahua, Mexico. She wrote *Bordeando la violencia contra las mujeres en la frontera norte de México* (2007) along with numerous articles on femicide and a coauthored a chapter with César Fuentes on the spatial aspects of femicide in *Violencia contra las mujeres en contextos urbanos y rurales* (El Colegio de México, 2004).

Guillermina Gina **Núñez** (PhD, University of California at Riverside) is Assistant Professor of Anthropology at the University of Texas at El Paso. She teaches courses on urban anthropology, applied cultural anthropology, and ethnographic research methods. She has published articles on immigration, border surveillance, multiple identities at the border, and service-learning. She is working on a book on *colonias* in New Mexico.

Tony **Payan** (PhD, Georgetown University) is Associate Professor of Political Science at the University of Texas at El Paso. He teaches courses on U.S.-Mexico relations, international law, and Mexican politics. Payan is the author of many articles and two books on the U.S.-Mexico border in 2006, including *Cops, Soldiers, and Diplomats.*

Sergio **Peña** (PhD Florida State University in Urban Planning) is Research Professor at El Colegio de la Frontera Norte in Ciudad Juárez. He is the author of a monograph and several articles on urban planning. He has taught urban planning and is teaching American Government at the University of Texas at El Paso.

Rosalba **Robles** Ortega (M. A., Universidad Autónoma de Ciudad Juárez) is a Research Professor at the Universidad Autónoma de Ciudad Juárez in the Department of Humanities and the Institute of Social Sciences and Administration. She has published nine articles on women, gender, and domestic violence. Robles is completing her dissertation in social sciences, specializing in women's studies and power relations, at the Universidad Autónoma Metropolitana, Unidad Xochimilco.

Kathleen **Staudt** (PhD, University of Wisconsin) is Professor of Political Science at the University of Texas at El Paso and *Investigadora Visitante* at El Colegio de la Frontera Norte (2008–2009) in Ciudad Juárez. She teaches courses on the border, democracy, public policy, and women and politics. Staudt is the author of 13 books, 5 of which focus on the U.S.-Mexico border. Her coedited collection, with Tony Payan and Z. Anthony Kruszewski, titled *Human Rights along the U.S.-Mexico Border: Gendered Violence and Insecurity,* was published by the University of Arizona Press in 2009.

INDEX

accountability 177–8
agricultural workers 151, 168
Amnesty International 30, 60, 77, 78–9, 81
Anderson, Benedict xiii
Anzaldúa, Gloria xv
automobile harness production 119–43

Baudrilland, Jean 23, 24, 25, 27, 29, 30, 31, 34
Bermudez International Group 94, 103–4
border xi, xii, 1–2; collaboration 140, 142, 218, 227, 230–1; security xii, xix; studies xiii, xv, xix
business model 175–8, 182

Calderón, President Felipe 23, 24, 36
Cameron, D and E. Frazer 45–6, 53, 56
capitalist discipline xii, xv
Caputi, Jane 45
Cardona, Julian 46
cartels xvi
Chamizal Agreement xiii
citizenship 84, 148, 149, 156, 163, 166–8, 220, 229. See also human rights, immigrants and immigration
civil society 25, 29, 49, 73, 74, 132,192. See also Industrial Areas Foundation, labor

unions, nongovernment organizations
Colegio de la Frontera Norte (COLEF) xviii
colonias 62, 80, 113, 147–73
convenientia 43–70
crime and criminal networks 30, 34, 37. See also domestic violence, drug trafficking, femicide, *feminicidio*, homicide, violence
culture 151–5

democracy 174, 175, 176, 187–91, 222, 223–4, 227, 228; deficit of 239
domestic violence 55, 71–89
drug trafficking xiv, xvi, xix, 3, 14, 25, 26, 28, 31, 33, 34, 38–9. See also cartels, crime and criminal networks
dual cities 97, 110

economic marginality xv–xvi, xx, 76, 173, 174, 176, 183, 184, 186, 201, 221, 150, 155, 159, 160. See also employment-centered poverty
education xvii, xix, xx, 173–94, 195–214
El Paso xiv, 11–12, 24, 26, 27, 32, 33, 39n7, 48, 50, 52–4, 72–89, 100–1, 108, 113, 159, 173–54

employment-centered poverty 96, 129–36, 158
environmental disaster 162
European: manufacturing 137n8; Union 201, 234, 241n5
export-processing factories xi, 8, 25, 46, 47, 93–5, 119–143, 201. See also automobile harness production, global manufacturing, *maquiladoras*

federal government xxi, 36,177, 239
femicide xv, xvi, xix, 23, 29, 30, 33, 38n1, 71, 75, 77, 80. See also *feminicidio*
feminicidio 43–70. See also femicide
feminist 43, 49
Flores, Carlos 26
Foreign Direct Investment (FDI) 3, 8, 9, 11, 30, 64, 103, 110, 113
Foucault, Michel 44, 49. See also *convenientia*

gender xiii, 44–5, 51, 59, 64, 73, 76, 102. See also feminicide, *feminicidio*, women
Giddens, Anthony 75–6
global capital xii, xv
global manufacturing xv, xviii. See also automobile harness production, export-processing factories, globalization, *maquiladoras*
globalization 1–16, 23, 26–6, 35, 93–117, 175
globalizing cities 3, 6–9
Gramsci, Antonio 74–5
governance, cross-border 217–44. See also democracy, federal government, state
Guadalupe Hidalgo, Treaty of xiii, xiv

guns and gun smuggling xiv, xvi, 29, 34, 35, 39n10

Harvey, David 7, 48
Hill, Sarah 154
homicide xvi, 23–4, 25, 28, 29, 33
housing 147, 149, 151, 154, 159, 162–3, 165, 166
human rights xvi, 149, 166. See also Inter-American Court of Human Rights

ideologies of competition 174. See also capitalist discipline
immigrants and immigration xii, xv, xvi, xix, xx, 47–8, 84, 108, 122–3, 127–9, 130, 137n8, 147–73, 166–8, 174, 221, 223, 228
Immigration Reform and Control Act 151–2
Industrial Areas Foundation 177, 187–91
inequalities xv, xxi, 5, 76, 96, 102, 108–10, 174, 222, 2223
informal economies xiii, xix, 98, 160, 192
insecurity 27, 28–9. See also employment-centered poverty
Intercultural Development Research Association 186
Inter-American Court of Human Rights 64–5, 87
International Boundary and Water Commission 232
international division of labor 5, 6, 120–1. See also globalization
International Organization for Standardization (ISO) 122, 123, 127, 132, 175

Japanese corporations 122–3, 127–9, 130, 137n8

Juárez, Ciudad xi, xiv, xv, xvi, xxii, 11–12, 23–39, 43–4, 46–8, 50–4, 71–89, 160; education 182–3, 195–214. See also automobile harness production, *maquiladoras*, Paso del Norte region

labor 119–143. See also employment-centered poverty; *maquiladoras*
labor unions 119, 130, 131, 138n12, 138n16, 138n17, 174, 180, 181, 190, 195
language of business 173, 175–8
Las Cruces 50–2, 54–8
Latin America 28–9, 179
law enforcement xii, xvi, 29, 30–1, 44, 45, 71–89, 223, 233; as government 227, 233–4, 237. See also border
Limited English Proficient (LEP) 178, 183, 184, 185
local land market 28–9, 152, 161–2, 165. See also property and real estate
Lomas de Poleo 54–5, 106, 114n7
Low, Setha 148, 153
Lugo, Alejandro xiii, 119, 132

Marcuse, Herbert 97
Martínez, Oscar xiv, 225
maquiladoras xi, xx, 3, 8, 9–12, 15n1, 16n3, 48, 55, 60, 71, 76, 108, 113, 119–43, 151, 160, 175, 223, 227, 228, 236. See also automobile harness production; education; export-processing factories; Juárez, Ciudad
Mexico 8–12, 24–26, 28, 33, 34–5, 36, 37, 46, 47, 60, 63; labor law 136, 137n9; local government 95, 104, 113, 114. See also state

migration xii; seasonal 156, 160, 164. See also immigrants and immigration
militarization xvi, xix, 166
military xvi, 26, 29, 31, 34, 36
money laundering 35, 37
Morales, Cynthia 51
murder. See femicide, *feminicidio*, homicide
Municipal Institute of Planning and Research (IMIP) 113

neoliberalism 28, 221
Nevins, Joseph xv
New Mexico 94, 95, 147–73. See also Las Cruces, Paso del Norte Region
No Child Left Behind 176, 177, 188, 195, 196, 205
nongovernment organizations (NGOs) xii, xxi, 3, 13, 14, 43, 46, 49, 55, 56, 60, 79, 149, 154, 162, 165, 169, 188. See also civil society, democracy, Industrial Areas Foundation

Obama, President Barack 24, 35, 36
Olson, Joy 33, 34
Ortega, Steve 217, 233

Paso del Norte Group xiv, xviii
Paso del Norte region xiii, xiv, xix, 1, 2, 43–70, 93–117, 147, 148, 151, 157, 167, 175, 127–44. See also El Paso; Juárez, Ciudad; Las Cruces; New Mexico
police impunity xvi, 55, 63, 66n13. See also domestic violence, femicide, *feminicidio*, homicide, law enforcement, state, violence
Portillo, Lourdes xv
power 154–5, 165–6, 167
property and real estate 93–117, 152, see local land market

public services   93, 95, 107–113,
    152–3, 158, 159, 160–2

Rico, Nieves   45

Salama, Pierre   28
San Diego   1
Sanders, Bill   106
Sassen, Saskia   xii, 4, 12, 13, 25–6,
    27, 44, 46–7, 49, 50, 56, 63, 64,
    71, 72–3, 87, 94, 95, 147, 174,
    191, 219–24, 229
sex trafficking   48, 55, 66n13,
    63
sexual violence   43–70. See also
    femicide, *feminicidio*
Sharlach, Lisa   45
Smith, Jackie   3
space   xii, 2, 5, 6, 7, 25,
    26, 27, 28, 33, 58, 149,
    238; culture   150–5,
    163; democratic   175;
    denationalized   xii, 122;
    neighborhood school-feeder
    pattern   184. See also border,
    convenientia
standards, world class   xii, xiv,
    xvii, xix, xx, 173; educational
    standardization and standardized
    testing   175, 182, 187, 196. See
    also International Organization
    for Standardization (ISO)
state   xi, xvi, xxii, 24, 25, 26,
    49, 72, 220; absent   xii,
    xix, 28, 49, 63, 121, 132;
    impunity   44; shrunken   xii,
    97; swollen   xii, xiv, xix.
    See also border, democracy,
    law enforcement, Mexico,
    Territory Authority Rights
    (TAR), United States
Staudt and Coronado   xii

Territory Authority Rights
    (TAR)   219–20, 225, 227, 239.
    See also human rights, space
Texas   148, 174, 176, 177
Tijuana   1, 11
transborder networks   3, 98,
    105, 113. See also
    nongovernment organizations,
    globalization
transnational urban systems   1–16,
    54–5, 219
transportation   1, 99, 106;
    advantage   10

United Way   132
United States   9, 10, 23–39,
    43–70, 71–89; education
    176–8, 195–6; as largest drug
    consumer   33, 34, 75; as source
    of guns in drug trafficking   35;
    corporations   122–3, 126,
    127–8, 130, 131. See also
    automobile harness production

Vallina family   104–6
violence   xv, 23–39, 43–70, 71–89;
    gender-based   xvi

Ward, Peter   154, 164
Washington Valdez, Diana   54
Wolf, Eric   168
women   xv, 43–70, 122, 126,
    132, 134–5, 138n19. See also
    domestic violence, femicide,
    feminicidio
workers' voices   133–6
World Bank   180, 182

youth   xxi

Zaragoza family   106, 114n7.
    See also Lomas de Poleo